QUERYING CONSENT

QUERYING CONSENT

Beyond Permission and Refusal

EDITED BY

JORDANA GREENBLATT AND KEJA VALENS

RUTGERS UNIVERSITY PRESS

New Brunswick, Camden, and Newark, New Jersey, and London

Library of Congress Cataloging-in-Publication Data

Names: Greenblatt, Jordana, 1981– editor. | Valens, Keja, 1972– editor.
Title: Querying consent : beyond permission and refusal / edited by Jordana
Greenblatt and Keja Valens.
Description: New Brunswick, New Jersey : Rutgers University Press, [2018] | Includes
bibliographical references and index.
Identifiers: LCCN 2017056002 | ISBN 9780813594149 (cloth : alk. paper) | ISBN
9780813594132 (pbk. : alk. paper)
Subjects: LCSH: Sexual consent—Social aspects. | Age of consent—Social
aspects. | Consent (Law)—Social aspects.
Classification: LCC HQ32 .Q47 2018 | DDC 176/.4—dc23
LC record available at https://lccn.loc.gov/2017056002

A British Cataloging-in-Publication record for this book is available from the British
Library.

∞ The paper used in this publication meets the requirements of the American
National Standard for Information Sciences—Permanence of Paper for Printed
Library Materials, ANSI Z39.48-1992.

www.rutgersuniversitypress.org

Manufactured in the United States of America

For all those who would say yes to the impossible, the improbable, and the forbidden

CONTENTS

FINE PRINT
A Foreword

JOSEPH J. FISCHEL

The young boy Kyle, in the 2011 premiere episode of season fifteen of Comedy Central's cartoon *South Park*, finds himself sewed mouth to anus to two other equally ill-fortuned human beings. This grotesque assemblage is to serve as the battery for the humancentiPad, a new product soon to be released by Apple that promises, as Apple always does, to revolutionize everything about the way we anything.

What happened? Kyle consented. Kyle, a metaphor for the rest of us, accepts the iTunes license agreement without reading its terms and conditions, terms and conditions that permit Apple to stitch human orifices into other human orifices for technical progress. As a cartoon Steve Jobs insists a little too defensively, "They all agreed!" Whereas in *Human Centipede*, the horror film *South Park* satirizes, the sewn subjects are kidnapped in their sleep, against their will, and without their consent, here in *South Park*, Kyle and his companions composing the singular gastric system of the humancentiPad signed off to their own debasement. In the parlance of 2017, they even consented affirmatively: they clicked a pop-up agreement validating their prior agreement.

Several of the entries in this impressively interdisciplinary volume, *Querying Consent: Beyond Permission and Refusal*, anatomize how consent is so often not the remedy for unjust social arrangements, for the dehumanization of humanity, but the cause—or worse, the alibi. If we consented, so goes the thinking, it must be OK. Inspired by Marx, Marxists, and critical theorists from one side and feminist and queer theorists from another, some of the chapters in this collection ask, *Why did we consent to this?* Today, especially in proximity to sex, consent is proffered as a solution. If we get consent right, sex will no longer be wrong. But we consent to deadening and underpaid jobs, toxic intimacies, medical (mal) practices, cultural memes, and bad art—not to mention so much unwanted and unpleasant sex. We consent to our own attrition, whether or not we wish to.

It is the very fineness of fine print that affirms to us consumers, clients, users, and patients what we already know to be true—nobody reads the agreements. Why? Because we have no other options than the one in front of us; because we waste time investigating whatever alternative options we might have when time is the always vanishing, ever precious commodity of late capitalism; because we trust that the big bad corporations or pharmaceuticals will not do anything *that* bad even though they usually do; because, as *South Park*'s Cartman observes, "everyone knows that everything but Apple is stupid"—and who wants to be on the wrong side of savvy, mouth-to-anus obligations notwithstanding? In the face of too little time and too much information, in a world where for an elite few the choices are so many as to be dumbfounding while for the rest of us the choices are so limited as to be nonexistent, what is consent good for, if anything? The contributions of *Querying Consent*, in their engagements with literature, pedagogy, digitalization, biomedicalization, and beyond, interrogate the allegedly transformative force of consent, whether consent to sex or to school, to medicine or to art, in imaginaries online or off.

If Apple is the poison, it is also the medicine. Indeed, it is only the Apple geniuses who are qualified to save Kyle from his own consent to Apple, and the solution requires Kyle's father to sign an Apple contract with no choice but to "agree" to its terms and conditions to rescue his son. Think ideological corporate apparatuses. Think totality.

The contributions of *Querying Consent* explicitly or implicitly approach the problem of the totality, the a priori: not only the *Why did we consent to this?* but the *When did we?* If consent provides an answer—to extant social, sexual, or economic inequalities—it tells us nothing about the question. Who decided upon these terms and conditions? We consent or not to *x*, *y*, or *z* in the already built world. But what if we wish to build new worlds?

Unlike several of the authors included in this volume, I do not hold that dominant discourses of consent presuppose a subject whose desires are transparent to herself, unidirectional and unequivocal. To the contrary, while the subject must be informed and competent to this or that degree, a performance of consent in fact ratifies that any outstanding ambivalences, hesitations, or untidy desires are irrelevant as a matter of liability. But not as a matter of ethics. This is why *Querying Consent* is such a necessary intervention. Collectively, the contributions call upon us to imagine kinds of ethical attunement to objects, ourselves, and nonhuman animals that consent, as a guarantor of limited liability, may mystify.

Likewise, a few of the scholars herein point to a paradox of consent: that whatever our initial agreement—whether to sex or to text—we can never know in advance what will happen next; how we will change or not; how words, things, or bodies may move us; how our bodyminds will expand, contract, or remain the same. We might call this the problem of penetration and prolepsis. We can consent to the possibility of a perturbance but predict neither its caliber nor its consequence. And openness to perturbance, to a not-rote feeling worth having, requires a certain willingness to be violated. One must read the text, the "agreement," and not just click through it.

The humancentiPad snags on a glitch before it can launch. Steve Jobs and his Apple team cannot get "it" to read over license agreements before "it" signs them. We humans are incorrigible, refusing to review the agreements to which we agree. The dimwittedness that authorizes humans' very envelopment into the technological apparatus now presents a flaw for the gadget, not the person. Of course, Apple has helped generate the problem it needs to solve: slavish, appetitive human subjects for whom contemplation, deliberation, and most of all reading are not only inconvenient but nearly incompatible for our iLives. Nonreading lubricates mass-scale sociality, human connectivity that is instant and everywhere yet amounts to little more than shitting in each other's mouths.

Querying Consent: Beyond Permission and Refusal beseeches us to be reading subjects once again but without nostalgia. As Apple put it years ago, *Querying Consent* wants us to think different. A reading subject suspends consent. A reading subject cannot be a consenting subject. Or rather, even or especially when we read the fine print, it is only once we soften our attachments to the safety, sovereignty, and mastery falsely promised by consent that we position ourselves elsewhere, to learn a new thing or two.

Querying Consent is a fine print. I found myself opened by and then opened to its precise provocations.

Parodying what we now call "trigger warnings," the *South Park* episode opens with a caution to its audience: "The following program contains coarse language and due to its content it should not be viewed by anyone."

Querying Consent contains challenging ideas and, due to its content, should be read by everyone.

QUERYING CONSENT

INTRODUCTION

The Subject of Consent

JORDANA GREENBLATT AND KEJA VALENS

Questions of consent—what it means, who can give it and when, what it entails, and when it applies—have sprung to prominence in the first decades of the twenty-first century in a series of highly public incidents, from the Donald Trump sexual assault allegations and "grab 'em by the pussy" tape; to the quickly spiraling number of women speaking out about assaults by the likes of Bill Cosby and Canadian radio and television personality Jian Ghomeshi; to revelations of serial sexual abuse committed by British television and radio personality Jimmy Savile, American football coach Jerry Sandusky, and Canadian hockey rink employee Gordon Stuckless; to the Stanford rape case, the lenient sentence given to perpetrator Brock Turner, and his father's notorious "twenty minutes of action" statement. Consent—primarily on the sexual register—is in the public eye. But of course, consent operates far beyond the sexual arena. We "click yes" so often it has become a reflex, even as warning flags are repeatedly waved about the dangers of granting access to the use of our personal information to online services such as Facebook. Consent arises again in controversies about the use and usefulness of trigger warnings, generating both passionate attacks and defenses that frame trigger warnings alternately as the height of millennial entitlement or valuable tools for self-care. And with every new biomedical procedure, drug test, or research project, there is a new "consent form" and new fine print that few people read, except when, strikingly, there isn't.

Do we just need to double down on consent, make ever more clear how exactly yes means yes or no means no, ensure that more people are more able to give, or deny, more informed consent? What if we look instead at the—perhaps inherent—limits, paradoxes, and problems with the ways that consent defines ideas and categories of personhood, citizenship, and property? Consent is a powerful tool in the acquisition and preservation of humanity, bodily integrity, property, and the recognition of alterity. But both in theory and in practice, consent also reinforces social norms and entrenched power dynamics.

Consent positions bodies and desires within or outside of institutions, discourses, and structures of cultural intelligibility, agency, and property. It is used to map and regulate sexual desire, gender relationships, global positions, technological interfaces, relationships of production and consumption, and literary and artistic interactions. Placing consent's anxious historical boundaries into conversation with new questions about its conceptualization and the often contradictory ends and means through which it works, *Querying Consent* explores consent, in all its dramatic malleability, as a social, legal, cultural, economic, biomedical, and literary construct that serves actively to produce and to reinforce borders between categories of social activity and between acceptable and unacceptable desires and social subjects.

The social contract places consent as the decisive act of citizenship even as the social construction of consent operates to produce contested boundaries of desire, determining certain desires and voluntary acts as incompatible with the acceptable social subject. In a notorious legal example, the Spanner Case, a group of gay male sadomasochists were successfully prosecuted for assault despite the objections of their willing sexual partners. In rejecting the Spanner defendants' appeal to the British House of Lords (Regina v. Brown), Lord Templeman famously wrote, "Pleasure derived from the infliction of pain is an evil thing. Cruelty is uncivilized." However, progressive political projects have been no less inclined to map and regulate the borders of acceptable desire. Sadomasochism has historically been a particularly contested issue within feminist discourse. Multiple political projects—from feminism to black power to gay pride—deploy concepts of false consciousness that construct limits to what one can consent to and who can grant consent that effectively exclude certain subjects from "civilization," however idealized and self-consciously politically progressive such "civilization" may be.

For Immanuel Kant, consent delineates ethical interaction. The ability to consent marks competency, freedom, and knowledge because it involves being an end in itself rather than only a means. Indeed, ends provide interpretive lenses for means, which are often discursively categorized as useful or abusive, emancipatory or exploitative, measured or violent depending on their ends. However, Audre Lorde's cautions about using the "master's tools" to dismantle "his house" indicate how means can also (ideologically and materially) constrain their ends through complex interplays of power/knowledge that restrict what—and who—can be means or ends. And Elaine Scarry's formulation of consent as granting active powers to seemingly passive bodies—thus troubling the very distinction of active and passive—directs us to reconsider how our notions of agency, citizenship, and Kantian ethics may work to shore up the power of the active against the subversion of that power that consent may give to the passive. Who can instrumentalize what and whom and who can instrumentalize (aspects of) themselves—how, when, and to what ends—determine how bodies and lives are permitted social subjectivity. Who can (withhold) consent to what and to whom, when, and how may determine as much as it is determined by being an end in itself.

At the basis of both the social contract and the categorical imperative, consent relies on and enforces liberal ideas—and ideals—of the subject. First and foremost, consent relies on the idea of the coherent subject—the self who is one self and is of one mind, a mind that it can and does know. The subject is expected to remain consistent through time in order to engage in consent interactions: it must continue to be the same self that wants the same things, or at least know when its desires have changed. It must remain the same self who once agreed to a contract or waiver for contracts and waivers to have any validity. Yet this very idea of the subject contradicts poststructuralist models of subjectivity and biopolitical understandings of bodies (politic), not to mention the strands within queer theory (i.e., Leo Bersani) and French feminist and/or poststructuralist theory (i.e., Roland Barthes, Hélène Cixous) that present the subject as shattered by sexuality, eros, bliss, jouissance, the sublime, or other transcendent experiences. How can one give ongoing consent if one is shattered by the experience to which one consents?

At the same time, the shattering, denial, or absence of human subjectivity has been a tool of control exerted on those inhabiting disempowered social locations, including women, people of colour, the colonized, children, and the insane, as well as all manner of nonhuman animals. Dehumanized, they are subjected to the will of those whose human subjectivity is accepted and to contracts in which they are not the subjects but the objects of exchange or confinement. The role of ensuring and expanding valid consent in protecting human status has made it difficult to consider consent as a tool of social regulation, but consent embodies the double edges of subjectivity and subjection. Obtaining the ability to consent means entering a fully human state, which also polices its borders and subjects its members to its laws. Conversely, assessing members of a given social category as too disenfranchised to meaningfully consent may well sometimes further dehumanize them and subordinate their assessments of their own will or willingness to the assessments of other, more accepted subjects. If we read certain subjects' assenting and dissenting experiences as equally coerced, even if that subject experiences them differently, could our assessment not then simply further entrench their subjection?

Querying Consent addresses the most uncomfortable questions about consent today: What might be the benefits of consenting to pain and/or submission? What if the subjected are understood not as refusing consent but as searching for the forms of social recognition that legitimate them as able to grant consent? If consent rests on notions of the human and the citizen, what happens to it when those concepts shift? Can a cyborg consent? Are we all consenting citizens of Rebecca MacKinnon's "Facebookistan"? How are notions of personhood challenged and reshaped through the arguments about consent? Grounded in theoretical explorations of the entanglement of consent and subjectivity across a range of textual, visual, multi-, and digital media, *Querying Consent* begins by considering relationships between consent and agency—or consent's conditions—before moving on to trace consent's outcomes through a range of investigations of the mutual implication of personhood and (self-)ownership through the locus of consent.

The first two sections of *Querying Consent*, "Consent, Power, and Agency" and "Consent, Violence, and Refusal," explore interpersonal negotiations of the limits of consent, as well as the ways that political and social power operate through, constrain, and may be contested by various forms of consent. The chapters in this section engage in new theorizations of consent, considering it at its intersections with violence, gender, dissident sexuality, race, aesthetics, spirituality, social control, and the nation. They pursue these questions through the venues of literature, film, music, and legal texts in conversation with a range of critical frameworks, including queer theory and political philosophy.

The chapters in "Consent, Power, and Agency" investigate situations in which consent is paradoxically both active and questionable. The intersection of the perverse, the erotic, and religious submission serves as our entry point; both Karmen MacKendrick and Amanda Paxton investigate apparently simultaneous assertions and relinquishments of agency through consent in spiritual practice. MacKendrick explores the inherent contradictions of confession: the confessing subject must be both willing *and* resistant in order to achieve the combination of shame and modesty necessary for the pleasure of confessional self-exposure. Seeking to perceive itself as perceived, her chapter maintains, the confessing subject cannot confess its desire for confession, which can only be maintained by self-exposure's necessary incompletion. Paxton's investigation of the sadomasochistic erotics of the feminized soul's submission to the masculinized deity in Catholic Victorian poetry elucidates a similarly contradictory juxtaposition of religious relinquishment and exertion of will. Identifying two models of the feminine soul—one null and one agential—Paxton's chapter positions the relationship between the human soul and the divine as necessarily sadomasochistic when it is grounded in the latter model, which requires the soul to *willingly* relinquish its will in a consensual act of religious submission to the divine.

Paxton's interest in sadomasochism is echoed in Jordana Greenblatt's chapter, which draws parallels between the erotics of literary genre and the law's regulation of social and sexual categories. Greenblatt positions genre-deviant contemporary literature as asking readers to consciously consent to reading, a process of consent that is often elided in more conventional literature. Her chapter frames this elision as reinforcing a normative reading subject-citizen, the citizen-subject who is constructed and reinforced through the genre distinctions that case law constructs between types of sexual and social interaction (i.e., sex vs. sport, commerce, etc.). Turning away from the pleasures of submission, Keja Valens's chapter investigates whether it is possible to consent to abuse—to violence that one does not enjoy for its own sake. Exploring literature and music of the Harlem Renaissance, Valens draws on works in which women represent remaining in violent relationships as an agential choice and evaluates whether these creative representations meet criteria for consent predicated on the ability to leave, whether or not one chooses to do so.

The second section of *Querying Consent*, "Consent, Violence, and Refusal," engages explicitly with the intersection of sexuality and nonconsent, exploring the refusals associated not only with sexual assault but with its aftermath. Rather, however, than assuming a standard order where refusal or absence of consent is followed by the violent seizing of persons who thus become victims, the chapters in this section consider how to read sexual consent in the aftermath of political violence and how refusal, resistance, or insurrection might serve as a response to the violence of ignoring consent.

Justine Leach explores discursive mobilizations of rape and sexual consent in relation to histories of colonization, investigating the prevalence of rape as a trope for imperial expansion. Interrogating the appearance of this trope in North African literature, specifically Tayeb Salih's *Season of Migration to the North*, Leach's chapter highlights the ways in which its seeming categorical stability is undermined in texts in which the sexual interactions between characters do not map comfortably onto Western ideas of il/legitimate sex—often because the depicted interactions involve subjects or relationships in which nonconsent is unintelligible. The intelligibility of both consent and nonconsent is at issue again in human-animal relations. Kimberly O'Donnell takes on the ways that humanist- and human-centric consent is challenged by thinking about how we read the consent or nonconsent of "companion" animals. Drawing on Ahmed's theorization of will and Jacques Derrida's and Donna Harraway's works on the animal, O'Donnell suggests that willfulness, as embodied disagreement or affective dissonance, offers a framework for alternative kinds of agency and companionability and allows the elaboration of an embodied ethics of discord.

Brian Martin's chapter takes the contemporary power dynamics of the classroom and the university as its focus. Responding to the recent debates about trigger warnings and college syllabi, Martin asks whether the pedagogical value of texts that depict sexual violence in order to critique misogyny might conflict with the strategies available for protecting student survivors of sexual assault from psychological harm. Investigating the mechanisms by which literature that depicts sexual violence works to critique it, Martin's chapter questions whether the inclusion of content warnings necessarily results in decreased student engagement with individual course readings. In the final chapter of "Consent, Violence, and Refusal," Caroline Godart also explores potential variation of goals and effects in creative work that depicts sexual violence. Exploring Abdellatif Kechiche's *Blue Is the Warmest Color*, Godart simultaneously attends to the director's alleged abusive treatment of the young actresses on set, along with the filmic gaze that denies difference, and recognizes the film's occasionally profound approach to alterity in its scenes that do not depict sex. Ultimately, Godart draws on the work of Luce Irigaray to call for a mode of respect for alterity that allows the other to explore who she is and what she wants and thus gain the capacity to say yes to her own needs and desires.

The final section, "Consent, Personhood, and Property," examines the contractual nature of consent, the ways that consent divides—and blurs the division—between persons and possessions. Exploring the tense and often oxymoronic relationship between persons and property, this section investigates how property is framed in relation to personhood through the locus of consent. Validated through the construction of self-as-property, consent is also at times elided, at times conditionally validated in dispersing this property to others through economic relations of labour, corporatized biomedicine, and technological extensions of the self. The chapters in this section consider the intersections of consent formations, property, and the person as they relate to labour and capital, citizenship, social media, biomedicine, disability, and the ethics of artistic production.

Consent and (self-)ownership mobilize the work of the third section of *Querying Consent*, particularly its first three chapters. Drew Danielle Belsky explores the ethics of artworks that incorporate marginalized and disabled participants as informants and/or material, but not as artists or implied audiences. In problematizing the tendency of artists engaged in such projects to mobilize social scientific discourses while remaining unbeholden to the ethical and legal requirements of social science disciplines, Belsky's chapter seeks to reformulate how informed and participatory consent are enacted in both the social sciences and the arts. Further exploring the intersection of self-ownership and artistic production, Annie Pfeifer's chapter draws parallels between Henry James's representation of hoarding in his writing and his attempts to control his work postpublication, both editorially and materially. With attention to James's 1909 attempt to burn his papers and manuscripts, Pfeifer frames hoarding as a type of possession that circumvents the standard consensual, contractual relationship between individuals and private property. While hoarding is often read as marking the hoarder's distance from competent personhood, Pfeifer reads the hoarder as a figure who challenges social and economic norms by operating outside of any framework of consent. Graham Potts's chapter investigates similar issues of media participation and (self-)ownership as they pertain to biomedicine and digital identity. Investigating the contradictions that emerge in projects of biodigital populations management, in which subjects attempt to control risk through participating in personalized digital genetic mapping while simultaneously ceding the right to their genetic information to private medical corporations, Potts questions the possibility for consensual liberal digital citizenship.

Questions of citizenship, self-ownership, and consent are the central concerns of the final two chapters in "Consent, Personhood, and Property." Analyzing Pfizer's notoriously procedurally flawed trial of the drug Trovan in Nigeria, Matthias Rudolf's chapter positions the capitalization of consent as fundamental not only to trials for new drugs, which become profitable insofar as they are able to generate consent that can lead to the drug's approval, but to capitalism itself. The fundamental inequalities between the (largely illiterate) trial subjects and those soliciting their consent, Rudolf argues, mark not only the failure to obtain legitimate consent in the instance of the drug trial itself but consent's fundamental fictionality. Meanwhile, Victoria Olwell's chapter explores the construction of subjects unable to formally enact such self-mastery. Like Pfeifer, Olwell turns to Henry James, examining his representation of the construction of the "minority" of girls. Through investigating the centrality of the developmental psychological narrative of consent to James's *What Maisie Knew*, Olwell elucidates how raising the age of sexual consent for girls in both the United States and the United Kingdom at the turn of the twentieth century also served to cement the exclusion of girls from civic processes predicated on the ability to consent.

The distinctly utilitarian focus of most engagements with consent—both popular and critical—makes sense given the contexts in which consent springs to public consciousness as well as the stakes when consent interactions go (deliberately or inadvertently) wrong. Indeed, many of the chapters in *Querying Consent* are concerned in part with these pragmatic elements (e.g., What effect does it have on our reading of a film if we know the director treated actors abusively? What responsibilities pertaining to consent accompany using members of marginalized groups as material for our artistic practices?). And yet, when we think consent only or primarily through the pragmatic lens of its utilitarian function, we both take for granted many of the social underpinnings that subtend the very notion of consent and abdicate a rich and vital area of intellectual inquiry. Our contributors refuse to approach consent purely as a pragmatic or utilitarian concern. Rather, they enter and open avenues of critical inquiry made pressing by consent's implication in constructions of the subject, agency, the civil, and property, not to mention the social itself. As consent becomes more and more a focus of public and intellectual discourse, it is increasingly imperative that its critical implications receive the serious inquiry they deserve. And so, querying not only what consent protects but what it enables, not only the measures of acceptance and refusal, but also what can be consented to and who can consent, we engage the subject of consent.

WORKS CITED

Kant, Immanuel. *Critique of Practical Reason.* Translated by Werner S. Pluhar, Hackett, 2002.

Lorde, Audre. "The Master's Tools Will Never Dismantle the Master's House." *Sister Outsider: Essays and Speeches,* Crossing, 2007, pp. 110–114.

MacKinnon, Rebecca. *Consent of the Networked: The Worldwide Struggle for Internet Freedom.* Basic Books, 2013.

Regina v. Brown et al., 1 AC 212. United Kingdom House of Lords. 1992. *United Kingdom House of Lords Decisions.* Bailii.

Scarry, Elaine. "Consent and the Body: Injury, Departure, and Desire." *New Literary History,* vol. 21, no. 4, 1990, pp. 867–896.

PART 1 CONSENT, POWER, AND AGENCY

1 · CONSENT, COMMAND, CONFESSION

KARMEN MACKENDRICK

I have many strange confessions to make, obviously—I don't necessarily want to make them, either. So I make them in a dark tongue, in the confusion of speech. This is how I defer them.

—Carl Watson, "To Be Blessed with a
Nightmare of Angels," in *Ritual Sex*

I'm convinced we're all voyeurs. We want to know secrets, we want to know what goes on behind those windows.

—David Lynch

Consent sets boundaries: I consent to *this* but withhold consent from *that*; I consent to *x* only on condition *y*. It requires knowledge: I can only really be said to consent when I am fully informed as to what is at issue and when I understand that information and its context. And that requires a rational subject: children or others with limited understanding are often unable to consent properly, so too those whose exposure to alternatives is too limited.

These are fairly commonsensical notions. What would it mean, though, if one consented to something improper and out of bounds? Especially, what would it mean if one were to consent to what makes problematic the boundaries of the very self that gives that consent? With those questions in mind, I explore here the workings of the will as it consents to both verbal and visual display beyond the bounds of propriety—or comfort—into the realm of humiliation. Outside the proper limits, we find marginal and abject pleasures and the complexity of claiming them without denying their humiliating character.[1] Wayne Koestenbaum happily declares, "I'm glad to belong to a community, however scattered, of souls who like to see rules (of linguistic propriety, of sexual propriety) turned upside down" (48). As this hints, among the best places to find twists in the will are the perverse pleasures of sex—and, I would add, the surprisingly similar pleasures of religion.

A common complaint against such pleasures as those involving submission, pain, or humiliation is that they can belong only to those who start out in sturdy, comfortable ego states—those for whom danger, obedience, or self-display that is not under one's own control is an *exception*. (Think, for instance, of the stereotype of the CEO as client of the dominatrix.) A mode of resistance or transgression that can only be undertaken by the relatively privileged would not be very subversive at all. However, as Kent Brintnall has pointed out, the desire for a stable and coherent self is strongly socially valorized, and as long as this is so, willing against that self—thus asserting the value of impropriety and self-loss, however temporary—is a resistant act.[2]

Let me begin with consent to verbal revelation beyond the bounds of propriety. The classical paradigm of verbal exhibition is the monastic practice of confession, which works to move the mysterious body toward the apparent clarity of speaking. The monastic abbot, who instructs and interprets the flesh, must also draw it into words, particularly where words emerge reluctantly. Often this reluctance is linked to something sexual; for instance, early monastic instruction is deeply concerned with "nocturnal pollution," knowledge of which one could and probably would wish to keep to oneself. One is compelled to tell what exceeds both modesty and the will, to tell of the flesh where it seems to be most clearly in excess of "mind" while retaining, and implicating, "self." The practice of confession moves on from the monastery to be taken up by psychoanalysis, social media, and those modes of entertainment that thrive on suggestions of scandal.

Throughout its history, confession has tended to pull itself apart in search of something elusive. As Virginia Burrus writes, "The act of confession is . . . at once assertive and yielding. . . . It is neither simply coerced nor simply voluntary but rather sits necessarily on the border of what is coerced and what is offered freely. . . . One must want, at least a little, to be broken, to be exposed, or the confession is sterile: it makes no truth. . . . One must also resist, at least a little, being overcome by this desire, or the confession, rendered glib by the promise of cheap grace, is equally fruitless" (3). This description draws our attention to a peculiarity of consent: we do not speak of consenting to what we would have done anyway. The very notion requires some resistance. Almost always, our attention is on the yielding, or even assertive, part of consent. Interesting things happen when we emphasize the resistant element as well. It would seem that the abbot or analyst or talk-show host has power, the monk or analysand or guest only the ability to consent or withdraw. But here we may draw on two well-known points made by Michel Foucault. First, power and resistance are mutually dependent (power exists only with pushback, and resistance, a power of its own, meets any imposition of power). There is, then, a necessarily double will about telling what might have been kept in silence. Michel de Certeau writes, "The secret localizes the confrontation between a *will to know* and a *will to conceal*" (98, italics in original). The secret stretches itself between hiding and revelation, between two incompatible desires—both within subjects and across them. And second, confession begins as a mode not only of self-revelation but of self-construction (the one who confesses both creates and resists the "internal" subject whose fleshly "truth" must be "externalized"). "Humiliation happens only in relation," Koestenbaum notes (11). So too does consent, and the two may tangle together.

Related to the tense pleasures of the confessional voice are those of seeing and being seen. There are plenty of exhibitionists and voyeurs who derive pleasure from the nonconsensual triumph of overriding another's will; my concern here is only the more complex case of at least slightly resisted display directed toward those who desire to see more than is held to be proper. Shame is exposure, one way or another. And the will to expose, to see and hear all the way into the psyche of the flesh, all the way into and under not just the clothing but the skin, is the will to know more of the body—to know its secrets.

In early optical theory, there is a mutual implication of seer and seen. Vision is understood to be neither purely active nor passive; it is an exchange moving across and between (Glick et al. 373–374). Rather than maintaining a disinterested aesthetic distance, vision entails a double penetration—all the more so before the flesh. Though it does not continue in physics, this idea reappears in psychoanalysis with Lacan, for whom gazing is at once anxious and pleasurable, active and passive: the object seen, without ceasing to be an object, nonetheless gazes back, tells me of my self (it makes me self-conscious). Lacan directly associates this reversible gaze with both the voyeuristic will to see and the exhibitionistic will to be seen (181–183).

This means that the demanding gaze seeks not only to see the improper nude body or to peer into the body's orifices and openings but also to reverse and thereby double the gaze. Bill Burgwinkle and Cary Howie write in *Sanctity and Pornography in the Middle Ages*, "In the case of the ecstatic or pornographic body, . . . we are encouraged to view the image . . . using a kind of surgical gaze that tries to touch the surface or even invade it, all with the intent of opening up the viewer him- or herself to potential invasion" (20).

Page duBois argues that "the logic . . . of some of our inherited beliefs about truth leads almost inevitably to conceiving of the body of the other as the site from which truth can be produced, and to using violence if necessary to extract that truth" (6). From the earliest traditions of Western thought, truth is created *as exposed*—we have to tear it out of matter, and especially out of bodies. Against this violent truth-seeking, mutual consent to exposure insists upon the undisplayable secrets of flesh, against the notion that secrets can all be told or seen. Rather than working to pin down a decisive truth, we may consent to seek both the satisfaction of knowing what can be told or seen and our own frustration at knowledge's necessary incompleteness. This desire is doubled; both seeing and hearing are reversible processes: the self is constructed in revealing confessionally what it is and has been; the penetrative gaze seeks to see within itself. To see most clearly, to hear in the greatest detail, we seek to unveil, to strip bare, even to get beneath the concealment of skin, to ask after the purity of the secretive soul. In all this seeking, we resist what shames us even when we masochistically seek it out.

To make sense of these odd claims about knowing, unknowing, and secrecy, let me offer a few examples from the intersecting annals of sanctity and perversity. Saintly flesh is sometimes revealed in ascetic nudity (such as that of desert saints who cannot be bothered with such frivolities as clothing), sometimes as the body is stripped in a step toward martyrdom. Early ascetics court nudity *for* its shamefulness, which necessarily leads them to resist it. Their nudity, easily seen as licentious by their opponents, is also an act of dispossession, less of clothing than of self-possession. It is an impropriety and the loss of a boundary. Asceticism seeks some truth of corporeality—a truth that sustains the will to know precisely by being unfindable. The abyss that gazes back seems always to be just one layer further in.

Burrus recounts a story strikingly reminiscent of a popular trope in humiliation pornography, in which the second-century monk Serapion "tests" the humility of a virginal devotee to God. First he insists that she appear in public, then that she disrobe and walk through the city. "When she protests that others will think her 'insane and demon-ridden,' he asks why she should care. She pleads with him: 'if you wish anything else, I will do it; for I do not boast that I have come to this point' (37.15). Serapion again translates her apparent modesty into a manifestation of pride, claiming that she considers herself 'more pious than others' . . . (37.16)" (Burrus 92).[3]

Like pornography, hagiography does not exactly report reality, but in their exaggeration and improbability, both give us a good sense of a wishful collective imaginary, and what we find writ large there hints at the hopes and pleasures of the lowercase "everyday." There are other saints' tales that make the parallel evident. One of my favorites, Angela of Foligno, writes that she "was plunged into an abyss of deep humility. . . . I saw so clearly the superabundance of my malice, iniquity, and sins that it seemed impossible for me to disclose them and make them known. . . . I was not ashamed, however, to confess in front of everyone all the sins I had committed. I even enjoyed imagining how I could make public my iniquities, hypocrisies, and sins. I wanted to parade naked through towns and public squares with pieces of meat and fish hanging from my neck and to proclaim: 'Behold the lowest of women, full of malice and deceit, stinking with every vice and evil'" (Angela of Foligno 219). Angela has no hesitation about public nudity but finds it not humiliating *enough*. She wants to make visible and public the sins that seem impossible to disclose, not to shame others, but to delight in their sneers. Such is the desire that Jean Baudrillard calls "the obscenity of the visible . . . obscenity of what no longer has any secret, of what dissolves completely in information and communication" (131). This is opposed to an older obscenity of the "hidden, repressed, forbidden, or obscure" (131). New obscenity would put an end to the secret, publicizing it at the very surface of the skin. give way to the seductive, or the new obscenity to the old: the body's secrets are stubborn. Angela might enjoy imagining her walk of shame, but as a mechanism of revelation, it remains imperfect.

The link of the secret to the shameful is an ancient one. What characterized the rites of ancient mystery religions was esotericism: they were not to be revealed to the uninitiated. This, of course, made many people want to know them. Among many exemplary passages, allow me to cite a particularly delightful instance from Tertullian about the Valentinians—of whom, historically speaking, it is not remotely true:

> These individuals care about nothing more than to conceal what they teach. . . . The fact that they keep silent about these mysteries makes them an object of shame. Consequently the mystagogues make entry difficult and perform long initiation rites before they accept the devotee; they put him on probation for five years in order to increase his anticipation by suspense and in this manner cause the awesomeness of their rites to match the desire which has been elicited. Their duty of secrecy is a natural consequence; they guard closely what they are finally to reveal. Then—the entire godhead of the sanctuary, the object of devoted sighs, the secret signed on all tongues: the image of a penis (ch. 1).

Tertullian's link of secrecy to shame to body is intriguing because it is not shame that silences but secrecy that makes the mysteries shameful. For all his errors about the Valentinians, Tertullian is on to something regarding shame and its mysteries. Seeking the unknowable through the forbidden, improper, obscene, or scandalous is not a fallacious conflation but a mystery incarnate in the flesh—even if not necessarily in the image of the penis, as such. The flesh is itself mysterious, not the veil over some greater mystery; it is with a sense of both sacrality and shame that we keep it under wraps.

The perverse, mystery-seeking gaze is greedy, refusing to stop at a fixed or confined truth, demanding further openings and revelations. In this refusal, in this demand for infinitude in the finite, the double character of the sacred is revealed. As Collette Peignot writes in "Story of a Little Girl," "Life soon managed to oscillate between these two poles: one sacred, venerated, which must be exhibited . . . ; the other dirty, shameful, which must not be named. Both more mysterious, more appealing, more intense than a bleak and unchanging life" (11). When the sacred is exhibited, it becomes the shameful, which must by definition be hidden (again), and so the oscillation continues, and so the desire demands.

The desire to know, to see the real secret beneath the skin, remains unsatisfied. By it, our conception of consent as something that takes place more or less contractually between clearly defined individual subjects is made problematic. We seem to have a powerful abbot, judge, or dominant who demands and seeks out truth, remaining nonetheless unsatisfied with what can be known. This demand seems to be imposed on the monk, saint, masochist, or submissive, who displays that limited truth reluctantly. But I propose that the double will to know and to question moves as consent does, across both of them, such that the propriety not only of their questions and answers, their removals and displays, their openings and peerings but even of their selves becomes a problem and that it is this to which they have consented, implicitly, in entering into their curious arrangements.

The inquisition may even open the skin itself—both through its given orifices and through created cuts. Saints slash or blister their skin, cut it open with whips or with chains bound around the flesh so long that the skin grows over them. Hagiographic depictions of asceticism can become pornographically detailed, while more overtly pornographic depictions and erotic practices of humiliation focus frequently upon the bodies' orifices—not always the expected ones—and upon opening them as widely as possible, as if to confess the interior of the body. Consider not just the spread legs of even the most vanilla pornography but such imagistic practices as ass gaping or nostril hooks too.

Shame, as Eve Kosofsky Sedgwick memorably points out (drawing upon the work of early affect theorist Silvan Tompkins), tends to contagion.[4] It also tends to reversibility, as Koestenbaum tells us: "The person doing the humiliation— aggressor, tyrant, bully, monolith, petty soldier, priest, poet—is humiliated by the act. (Even Jesus knew how to dish it out: he told Mary, Mother of God, 'Woman, what have I to do with thee?') And so the humiliator (the instigator) is besmirched, reflexively, by the act—if only in the eyes of the victim and the witness" (9). In the eros of humiliation, shame must exceed this typical structure. If the crowd turns away, appalled, from Angela or the desert ascetic; if the gaze upon the naked, opened flesh is neither lascivious nor curious but embarrassed into the urge to cover the revealed body; if the confessor finally asks the confessee to be quiet, the pleasure cannot work. It is here that the complications of consent and command may emerge most clearly. As I mentioned briefly earlier, it is true that there are those, such as flashers, who take nonconsensual pleasure in a show, however false, of their own strength. Their pleasure disregards other pleasures. The abbot and the monk, the saint and the judge, the submissive whispering secrets, the saint or sub in full bodily display must instead increase both the easy desire (to conceal) and the difficult one (to show). *This* is what they consent to—not simply to overcoming or destroying one will, ignoring one side of an agreement, or denying any desire.

Confession and display risk disgust because they play with interiority and exteriority, risking their confusion, opening, voiding, and reclaiming the flesh. Nothing is in its proper place. Both the one who exhibits and the one who looks are trying, with the desperation of all impossible desires, to see and to show. To see the mystery, to show the secret: to know what cannot be known. The body attracts the gaze; ears listen to the answers that construct its "inner" life, eager hands strip it bare; assistive technologies and divine interventions alike serve to open it up—yet it eludes us. Beginning in consent, the questioning, probing parties to these activities exceed its very possibility. The urgent search for revelation reverses: in revealing the body, we seek to invite within us the mystery that the mystic, martyr, or masochist seems to know so surely within her own flesh, so that we can know it too—only to find that the seeming is no more than that; this knowing is only in the elusive manner of the mysterious. It is easier just to ignore it. But sometimes easy is simply too boring.

Consent between individual, responsible parties, properly obtained, exchanges information (it is informed). When what is exchanged goes beyond knowledge, it muddles the parties involved as well. When the parties and the informedness are problematized, so is the very meaning of consenting. We cannot both connect and remain within ourselves: "Beings, human beings, can only 'communicate'—live—outside of themselves," writes Georges Bataille. "And as they must 'communicate,' they must want this evil, defilement, that, placing being at risk in themselves renders both being and themselves penetrable to one another" (*On Nietzsche* 39).

Such communication is closer to our model of a communicable disease than to the simple transfer of data. Fully self-contained beings do not communicate; for communication, boundaries must be broken—but not all breaking is equal, as Bataille points out: "These burning courses only replace the isolated being if that being consents, if not to annihilation, at least to risk itself, and in the same movement, to risk others. . . . By destroying in myself, in others, the integrity of being, I open myself to communion" (*On Nietzsche* 40).

Consenting to this disruption, we may also feel disgust and horror, such as we feel at the gaping wound—not least where the impurity of disgust is tinged with desire. Bataille further declares, "So, what attracts desire in the being of flesh is not immediately the being, it is its wound: it is a point of rupture in the integrity of the body, . . . a wound that puts its integrity at stake, its rupture, which does not kill but desecrates" (*Unfinished* 29). But we know that, often as not, wounds will make us turn away. After all, points of rupture or leakage are widely linked to disgust. When we have not consented to their infliction, we are likely to be repulsed and horrified. Wholeness disrupted is interesting; the altogether broken is sad. But where there *is* tension between disruption and desire, the two pulls exist with one another. The speaker and the interrogator, the seer and the seen, struggle to bring into speech and visibility the secret that is too intimate and too immense, too deeply embodied, to be said or seen at all.

No confession is so thorough as to touch upon everything, and this incompleteness keeps secrets. Confession in the pastoral context is meant to contribute to the power of order and regulation, of discipline; this is the potential utility of it, a utility always exceeded by the untouchable, undisciplinable secret. Likewise, visible bodies are bodies that may be regimented—such is the infamous work of panoptical power. Yet in other contexts, being caught in the gaze, confessing to humiliation, telling an embarrassing tale of oneself "momentarily deactivates the disciplinary power of confession and turns isolation into something like a membership card" (Halperin and Traub, "Beyond" 38). Humiliating exposure has strange effects: it may form a subject or divide it from itself; it may isolate or invite into membership. It is most interesting when it does not move in a single direction.

There are aspects of ourselves that we actively isolate. Leon Wurmser, in one of the first important works on the affect of shame, writes, "The power sphere around a person resembles territory in animals. There is also an inner limit covering this intimate area that one does not want to show" (62). But sometimes, one both wants and does not and so consents to trying. Michael Warner similarly writes, "In shame my exposure has witnesses (even if imaginary or internalized), but being witnessed separates me, abjects me" (293). I am both publicized and isolated. I both agree and resist.

Shame results from exposure, but more specifically from infringement upon the concealed. Part of pride, perhaps as distinguished from mere self-display, is that it may occur in the very fact of not sharing, in maintaining the Stoic dignity of the stiff upper lip. Wurmser continues, "If one person crosses another's outer limits, he violates the other's integrity, social prestige, and power" (62). When we think well of ourselves, we would like public opinion to measure up; more dangerously, we might assume that it does so. We might try to hide what shames or embarrasses us. If we cannot, our pride suffers. It is hard to imagine anyone consenting to having that good self-opinion overturned.

Fortunately, matters are not always so simple. In "Sex, Shame, and Disability Identity," Tobin Siebers notes, "Shame is terrifying because it relies on public exposure: the etymology of 'shame' derives from a pre-Teutonic word that means 'to cover oneself,' covering being a natural expression of shame. But shame is also a sumptuous emotion. To stand out in public has its own delights. The feeling of shame, then, turns on the movement between the private and public realms" (205). Inside cuts through to outside; the outside peers all the way in. It is not just that shame may be one *or* the other, horrifying *or* sumptuous. It cuts both ways. Burrus writes, "Shame does not merely guard the boundary between the public and the private, the political and the personal, the inter- and intra-subjective, but also constantly traverses those boundaries—even very nearly dissolves them" (152). And she makes a vital connection: "This traversal—this near-dissolution—binds shame tightly to the erotic. If the embrace of the stigma of identity represents a conversion that takes place within shame, so too does the plunge into the abjection of flesh-and-soul that undoes identity" (152).

Power is tangled and reversible here, too tangled to belong to an individual. Neither a pact between subjects nor an opposition of subject to object, the power relations of consensual shaming unsettle the very terms. Each party makes use of the other, in a way; each is the other's object, in a way; but they begin in agreement, only gradually, and consensually, moving past consent's proper boundaries. Sean Connelly notes that Peignot's texts, under her pen name Laure, "exhibit the paradoxical power inherent to the subject *itself* as a site of power that is both given up and returned as in self-sacrifice. The political struggle *for* power in Laure's writings is, in other words, the struggle *of* power inherent in the condition of subjection. . . . The speaking subject of Laure's poetry is always, at least in part, beyond the law in submission to the law" (28). In cooperating more fully than the demand ever imagined, Laure as a perverse subject eludes any will that might think itself in command of hers—and, more deeply, eludes self-command or self-mastery as well, simply by that cooperation. Like ascetic and perverse wills more broadly, the will that thus consents is too strong for simplicity. While she seeks out deeper humiliations, Peignot's commentators and translators emphasize her pride, even "insolence"; her translator Jeanine Herman goes so far as to argue that it is salvific (ix).

Not every will is susceptible to such movement. Those with unassailable pride will avoid any downward push. Those who start with minimal pride might find humility without too much struggle; as William Ian Miller argues, "The defense against humiliation is . . . the fear of humiliation or perhaps, more subtly, it is humility" (147). He connects this claim explicitly to the Christian, not least monastic, discourse: "In their earlier histories both words were intimately connected to one style of Christian moral discourse until well into the eighteenth century, whereas only humility remains an active part of that discourse today" (147). Unlike "self-esteem" of the sort that holds that one is all-deserving by virtue of existing, pride is falsifiable. Miller continues, "Vanity begs for humiliation. . . . Humiliation depends on the deflation of pretension" (137). This suggests a realization that one's pride was falsely grounded.

Miller's generally rich text becomes a bit squeamish and avoidant on the topic of "what were once referred to as perversions" (we are not given a more contemporary term for them): "But the pretension being deflated in that upside-down sadistic world is different. It is not the unmerited claim to a higher social status in the moral and social world than one justifiably merits; rather, the claim of the torturer, the concentration camp guard, the ideologues of ethnic, racial, and religious genocide, is that the humanity of their victims is a pretense" (165). The conflation of perversions with this group ignores questions of will and consent—in which that very pretense may be put into play. Nonconsensual pleasures are one-sided, presenting little or no threat to the pleased subject; "humanity" insofar as it entails secure subjectivity belongs to that subject alone. Complex pleasures that begin in consent and become so intense as to problematize the boundaries of knowledge and subjectivity are first mutual and intersubjective but go on to challenge subjectivity altogether. In a sense, both kinds problematize humanity, but the ways in which they do so are so different that the resultant pleasure differs as well—and consent as a starting point is the heart of that distinction.

Wurmser, like Miller, is happy to uncomplicate matters by pathologizing. He writes, "The masochistic position is reexternalized . . . in the form of shame: 'I am ridiculed, mocked, despised, humiliated.' The sexual nature of all this is massively repressed. . . . The masochism itself, of course, . . . is a poor defense against intensely competitive, envious striving" (174–175). This too assumes a fundamental hostility in the relation of humiliation (or, for Wurmser, in masochism more broadly) that fails to account for its consensual variants by assuming that there can be no pleasure here.

Hungry for reversible seeing, touching, knowing, we seek the truth in repeated query, in stripped bodies, in opened flesh, in commanded confessions, as if we could find the mystery in the forbidden publicizing of skin, as if the interior were somehow a secret site and not simply another shifting and changing layer. In this very elusiveness, however, the body, always withdrawing its truth from even the most sadistically or lasciviously attentive gaze, the most persistent interrogation, is a revelation of mystery: not of the answer to the question, but of the infinite immanence of the question itself. All people by nature desire to know—but some people by nature desire to want to know, possibly even more. Some desire is too strong to be satisfied by satisfaction.

Howie and Burgwinkle remind us of the "medieval sense that visual penetration always goes both ways" (38). But this penetration runs into something, not quite a barrier, not even quite a deflection, but the nonvisible, the unsayable. Abjection is not simply what is displaced or out of place, but at its most intense, it is the troubling act and instance of the wholly unplaceable, of what refuses inside or out, of the remainder that is nonetheless the trace of myself.

Impossibility sustains the possible. Never there yet, we want more. Bataille suggests, "Maybe the desire to know has only one meaning: to serve as motive for the desire to question" (*Unfinished* 33). Incompletion is built into desire: when we want to know, it is in order to direct the next interrogative. Obviously this is not always true; if I ask for directions to the train station, I am unlikely to be grateful if I am led into an indefinite series of questions. But it does seem to be true of the more intense desires that especially interest Bataille and that are my subject here. By pulling upon what can be told and shown only against shame and resistance, we sense what we cannot see, what we do not hear, secrets of flesh that words and images cannot quite hold at all. Shame, like eros, crosses boundaries, outside to in and vice versa. Abjection, further, violates the policy against reentry, through the ears and eyes as much as through the mouth, and so we cross more boundaries, enter the sacred, or play a little bit harder.

What we seek to see and hear, through that urgent reversible double gaze, through hearing our voices pulled out of ourselves, is not the shame written, if not on the flesh, at least on a placard hung around the naked body. It is not the opened ass, the bowed and hooded head, the walk on the leash. We seek, rather, to make the resistant into the speakable, into the knowable and properly conceptualizable, not into this irritatingly slippery confrontation with what eludes us—and we know that this is impossible. We gaze avidly at, or avidly draw the gaze to, shame and remnants and the very interior of the flesh—and we know this too is impossible. We keep asking questions, keep pushing for what will refuse to yield and answer. Yet only further questions open. We depend on it: the desire to know, too, may be bored by satisfaction.

And the will to know is also the will to be known, to turn upon oneself as the object of knowledge: to be *worth* knowing and worth infinite query. The most shameful option is not to be exposed but to find oneself neither listened to nor looked at, uninteresting. The shame of exposure pales in relation to the shame of invisibility. J. Brooks Bouson, in *Embodied Shame*, describes a scene from Toni Morrison's *The Bluest Eye*: "In the vacant gaze of the white store owner, Mr. Yacobowski, Pecola senses racial contempt. 'He does not see her, because for him there is nothing to see'" (61). As Wurmser has it, "If it is appearance (exposure) that is central in shame, disappearance is the logical outcome of shame" (81). But it is not the case that shame can simply *cause* one to disappear; the failure of one's appearance to register in the first place can be more shameful than any appearing. "The two risks," Wurmser adds, "are to offer oneself and be proved unlovable, and to merge or to conquer by sight and expression and be proved helpless" (96). Avoidance of both risks, of an appearance that puts an end to the need to know more and of a disinterest that keeps knowledge from being desired, keeps pride pulling on shame, keeps the paradox open and alive: we desire both to be seen and to be invulnerable, to be unseeable and to be before the eyes of all, to fascinate listeners endlessly and to keep our shame a secret. Exhibitionism and voyeurism both direct the gaze to what is "inappropriate," to what is not conventionally given for seeing; confession gives to the ear what may only be whispered—or spoken under seal. They give a place to the out-of-place, the improper. In the face of shame, writes Burrus, "we both do and do not want to look" (14). And this double wanting is further complicated when we want to display what shames—and to keep the other from looking away. We want to display the shameful without shame's contagion. This demands that the viewer or listener consent to the display eagerly and with a willingness to be shameless before it. For this to be possible, the demands of desire must be especially strong.

"The *I*," writes Certeau, "appears in its dependency on the other. *I* cannot express itself except in the desire emanating from elsewhere. . . . *I* speaks only if it is awaited (or loved), which is the riskiest thing in the world" (187). This risk sustains a fine edge of anxiety, beyond that attending to the telling of flesh and of shame. But here too is the beauty of the secret's infinitude: there will always be more for the other to hear, more than I, even without withholding, could ever give. There is a promise given by those who demand to see and to hear and to abject: because theirs is an impossible desire, it will not turn away in disinterest.

Drawing upon Augustine, Burrus writes, "To receive a confession and thus claim to know another—to risk *acknowledging* another—is a hopeful extension of love in the face of the unverifiability of *veritas*. . . . Yet the point is not just that others have no way of verifying the actual state of one's heart or the true nature of one's intentions; one cannot know this with certainty oneself" (14). Even hesitation becomes a sign, the speaking voice resisting out of either willfulness or shame, out of the shameful impossibility of telling nothing but the truth. So too with uncovering, opening, the resistance not only of the hand and eye but of the orifice too. Struggling to give the truth of the self that it makes, speech under confessional interrogation is both the most intimate speaking (the stripped, the confessed, the humiliated, the shameful) and not intimate at all, because the I eludes, because the I stripped bare *is* no core of self but pure elusion: because there is no core, only the murmurous voice of no one, the secret of speaking. Where part of pleasure is in desire, the inexhaustibility and incompletion become themselves desirable. By them, consent is still more complicated: I agree knowing that the "I" who agrees is neither static nor permanent and will be other than the "I" continually emerging.

Humiliation involves a sort of monsterizing, an abjection, pushing to the margins what nonetheless remains at the heart of that "I," intensifying the gaze. The sacred, like the secret with which it is entangled, might appear to us as what is buried within but likewise as what has been pushed outside of the resealed self—as the abjected. It has no proper where, any more than it might be properly named—but it is invariably of the flesh.

In an introductory note to her work, Bataille describes Peignot as being "as inconceivable on a scale of real beings as a mythical being," because "she tore herself on the thorns with which she surrounded herself until becoming nothing but a wound" (Bataille, "Notes" 87). When there is nothing but a wound, we peer eagerly or anxiously or voyeuristically in, eager to see more—but there is only more wounding to see; the deepest secret conceals itself or refracts only onto more secrecy. L. Bernd Mattheus, who translated Peignot's work, writes of this passage, "Laure herself as something sacred, untouchable and incomprehensible?" (428). The untouchable is kept pure, uncontaminated by whatever contact might impart. But as Milo Sweedler's commentary on the same passage reminds us, the untouchables are also the lowest of castes. By their abjection, their exteriorization from the rest of human collectivity, impurities are removed and kept away. Purity and danger intersect in what is not touched, what may not be touched, what is kept carefully from touching—even if it is glimpsed through a wound. "The sacred is what cannot ultimately be touched, rejoined, repaired or redeemed," write Howie and Burgwinkle (39). Purity and danger both are perhaps at their strongest in what is never quite glimpsed any more than it is quite heard, in the mystery or the secret, in what remains after we would swear that all has been said, that there is nothing left to see, to say, to show. The *remainder*, a concept that philosophy takes up primarily from Julia Kristeva's discussion of abjection, is that which is within identity and representation and yet eludes them. At the heart, it attracts us as unknowable; at the limit, it repels us in its familiarity.

In the double penetration of the gaze, in the reversibility of shame, but also in the enticement of the desire to know as it is drawn to the unknowable, in the desire to escape the boundaries of the very self, humiliation entices without satiation, draws without the satisfaction of ending. There is no completion. We might suspect the secret of being simply absent—that is, of being a fiction, indeed a lie. But the absence of the secret is not of a sort that reduces it; rather, it is at the heart of its presence. No wonder we are so unsuccessful in pushing it away. "There is nothing secret, anywhere," writes Maurice Blanchot. "This is what the secret always says.—All the while not saying it. For, with the words 'there is' and 'nothing,' the enigma continues to rule, preventing settling and repose" (in Massie 47).[5] The mystery remains: in our remains, in our remainder—the site and nonsite of our abjection, our introjection of otherness, our extrajection of self, our own impossible divinity.

This does not mean that there is some *thing* that is the secret, whether that thing is a fact or a technique or an object; as Blanchot reminds us, that there is no thing is as enigmatic as any thing can be. It means rather, I suspect, that the secret has the character of retreat or regression, that it always pulls further away from the known (and thus beyond or behind those once-secrets that we have come to know); we cannot track it down because its pushed-away abjection only tugs it more tightly into the heart of ourselves and our knowing.

The secret, pure and dangerous, remains untouchable by senses or words. Secrecy is kept. But by its own elusion, secrecy also keeps desire. That secrecy must entangle itself with other modes of desire is so widespread a notion that the naughtiness of the confessional is an early pornographic commonplace (Burton xxi). This secret, inseparable from any said, is what we reach for most urgently in confession, interrogation, the search for the heights and depths of the sacred. And all speech desires, even speech barely exteriorized past resistance. Certeau declares, "This volition does not have speech for object. . . . It defines the act of speaking. It *is* what all speaking says: to say is to want" (175).

The secret that there is no secret—drawn to the flesh that speaks it—twists just enough to reveal the secret that there are always more secrets. All people by nature desire to know, but some people perversely desire to have that desire gratified, frustrated, and sustained. In the play between the unsayable and the not-to-be-said, the unshowable forbidden and the invisible secret, a mystery is drawn out, and it draws us in, in a reversible and no longer perfectly closable opening. The secret would be lost, the silence broken, by the telling. Body displayed, flesh broken tells the very secret that it keeps. Against the production of the truth, we use its own will to knowledge. These pleasures allow us a quite unusual experience of consent: the knowing, informed, and agreeing subject is reminded of, and indeed consents to, its necessary obverse: the mystery, the beyond-knowing, the rupture of subjection, and the agreement to resistance itself.

NOTES

1. And we do want to deny that character. Even a subtle thinker like Wayne Koestenbaum declares, "Humiliation, if passed through the masochistic centrifuge, becomes joy, or uplift—all emotional dissonances resolved" (2). But it is precisely the irresolution, the dissonance sustained, that I think makes such pleasure intriguing—and powerful. (In fairness, Koestenbaum goes on to qualify this claim considerably.)

2. This is a point that Brintnall has raised in conference and symposia Q&A sessions as well as in private communication.

3. Cross-references are to Palladius.

4. See especially 33–38.

5. Massie slightly modifies Ann Smock's translation *The Writing of Disaster* (Blanchot 137).

WORKS CITED

Angela of Foligno, Saint. *Angela of Foligno: Complete Works*. Translated by Paul Lachance and Romana Guarnieri, Paulist, 1993.

Bataille, Georges. "Abjection and Miserable Forms." *More & Less*, translated by Yvonne Shafir, edited by Sylvere Lotringer, Semiotexte/Autonomedia, 1999, pp. 8–13.

———. "Notes." *Laure: The Collected Writings*, by Colette Peignot, translated by Jeanine Herman, City Lights Books, 1995, pp. 86–94.

———. *On Nietzsche*. Translated by Stuart Kendall, SUNY, 2016.

———. *The Unfinished System of Nonknowledge*. Translated by Michelle Kendall and Stuart Kendall, edited by Stuart Kendall, U of Minnesota P, 2001.

Baudrillard, Jean. "The Ecstasy of Communication." *The Anti-Aesthetic: Essays on Postmodern Culture*, edited by Hal Foster, Bay, 1995, pp. 126–134.

Bell, Rudolph. *Holy Anorexia*. U of Chicago P, 1987.

Blanchot, Maurice. *The Writing of the Disaster*. Translated by Anne Smock, U of Nebraska P, 1995.

Bouson, J. Brooks. *Embodied Shame: Uncovering Female Shame in Contemporary Women's Writings*. SUNY, 2009.

Burgwinkle, William, and Cary Howie. *Sanctity and Pornography in the Medieval Culture: On the Verge*. Manchester UP, 2010.

Burrus, Virginia. *Saving Shame: Martyrs, Saints, and Other Abject Subjects*. U of Pennsylvania P, 2007.

Burton, Richard D. E. *Holy Tears, Holy Blood: Women, Catholicism, and the Culture of Suffering in France, 1840–1970*. Cornell UP, 2004.

Certeau, Michel de. *The Mystic Fable, vol. 1: The Sixteenth and Seventeenth Centuries*. Translated by Michael B. Smith, U of Chicago P, 1995.

Connolly, Sean. "Laure's War: Selfhood and Sacrifice in Colette Peignot." *French Forum*, vol. 35, no. 1, winter 2010, pp. 17–37.

Derrida, Jacques. *The Animal That Therefore I Am*. Translated by David Wills, edited by Marie-Louise Mallet, Fordham UP, 2008.

duBois, Page. *Torture and Truth*. Routledge, 1991.

Glick, Thomas F., et al. *Medieval Science, Technology and Medicine: An Encyclopedia*. Routledge, 2005.

Halperin, David M., and Valerie Traub. "Beyond Gay Pride." *Gay Shame*, Halperin and Traub, pp. 3–40.

———, editors. *Gay Shame*. U of Chicago P, 2009.

Herman, Jeanine. Introduction. *Laure: The Collected Writings*, by Colette Peignot, translated by Jeanine Herman, City Lights Books, 1995, pp. vii–ix.

Kelly, Daniel. *Yuck! The Nature and Moral Significance of Disgust*. MIT, 2011.

Koestenbaum, Wayne. *Humiliation*. Macmillan, 2011.

Lacan, Jacques. "The Partial Drive and Its Circuit." *Four Fundamental Concepts of Psychoanalysis*, translated by Alan Sheridan, edited by Jacques-Alain Miller, W. W. Norton, 1998, pp. 174–186.

Massie, Pascal. "The Secret and the Neuter: On Heidegger and Blanchot." *Research in Phenomenology*, vol. 37, no. 1, 2007, pp. 32–55.

Mattheus, L. Bernd. *Georges Bataille: Eine Thanatographie*. Matthes & Seitz, 1984.

Miller, William Ian. *Humiliation: And Other Essays on Honor, Social Discomfort, and Violence*. Cornell UP, 1995.

Palladius. *Lausiac History*. Translated by Robert T. Meyer, Newman, 1964.

Peignot, Colette. *Laure: The Collected Writings*. Translated by Jeanine Herman, City Lights Books, 1995.

———. "Story of a Little Girl." *Laure: The Collected Writings*, by Colette Peignot, translated by Jeanine Herman, City Lights Books, pp. 1–36.

Sedgwick, Eve Kosofsky. *Touching Feeling: Affect, Pedagogy, Performativity*. Duke UP, 2003.

Siebers, Tobin. "Sex, Shame, and Disability Identity: With Reference to Mark O'Brien." Halperin and Traub, pp. 201–218.

Tertullian. "Tertulliani Adversus Valentinianos." Translated by Mark T. Riley, 1971, *Gnostic Society Library*, gnosis.org/library/ter_val_riley.htm.

Thompson, Anne B. E., et al. "The Life of St. Thais: Introduction." *Saints' Lives in Middle English Collections*, edited by Anne B. E. Thompson, Robert K. Upchurch, and Gordon Whatley, Medieval Institute Publications, 2004, *Robbins Library Digital Projects*, University of Rochester, d.lib.rochester.edu/teams/text/whatley-saints-lives-in-middle-english-collections-life-of-saint-thais-introduction.

Warner, Michael. "The Pleasures and Dangers of Shame." Halperin and Traub, pp. 83–96.

Wurmser, Leon. *The Mask of Shame*. Johns Hopkins UP, 1981.

2 · THE GENDER OF CONSENT IN PATMORE, HOPKINS, AND MARIE LATASTE

AMANDA PAXTON

In Victorian England, questions of consent were often questions of gender. Although popular discourse contrasted ideals of genteel middle-class British domesticity with Orientalized images of concubines subjugated within "seraglios,"[1] the standing allotted to married women under English common law led some nineteenth-century critics to describe marriage as its own type of domestic thralldom.[2] For most of the nineteenth century, a married woman was denied legal personhood, her property and body being subsumed under the legal protection and identity of her husband in a system known as coverture, dating from medieval common law. Under coverture, a woman's consent to marriage effectively transferred her control over her property and body to her husband. As William Blackstone defined it in his *Commentaries on the Laws of England*, coverture requires that "the very being or legal existence of the woman is suspended during the marriage, or at least incorporated and consolidated into that of the husband" (441).[3] Even after the Married Women's Property Acts of 1870 and 1882 allowed married women in England the right to own property and earnings, their rights to bodily autonomy remained contested. Due to a marital exemption governing sexual relations, a woman was legally unable to withhold consent to sex with her husband.[4]

The system received criticism from observers such as women's rights advocate Annie Besant, who noted that coverture leaves wives with "no power to consent" to, or resist, any incursion on their property or bodily integrity (11). Nonetheless, coverture retained a cultural currency not only from its historical tenure but also from a concurrent claim in Christian theology that depicted earthly marriage as a reflection of the soul's union with the divine: under this model, God is the Bridegroom, the soul the bride. Within this system of analogy, the consolidation of a woman's identity into that of her husband becomes a natural reflection of the divine order in which the soul surrenders to God, just as the Virgin Mary consents to God's will that she become the mother of Jesus. It does not take much to find echoes of coverture in Anglican priest and poet John Keble's call for the human soul to submit "to her immortal Spouse and King, / How He should rule, and she with full desire approve" (77).

Two Victorian poets whose works explore the tensions surrounding Christian nuptialism's spiritualized coverture are Coventry Patmore (1823–1896) and Gerard Manley Hopkins (1844–1889), Catholic converts who shared a lengthy correspondence. Patmore and Hopkins both figure the relationship of the divine and the individual as a marital bond. Whereas Patmore's divine marriage concurs with conventional Victorian codes that allot all rights to a woman's body to her husband and nullify a wife's capacity for consent, Hopkins's takes a more complex, relational view that posits consent as being continuously necessary within the union. The kernel of difference between the two models can be understood through a mystic whose writing found a notable Victorian Catholic readership and profoundly influenced both poets: nineteenth-century French lay sister Marie Lataste (1822–1847), whose memoirs and letters were first published in French in 1862 and whose biography appeared in English in 1877. Her work proves crucial to differentiating how each man figures the capacity for an individual soul to consent to erotic mystical union and the extent to which their respective theorizations of divine marriage reinforce or challenge the norms governing legal marriage.

The visions involving the Virgin Mary that Lataste recounts in her memoirs fascinate both Patmore and Hopkins. Patmore shares Lataste's interest in Mary as a cavity necessarily available to masculinized spiritual colonization. In his 1877 collection of odes, *The Unknown Eros*, he allegorizes the bond between the Christian God and humanity as a marriage between the classical personages Eros and Psyche. The relationship turns on the vacancy of Psyche and its reflection of the nothingness of the Virgin, both women serving as representatives of humanity's feminized position in relation to the masculinized divine. In both cases, feminine subjectivity is refused in the marriage bond, negating the issue of consent. Conversely, Hopkins takes as his guiding current Lataste's focus on grace, the Christian doctrine concerning the potential of individual will to work in tandem with divine will. Like Patmore, Hopkins often envisions a gendered relationship between a masculinized god and a feminized soul. Hopkins, however, finds inspiration in Lataste's writings about libidinally charged consent, the "sigh of desire" required from the individual in order to receive the pleasures and pains of the divine. The now-obscure French mystic presents a fulcrum by which to measure these two theological models and to shed light on both conservative and unexpectedly radical modes of theorizing consent within nineteenth-century Catholic discourse.

PATMORE'S CELESTIAL CONCUBINES

Patmore is now primarily associated with his poem *The Angel in the House*, the first book of which appeared in 1854, the second in 1858. An attempt to voice the spiritual majesty that Patmore identified in marital love, the verse narrative depicts the marriage between the characters Honoria and Felix. The solemn centrality of marriage to Patmore's vision of the universe is reflected in the lines "The nuptial contrasts are the poles / On which the heavenly spheres revolve" (26); today, however, the poem is largely remembered for its saccharine depictions of domesticity and its preternaturally self-sacrificing heroine.[5] Writers such as John Ruskin, Robert Browning, Dante Gabriel Rossetti, and Alfred Lord Tennyson admired the book, with the latter congratulating Patmore on having written "a poem which has a fair chance of immortality" (qtd. Champneys 1:165). More than 250,000 copies had been purchased by the time of Patmore's death (Heideman 181). In 1862, Patmore's first wife, author Emily Augusta Andrews (pseud. "Mrs. Motherly"), who reportedly provided the inspiration for Honoria, died of tuberculosis. Two years later, the poet would join other Victorian writers such as Aubrey de Vere and Alice Meynell in converting to Roman Catholicism and would marry Marianne Caroline Byles (1822–1880), a wealthy Catholic convert.

With Patmore's conversion came what superficially resembles a new brand of poetry: *The Unknown Eros*, issued in 1877.[6] Far from the trite tetrameter of *The Angel*, the metrically complex odes of *The Unknown Eros* were intended to move beyond *The Angel*'s preoccupation with earthly Protestant marriage to the heavenly marriage between God and the soul, figured as the relationship between the central characters, the classical god Eros and human Psyche. *The Unknown Eros* won Patmore some favour from a small group of Catholic aficionados including Lionel Johnson, Alice Meynell, Francis Thompson, and Aubrey de Vere, but its obscure style and imagery left most readers confounded.[7]

Despite the stylistic differences between *The Angel* and *The Unknown Eros*, the gendered dynamics within Patmore's depictions of marriage remain similar, his conversion notwithstanding. J. C. Reid notes that, whether writing as a Protestant or a Catholic, "Patmore had always in mind the supernatural experience which runs through and beyond marriage" and that the change from the earlier text to the later is one not of philosophy but of "tone and emphasis" (167). The theological vision underlying both texts finds its basis in marriage's centrality to Patmore's understanding of metaphysical truths, seen in his claim that "all knowledge, worthy of the name, is nuptial knowledge" (*Rod* 65). For Patmore, marital union constituted the supreme analogy by which humanity could understand the cosmos. First, heteronormative Victorian marriage contained a gender duality that aligned with Patmore's own patriarchal metaphysical gender hierarchy. Second, the feminization of matter in his cosmic architecture rendered the mystery of Christian Incarnationalism—the doctrine that Jesus is a divine being born of a human woman—apprehensible through the metaphor of a marital contract between God and Mary, the mother of Jesus. The fascination with the body, marital sexuality, and Incarnationalism leads Patmore to an equal captivation with Marianism, the Christian devotion to the Virgin Mother, a focus that he articulates alternately directly and tacitly. As the mother of Jesus, Mary becomes a symbol of flesh, womanhood, and matter in Patmore's theology. His 1895 collection of aphorisms and meditations, *The Rod, the Root, and the Flower*, exposes this metaphysical model: "God is the great, positive Magnet of the Universe, and whatever, in the Universe, aspires to approach Him must assume the negative, the feminine, or passive and receptive aspect. He repels and rejects His own primary aspect. He says to His own: 'Thy Maker is thy Husband'" (118). Equally, for Patmore the metaphor is never far removed from marriage's status as a legal agreement: an ode in the 1877 collection detailing the coupling of the first man and woman in the Garden of Eden is tellingly called "The Contract."

In spite of his apparent radicalism in championing sexuality as a reflection of metaphysical truths (rather than an indicator of humanity's fallen nature), Patmore insists on legitimizing sexuality through the socially sanctioned institution of heterosexual marriage. His determination reaches levels of improbability in the final ode in *The Unknown Eros*, in which the bond between God and the Virgin Mother is described in terms befitting a Victorian domestic frieze (or perhaps more appropriately, a scene from *The Angel*): theirs is an "ever seal'd wedlock so conjoint with bliss," and the divine is said to enjoy the "married smile" of his spouse, Mary (206, 207).

Similar to the marriage contract in Victorian England, Patmore's metaphysical marriage implies a relationship between unequal parties. In fact, many of the inequalities found in the legal formulation of marriage arise in his writing; specifically, both *The Angel* and *The Unknown Eros* imbue marital union with a gendered dynamic predicated on a spiritualized coverture in which the female partner is subsumed into the identity of the male, her right to consent nullified, her identity and will dissolved into his. Notably, a scene in *The Angel* in which Honoria accepts Felix's marriage proposal is titled "The Abdication," and is marked by the diminishment of the heroine from the status of "queen" to "pet fawn by hunters hurt" (158, 159). Whereas the unmarried woman maintains her right to determine whether or not to accept her suitor, the moment of her acceptance diminishes her status into nonhuman property.

The depiction of earthly marriage as a metaphysical analogy constitutes a central rhetorical trope in *The Angel*. However, when he turns in *The Unknown Eros* to representing marital union *with* the divine, Patmore joins a Catholic tradition in which such depictions are commonplace.[8] Specifically, Frederick Page proposes that the preoccupation with the Virgin Mary in the 1877 edition of *The Unknown Eros* might be attributed to Patmore's reading of Lataste. In an undated note collected in his memoirs, Patmore writes, "I am just now reading the Life of a peasant girl, Marie Lataste, who died only a few years ago. Her life was all grace and miracle, and her writings full of living sanctity and vigorous perceptions of things hidden to the wise" (qtd. in Champneys 2:80). Although it is unclear when exactly Patmore read Lataste's memoirs, there is indeed a theological resemblance between the thinkers, particularly their Mariology, the theological study of the Virgin. This likeness plays a significant role in Patmore's figuration of consent within the divine marriage.

Born in Mimbaste, a village in Landes, Lataste came from a modest background and had little education. In 1844, after years of visions in which she reported seeing Christ in the flesh on her church altar, she joined the Society of the Sacred Heart as a lay sister. The vividness of her mystical accounts led her spiritual director, Father Pierre Darbins, to collect, edit, and publish her memoirs, reflections, and letters in 1862, issued in a three-volume edition titled *La Vie et les oeuvres de Marie Lataste*. In 1877, an English account of Lataste's life was published, followed by translations of her meditations and letters, the third and last volume appearing in 1893. Lataste's memoirs of her visionary encounters with Christ enjoyed what Christopher Devlin calls "discreet popularity in Catholic literary and religious circles" in France and England (325). A review of the French edition of her work in *The Dublin Review* praised her "humility, her obedience, and, which was painfully tried, her dread of all illusion" (Rev. of *La Vie* 233). Indeed, her name had become recognizable enough to serve as a talisman in England in 1877, when the preface to a new edition of Julian of Norwich's *Revelations* included a respectful comparison between the two mystics (Collins xx).

Some controversy exists as to the extent of Lataste's influence on Patmore's work. Page suggests that Lataste provided the inspiration for Psyche in *The Unknown Eros* (125), whereas J. C. Reid notes that "there is so little in her writings which may not be found in St Thomas Aquinas, St Augustine and St Bernard, that it is difficult to agree that she played quite so important a part in the writing of *The Unknown Eros*" (103). Reid's skepticism as to Lataste's originality appears to be at least partly valid. A reviewer of an 1863 edition of her work asserts, "What has proceeded from the pen of this poor uninstructed girl seems quite beyond the unassisted powers of one so circumstanced" (Rev. of *La Vie* 233). If this seemed the case, it may have been because much of the material appeared to some readers to have been directly taken from Aquinas's *Summa Theologica* (Poulain 339, qtd. in Reid 104). Nonetheless, several elements of Lataste's theology certainly appealed to Patmore, not least of which was her immersion in a sensory and sensual mysticism that was contiguous with the tradition of medieval women's Christian mysticism.[9] Her depictions of Christ as a divine spouse (particularly in Book XI of the second volume of her writings) no doubt spoke to the poet's own nuptial philosophy.

A further element of similarity between Lataste and Patmore arises in Lataste's description of the Virgin Mary. In a key account of a conversation with Jesus concerning the Annunciation,[10] Lataste notes Jesus's explanation for Mary's reticence when approached by the angel Gabriel: "There was a struggle between her humility and the words of the celestial messenger" (184, qtd. in Devlin 331, my translation). At the moment that she was to be exalted as the mother of God, "Marie was thinking of nothing but humbling herself before God; and her humility left her speechless and she was confounded in her nothingness at the moment that God was going to exalt her through His divinity" (184, qtd. in Devlin 331, my translation).

Throughout *The Unknown Eros*, the nothingness inherent to Mary, and her humble acceptance thereof, enable her receptivity to divine presence: "Vast Nothingness of Self, fair female Twin / Of Fulness, sucking all God's glory in!" (204). Adrian Grafe terms this fixation on female emptiness "kenotic Marianism,"[11] which he describes as symptomatic of Patmore's theology: "The poet views the relations between God and man, culminating for Patmore in the Incarnation, and man's entire spiritual life, through the prism of this analogy, which works both ways" (105). To be sure, Patmore's Marianism is concerned with legitimating the body in a way that was at odds with much Victorian Christianity. Grafe's language, however, uses a misleading gender neutrality: by interpreting Patmore's kenotic Marianism in terms of its relevance to the relationship between God and man, he overlooks the specifically gendered underpinnings of the marital analogy, particularly within the system of coverture.

In Grafe's reading, Mary is a representative of humanity, her role as an empty vessel enabling the infusion of the divine into the mortal body. Importantly, however, her "nothingness" is an intrinsically gendered quality, evident in Patmore's attribution of it to Psyche, who is representative of humanity in divine marriage in many of the odes in *The Unknown Eros*. In the world of the odes, the "nothingness" of Psyche constitutes her "giddiest boast," the "charm for which he loved her most" (138). Psyche is compelled to accept the inequality of her partnership with Eros and to submit herself for use at the hands of the masculine god. Not to do so would be to violate the contract of mystical marriage, a contract that is unmistakably predicated on Victorian legal constructions.

Psyche's mother advises her that the terms of divine marriage require that the "nothingness" inherent in her own fallible humanity be made sexually available at all times to her divine husband:

All he ask'd, for making her all-blest,
Was that her nothingness always
Should yield such easy fee as frank to play
Or sleep delighted in her Monarch's breast[.] (138)

In somewhat puzzling phrasing, "nothingness" appears to be imbued with some kind of will, its capacity to "yield" to the caresses of the divine implying a corresponding ability not to yield. The implied power to withhold consent, however, is negated by the warning that follows, in which Psyche's mother invokes threats of celestial litigation:

What if this reed,
Through which the King thought love-tunes to have blown,
Should shriek, "Indeed,
I am too base to trill so blest a tone!"
Would not the King allege
Defaulted consummation of the marriage-pledge,
And hie the Gipsy to her native hedge? (138–139)

In what is meant to be a girlish moment of confidence, the representative of humanity is advised that, just as a woman's right to consent is precluded within earthly marriage, so it is in sexual metaphysics. To refuse the affections of the divine lover would be to violate the terms of mystical marriage.

The punishment for this failing, in its metaphysical form, is unstated; the bizarre image of a heavenly family court in which the claims of God are opposed to those of the soul is not far off. Nonetheless, the salient implications of the threat are not of litigation but of the inescapability of the "voidness" that legally defines a married woman. Psyche's voidness equates to the nothingness that a wife becomes under coverture, in which the "legal existence of a woman is suspended" (Blackstone 441). As on the ground, so in heaven: nothingness is a gendered (non)space inhabitable only by women, rendering them incapable of consent. The celestial marriage as Patmore depicts it reflects the same paradox inherent to earthly marriage: although the union can only be legally enacted through the consent of both parties, a wife's legal power of consent dissolves with her consent to the marriage itself. Elaine Scarry locates this phenomenon as a marker of heterosexual marriage, in which "the promised reciprocal transfer of rights over the body has historically tended to be one-directional, favoring the man" (Scarry 886).[12]

Moreover, as a vessel of "nothingness," Psyche is also devoid of desire. Her submission need not be willing or eager; it must merely be automatic. Robin West uses similar terms when describing historical laws governing marriage in the United Kingdom, noting that a wife's "pleasure and desire likewise were either irrelevant or their importance minimized by social norm. It was her *availability* that was expected of her, and that defined her sexual being, not her rapturous participation" (236). In this light, the fact that Psyche's nothingness, her inability to withhold consent, is the "charm for which he loved her most" takes on chilling implications (138). The "nothingness" inherent in the status of the married woman persists in the heavenly union, defines her incapacity for self-determination, and provides for Patmore a metaphysical legitimation of the laws of Victorian matrimony.

HOPKINS'S CORRESPONDENCE OF CONSENT

When Patmore and Hopkins were introduced at Stonyhurst College in July 1883, the former was an established poet visiting the school for speech day and the latter was a Jesuit priest (having converted to Catholicism in 1866, joined the Society of Jesus in 1868, and received priestly ordination in 1877) teaching at Stonyhurst, who showed a great interest in poetry. The Jesuit, of course, would not achieve poetic recognition until 1918, when his friend Robert Bridges published a posthumous collection of his poetry. Hopkins was a reader and admirer of Patmore's, and the two maintained a correspondence until Hopkins's death in 1889. In a letter, Hopkins declared to Patmore, "Your poems are a good deed done for the Catholic Church and another for England, for the British Empire" (*Correspondence* 2:785).

Jude Nixon credits Patmore directly with the sexism he finds in Hopkins's "The Candle Indoors" (136), a domestic idyll in which we find a wife "eagerer a-wanting Jessy or Jack," the male figure equated with the "master" (ll. 7, 11).[13] The question of whether Hopkins absorbed deterministic gender conventions directly from Patmore remains open for discussion, but the sentiment of domesticated femininity awaiting masculine mastery is certainly common to both writers. In fact, Hopkins sometimes took issue with Patmore for being lenient in prescribing wifely consent and submission. In a letter discussing *The Angel*, Hopkins objects to a section in which the speaker observes that a wife calls her husband "lord" "not by least consent of will" but by virtue of custom (*Angel* 298). "But he *is* her lord," Hopkins balks, "if it is courtesy only and no consent then a wife's lowliness is hypocrisy and Christian marriage a comedy, a piece of pretence" (*Correspondence* 2:607).

Like Patmore, Hopkins was drawn to marital figurations of the relationship between the human and the divine, a tendency most famously found in his magisterial poem "The Wreck of the Deutschland" (1875–1876), which commemorates an 1875 shipwreck that took the lives of five Franciscan nuns journeying to Missouri to escape the oppressive anti-Catholic Falk Laws in their native Germany. The poem details the death of one particular nun who was said in survivors' accounts to have cried out during the storm, asking Christ, described as her "lover," to "come quickly" (ll. 195, 190). In many ways, the dynamics at work in this text appear to conform to the Patmorean model of the heavenly marriage that replicates earthly standards. As Margaret Johnson observes, "Gender distinctions which are implied by the metaphor of marriage are maintained rigorously by Hopkins. Christ is hero and protector: Christian humanity, represented by the nun, accepts whatever of good or woe he bestows, trusting him for deliverance" (121). In his personal notebooks and later poetry, however, Hopkins reveals a more theologically complex nuptial metaphor that challenges and even inverts the legal norms of consent within Victorian marriage.

Hopkins shared Patmore's enthusiasm for Lataste's work, which he first encountered in 1878 at a retreat at Beaumont (Devlin 325).[14] He went on to transcribe lengthy passages from the second volume of her writings and to refer to her at numerous points in his meditation notes on the Ignatian *Spiritual Exercises*.[15] Critics have noted Hopkins's particular attraction to Lataste's appreciation of suffering as an act of faith. Alan M. Rose argues that Hopkins's embrace of suffering in "Carrion Comfort" echoes admonitions of Lataste's, citing her contention that "the just man regards his persecution as the instrument which God employs to punish him. He considers less the rod which smites him than the sovereign hand which holds it, and receives each stroke with patience and submission" (qtd. in Rose 211). And to be sure, a key component in Lataste's affective devotionalism is patient submission to suffering. She is reported to have said to her Mother Superior, "I cannot satisfy the intense desire which I feel to consume myself for my God. Must I respond so ill to all the love which He deigns to show to His weak creature? Ah, if people did but know the good which comes to a soul from the love of the cross and of humiliation! Our Lord has vouchsafed to teach me this" (Darbins 293).

The import of patient suffering in devotional practice and faith life was also integral for Hopkins, and obedience to authority defined Jesuit practice.[16] Nonetheless, his retreat notes on Lataste do not dwell on her interest in virtuous misery. Instead, they contain an extended consideration of humanity's capacity to consent actively to the will of God, prompted by Lataste's discussion of grace.

Among the passages that Hopkins transcribed is the conversation with Christ described earlier, in which Lataste records Christ's account of Mary's anxiety provoked by her "nothingness" and consequent unworthiness to bear the Son of God. Like Patmore, Hopkins reflects in his own writing on the "nothingness" of the Virgin Mother; unlike Patmore, however, he notes that the Incarnation redeemed her "from the nothingness" (*Sermons* 170). The difference is a key indicator of a more wide-ranging distinction between each writer's relationship to Lataste's work. Whereas Patmore's Mariology entails a perpetual vacancy within the role of heavenly bride and a commensurate inability to exercise free will, Hopkins struggles with the theological implications of continued consent on the part of Mary and the individual. His notes on the Ignatian *Spiritual Exercises* and his poetry reveal a complex vision of consent to the divine Bridegroom as predicated on mutuality, desire, and continued dialogue. At the heart of his Marianism lies a heavenly bride—be it the Virgin Mary or a feminized humanity—that retains a capacity to consent or dissent at any moment.

Notably, in the conversation transcribed by Hopkins, Jesus also informs Lataste that the salvation of the world depended on the singular consent of the Virgin to the Annunciation—that is, her response as a freely willed subject. Jesus notes, "I was able to incarnate myself in Mary, but her consent was needed" (188, qtd. in Devlin 332, my translation). "What power, what grandeur communicated to Mary!" remarks Lataste's Jesus (188, qtd. in Devlin 332, my translation). Regardless of her "nothingness," it seems, Lataste's Virgin Mary is endowed with the power to consent or dissent, a power that, in Hopkins's theology, appears to extend even to humanity in its fallen state. Whereas the woman, consenting to secular marriage, forfeits her power to withhold consent thereafter, the divine marriage envisioned by Hopkins entails a more complicated and reciprocal development.

In his meditation "On Personality, Grace and Free Will,"[17] Hopkins invokes Lataste's discussion of grace, a Christian doctrine conceived of as a gift enabling the individual's conversion and salvation, which God extends *in potentia* to humanity. Of particular interest to Hopkins is the vexed theological question, famously tackled by Augustine, of the interaction between grace and free will. In Augustine's formulation, grace takes various forms, of which Hopkins discusses two in depth: prevenient grace and concomitant (sometimes called cooperative) grace. Prevenient grace, as its name suggests, is held to precede conversion and enable humanity to accept God's offer of sanctity by making it "free from sin" and what Augustine takes to be its occluding effects (167). Concomitant grace, conversely, entails the cooperation between humanity and the divine by which humanity might sustain its salvation through its own continuous self-determination. In Augustine's words, "By working along [with us] He perfects what He began by working [in us]" (169).

Lataste demonstrates considerable interest in consent on the part of humanity to God's grace. In another dialogue, Jesus explains to her, "God gives graces, but He gives them freely, and man, in giving or refusing correspondence to these graces, freely damns or saves himself" (54–55, qtd. in Devlin 328, my translation). In his reflections on Lataste's discussion of grace, Hopkins puts forth an understanding of prevenient grace based on a possible-worlds model, in which the Christian God, standing outside of time, is privy to the infinite possibilities contained, but not yet actualized, in the existence of the individual.[18] Hopkins speculates that, from this vantage point, God is able to choose a moment within the as-yet-unrealized potentialities within the individual "where the creature has consented, does consent, to God's will. . . . It is into that possible world that God for the moment moves his creature out of this one or it is from that possible world that he brings his creature into this, shewing it to itself gracious and consenting" (*Sermons* 154). Such a model of consent differs from Patmore's metaphysical marriage in that it is not predicated on a specific temporal moment of assent from which the individual loses all further capacity for self-determination. Instead, the moment of consent is founded on a future moment in which the individual has already consented. This "possible" future moment is then transposed into the present, delivering the believer with the momentary gift of having consented but requiring full consent to continue.

Rather than annihilating the autonomy of the individual (as in the case of a woman's consent to marriage under the system of coverture), this initial act of grace represents what Hopkins terms a "forestall." The neologism indicates a preliminary moment of consent that anticipates the willed and consciously continued consent that may follow, an outcome determined by the individual. For Hopkins, "prevenient grace . . . *rehearses* in us our consent beforehand, when for the moment we find ourselves to have consented, without finally consenting" (*Sermons* 150). Another, indefinitely recurring consent is required from the individual, which must be actively given. Lataste notes that grace is not sufficient on its own, but requires a "correspondence" from the individual: "It is not grace that makes saints, but the correspondence to grace" (58, qtd. in Devlin 330, my translation).

Whereas prevenient grace relies on the action of the divine, concomitant grace is relational, predicated on the mutual and ongoing consent between the divine and the individual.[19] In contrast to Patmore's theology, which features a deity for whom humanity's inability to withhold consent is its greatest charm, Hopkins's philosophy finds in this correspondent consent "a greater blessing" since it is based not on constraint but on will (*Sermons* 154). In this mode of grace, then, the individual moves from being the object of the actions of the divine to being a self-determining subject in a relational model. The reciprocity that is only nominal within Victorian marriage models becomes instantiated in

Hopkins's metaphysical marriage. Moreover, this correspondence is not limited to one voluntary utterance; instead, it must be constituted and reconstituted indefinitely: "This is a prophecy, a forecast, not of the certain future, for it leaves us free still to discard and unmake that future" (*Sermons* 155). The rescindment of all future autonomy that accompanies a woman's consent to marriage under coverture is replaced by a requirement for continuously reconstituted consent, a structure more akin to Heidi Hurd's theorization of consent as "a subjective mental state" rather than a one-time token that is granted (125).

Moreover, Lataste's writing and that of Hopkins take desire to be a fundamental element in the correspondence to divine grace.[20] Lataste describes receiving the following advice from the Virgin Mother: "Thus, my daughter, each time you seek my Son with a great desire, you are sure to find Him" (200, qtd. in Devlin 333, my translation). Similarly, she reports Jesus advising her that desire itself constitutes prayer: "If you desire God and all that is of God, you will pray continuously; your life will be nothing but a life of prayer" (qtd. in Devlin 327, my translation). Hopkins too finds in desire a central component of the consenting relationship to the divine. In similar language to that with which he explains the "sigh of correspondence" required to consent to divine grace, Hopkins remarks that this assent must arise out of a "sigh of desire" from the believer (*Sermons* 156, 155). Consent is to be enthusiastic: "For there must be something which shall be truly the creature's in the work of corresponding with grace: this is the *arbitrium*, the verdict on God's side, the saying Yes, the 'doing-agree' (to speak barbarously)" (*Sermons* 154). Here Hopkins invokes the Latin term for choice, *arbitrium*, used in both theological and legal contexts.

The departure from standard Victorian doctrine is, once again, marked. West notes that, historically, women have commonly consented to sex that they do not desire, often in the context of marriage. She remarks that, within standard marriage laws, desire on the part of a wife is a moot point: "What lack of sexual desire within marriage did *not* constitute, for married women, was a good reason to resist the imposition of invasive, undesired penetration of their bodies by their husbands" (236). The legal context surrounding earthly marriage renders Hopkins's "sigh of desire" specifically remarkable in that it requires not only *consent*, or, in Patmore's terminology, "yielding," but also *will* on the part of the consenting soul. By infusing personal desire with power, Hopkins figures consent as a continuous process that the individual may choose to discontinue at any point. The sigh of desire must be present not only in an initial moment of consent but also throughout all subsequent moments as the believer is at any time able to "unmake" or dissolve that contract (*Sermons* 155).

Notably, whereas Patmore uses gendered language to describe his metaphysical marriage, Hopkins writes of the relationship between God and humanity in gender-neutral terms. Granted, gender-neutral language in the legal doctrine of the time often obfuscated gender inequalities; context, however, must be taken into account. For instance, Patmore's marked insistence on the gendered relationship between Psyche and Eros characterizes his metaphysics. God is inherently masculinized and has the privileges of a husband over the feminized soul. While resisting the temptation to read his philosophy purely biographically, I find it useful here to consider Hopkins's theology in light of what would now be termed his "homoerotic" desire. Although the category of homosexuality only took on the status of a personal identity (what Foucault would call a "species") in the late nineteenth century (Foucault 43), scholarship since the 1970s has drawn fruitful readings of Hopkins as a queer writer.[21] In his figurations of metaphysical marriage, Hopkins does not share Patmore's squeamish insistence on the heterosexuality of the coupling. Hopkins's consideration of the bond between humanity and the divine in terms of the contract of grace rather than of marriage leads to a wider margin available for the gender roles and personal freedoms involved. Instead of installing Victorian marital norms into the relationship with the divine, Hopkins invests a more liberal social contract between God and humanity, at times using the metaphor of the "divine commonweal, City of God" (*Sermons* 166) to describe the ongoing contract between humanity and God, predicated on mutuality.

Hopkins's Mariology, moreover, provides a far more complex portrait of the Virgin than does Patmore's, suggesting an uncoupling of femininity and nothingness in the metaphysical marriage. Rather than describing Mary in terms of emptiness, the speaker of Hopkins's "The Blessed Virgin Compared to the Air We Breathe" figures himself as a cavity that fills itself with her plenitude, whether she be "My more than meal and drink," or "This air, which by life's law, / My lung must draw and draw" (ll. 11, 13–14). In a virtual inversion of Patmore's gendered metaphysics in which the Virgin is a "Vast Nothingness of Self, / . . . sucking all God's glory in!" (*Unknown Eros* 204), Hopkins's presumably male speaker breathes in the incorporeal animating spirit of the Virgin. Although he writes in his notebooks of Mary's "nothingness," his portrait of her profuse and abundant substance belies any sense of her divestment of selfhood. If Patmore's Mary becomes yet another woman effaced by coverture, Hopkins's Virgin is charged with selfhood.

The attribution to the Virgin Mary of a level of independence and freedom of choice traditionally constitutes a point of contention between Roman Catholic and Protestant branches of Christianity. Donal Flanagan remarks that "it is because Roman Catholicism, as is revealed most clearly in its mariology, is a doctrine of human self-sufficiency in regard to salvation that Protestant Christians must reject it so decisively" (238). Karl Barth goes further, identifying Mary as a rival to her son based on her power to withhold consenting cooperation: "All this is what Mariology means. For it is to the creature creatively co-operating in the work of God that there really applies the irresistible ascription to Mary of that dignity, of those privileges, of those assertions about her *co-operatio* in our salvation, which involve a relative rivalry with Christ" (145). Ascribing rivalry to the mother-son relationship on the basis of Mary's capacity for voluntarism may appear to be anti-Catholic hysteria. And yet, the discomfort with the ability of a feminized party to exercise sustained personhood appears even in the metaphysics of a fervent Catholic convert like Patmore. In fact, although Patmore's later work embraces Catholic devotion to the Virgin Mary, conventional Victorian marital norms inform his view of this divine marriage contract in ways that echo Protestant panic over the veneration of Mary.

For Hopkins, by contrast, the metaphysical marriage does not necessitate that a celestial act of coverture be inflicted the moment that humanity consents to grace but rather entails an ongoing requirement for passionate voluntarism. Such an understanding gives new meaning to the words uttered by the speaker of "The Wreck of the Deutschland": "I did say yes, / O at lightning and lashed rod. / Thou heardst me truer than tongue confess / Thy terror, O Christ, O God" (ll. 9–12). As he describes his heart "flash from the flame to the flame then, tower from the grace to the grace," he signals a shift from the initial, dependent spark of prevenient grace to the subsequent, relational consent within concomitant grace (l. 24). The past tense of the declaration "I did say yes" indicates, then, only one moment of consent within a series of yeses, which the speaker is at liberty to revoke at any time. Like the nun who, already a bride of Christ, further consents to suffering at the hands of her God by crying for Christ to "come quickly," the speaker partners with his God in a relation of desire, correspondence, and consent. If Patmore transposes the legalities of earth to the heavenly sphere, Hopkins suggests that a heavenly mutuality might inform our earthly relations. At its most profound pressure points, Victorian theology can reveal possibilities for radical reimaginings of power, desire, and will.

NOTES

1. A notable example comes from Jane Eyre's flirtatious exchange with Rochester, who tells her that he "would not exchange this one little English girl for the Grand Turk's whole seraglio." Jane notes that the "eastern allusion bit me," and she retorts, "If you have a fancy for anything in that line, away with you, sir, to the bazaars of Stamboul, without delay; and lay out in extensive slave-purchases some of that spare cash you seem at a loss to spend satisfactorily here" (Brontë 229).

2. Perhaps most famously, John Stuart Mill observed, "Marriage is the only bondage known to our law. There remain no legal slaves, except the mistress of every house" (147).

3. Staggeringly, after detailing the entailments of coverture, including the fact that the law permits a husband to "restrain a wife of her liberty, in case of any gross misbehavior," Blackstone concludes by remarking that such provisions are "intended for her protection and benefit: so great a favorite is the female sex of the laws of England" (444).

4. The marital exemption would not be revoked until 1991, in the case of *R v. R*, 1991, UKHL 12.

5. In Susan Gubar and Sandra Gilbert's landmark study *The Madwoman in the Attic*, Honoria is described as a bland fixture whose "essential virtue . . . is that her virtue makes her *man* 'great'" (22).

6. Patmore had published nine odes privately and anonymously in 1868. From 1875 to 1877, he published additional odes in the *Pall Mall Gazette*, signing them "C.P." In 1877 he released an expanded version in the book *The Unknown Eros* (see Champneys 1:246).

7. The *Athenaeum's* review, while generally positive, ends with the assurance that "these odes are hardly likely to be popular" (Rev. of *The Unknown Eros* 377).

8. The Catholic literary tradition depicting divine marriage begins with Counter-Reformation writers such as George Herbert and John Donne and continues to include contemporaries of Patmore such as Francis Thompson and Frederick William Faber.

9. In the previously cited preface to Julian of Norwich's *Revelations*, the author claims that Lataste's writings are most closely aligned with the writing of Angela of Foligno by virtue of their emotional valences (Collins xx).

10. Lataste's theological writings are largely in the form of Socratic-style dialogues in which Jesus or the Virgin Mother explains doctrinal and theological points to her in conversation.

11. Grafe is invoking the Christological notion of kenosis, which understands Christ to have emptied himself of his divinity in order to make himself available to become fully human during his time on earth. The individual believer too strives to empty herself of will in order that God may function through her.

12. Mary Lyndon Shanley makes a similar point regarding the use of gender-neutral language in Victorian marriage laws, which presumably provide each spouse with equal sexual access to the other within the partnership: "The physiological differences between men and women often made it possible for a husband to force sexual relations on his wife while neither she nor the court could force them upon him: gender-neutral language marked very real differences in power between men and women" (178).

13. All references to Hopkins's poetry are from *The Poetical Works*.

14. For discussions of Hopkins's reading of Lataste and her potential influence on his thought, see Devlin, "Appendix II"; Pick 133ff.; Rose; and Downes, *Hopkins' Achieved Self* 128.

15. Designed as a retreat guide for members of the Society of Jesus, the *Spiritual Exercises* is a four-week manual written by Ignatius Loyola, the founder of the order. The *Spiritual Exercises* were central to Hopkins's life as a Jesuit, and the commentary on Lataste in his retreat notes speaks to the importance of her work to his thought at the time.

16. Downes notes that "the touchstone of Ignatian obedience is this: obedience to a superior is obedience to Christ" (*Ignatian* 27).

17. The title is given by Devlin in order to add coherence and structure to the notes compiled in *Sermons*. The section can be found on pages 146–159.

18. The idea of counterfactual possible worlds most likely comes from the medieval Franciscan theologian and Doctor of the Church Duns Scotus, who became central to Hopkins's thought after the poet encountered his work in 1872. For accounts of the importance of Scotus to Hopkins, see Devlin, "Appendix II"; Bowman; Hywel; Ward, "Philosophy and Inscape" and *World as Word*.

19. For further explanation of the distinction, see McGrath 356.

20. To conceive of prevenient grace as the arousal of desire is by no means unorthodox; Michael Purcell observes that one might speak of grace "in terms of the desire which the other excites in the same" (74).

21. Wendell Stacy Johnson provides an early examination of Hopkins's same-sex desires, as does Michael Lynch. More recent work includes that of Julia Saville and Michael M. Kaylor.

WORKS CITED

Augustine. *On the Free Choice of the Will, on Grace and Free Choice, and Other Writings*. Edited by Peter King, Cambridge UP, 2006.

Barth, Karl. *Church Dogmatics*. Vol. 1, no. 2. *The Doctrine of the Word of God*. Continuum, 2004.

Besant, Annie. *Marriage, as It Was, as It Is, and as It Should Be: A Plea for Reform*. Freethought, 1882.

Blackstone, William. *Commentaries on the Laws of England*. Edited by Thomas M. Cooley, vol. 1, Callaghan, 1884.

Bowman, Leonard J. "Another Look at Hopkins and Scotus." *Renascence*, vol. 29, no. 1, 1976, pp. 50–6.

Brontë, Charlotte. *Jane Eyre*. Edited by Richard J. Dunn, W. W. Norton, 2001.

Champneys, Basil. *Memoirs and Correspondence of Coventry Patmore*. George Bell and Sons, 1900. 2 vols.

Collins, Henry. Preface. *Revelations of Divine Love, Shewed to a Devout Anchoress, by Name, Mother Julian of Norwich*, Thomas Richardson and Sons, 1877, pp. xiii–xxi.

Darbins, Pascal. *The Life of Marie Lataste, Lay-Sister of the Congregation of the Sacred Heart*. Translated by Edward Healy Thompson, Burns & Oates, 1877.

Devlin, Christopher. "Appendix I: Marie Lataste." *The Sermons and Devotional Writings of Gerard Manley Hopkins*, edited by Christopher Devlin, Oxford UP, 1959, pp. 325–337.

———. "Appendix II." *The Sermons and Devotional Writings of Gerard Manley Hopkins*, edited by Christopher Devlin, Oxford UP, 1959.

Downes, David Anthony. *Hopkins' Achieved Self*. UP of America, 1990.

———. *The Ignatian Personality of Gerard Manley Hopkins*. University Press of America, 1990.

Flanagan, Donal. "Mary in the Ecumenical Discussion." *Irish Theological Quarterly*, vol. 40, no. 3, 1973, pp. 227–249.

Foucault, Michel. *The History of Sexuality: An Introduction*. Translated by Robert Hurley, vol. 1, Vintage, 1990.

Gilbert, Sandra M., and Susan Gubar. *The Madwoman in the Attic: The Woman Writer and the Nineteenth-Century Literary Imagination*. Yale UP, 1984.

Grafe, Adrian. "'Telling Secrets': Remarks on Coventry Patmore." *Cahiers Victoriens et Édouardiens*, vol. 52, 2000, pp. 99–119.

Heidemann, A. W. "Coventry Patmore." *Victorian Poets after 1850*, edited by William E. Fredeman and Ira Bruce Nadel, Gale Research, 1985, pp. 180–194.

Hopkins, Gerard Manley. *Correspondence*. Edited by R. K. R. Thornton and Catherine Phillips, Oxford UP, 2012. 2 vols.

———. *The Poetical Works of Gerard Manley Hopkins*. Edited by Norman MacKenzie, Oxford UP, 1990.

———. *The Sermons and Devotional Writings of Gerard Manley Hopkins*. Edited by Christopher Devlin, Oxford UP, 1959.

Hurd, Heidi. "The Moral Magic of Consent." *Legal Theory*, vol. 2, no. 2, 1996, pp. 121–146.

Hywel, Thomas. "Gerard Manley Hopkins and Duns Scotus." *Religious Studies*, vol. 24, no. 3, 1988, pp. 337–364.

Johnson, Margaret A. *Gerard Manley Hopkins and Tractarian Poetry*. Ashgate, 1997.

Johnson, Wendell Stacy. "Sexuality and Inscape." *Hopkins Quarterly*, vol. 3, no. 2, 1976, pp. 59–65.

Kaylor, Michael M. *Secreted Desires: The Major Uranians: Hopkins, Pater and Wilde*. Masaryk UP, 2006.

Keble, John. *The Christian Year: Thoughts in Verse for the Sundays and Holydays throughout the Year*. Rivington, 1827.

Lataste, Marie. *La Vie et les Oeuvres de Marie Lataste*. Vol. 2, Ambroise Bray, 1866.

Lynch, Michael. "Recovering Hopkins, Recovering Ourselves." *Hopkins Quarterly*, vol. 6, no. 3, 1979, pp. 107–118.

Maynard, John. *Victorian Discourses on Sexuality and Religion*. Cambridge UP, 1993.

McGrath, Alister E. *Christian Theology: An Introduction*. Wiley-Blackwell, 2011.

Mill, John Stuart. *The Subjection of Women*. Longmans, Green, Reader, and Dyer, 1869.

Nixon, Jude V. "'Death Blots Black Out': Thermodynamics and the Poetry of Gerard Manley Hopkins." *Victorian Poetry*, vol. 40, no. 2, 2002, pp. 131–155.

Page, Frederick. *Patmore: A Study in Poetry*. Oxford UP, 1933.

Patmore, Coventry. *The Angel in the House*. Macmillan, 1863. 2 vols.

———. *The Rod, the Root, and the Flower*. George Bell and Sons, 1895.

———. *The Unknown Eros I–XLVI*. George Bell and Sons, 1878.

Pick, John. *Gerard Manley Hopkins, Priest and Poet*. Oxford UP, 1966.

Poulain, R. P. A. *The Graces of Interior Prayer*. Translated by Leonora L. Yorke-Smith, Kegan Paul, Trench, Trubner, 1912.

Purcell, Michael. "Glimpsing Grace Phenomenologically: Prevenience and Posteriority." *Irish Theological Quarterly*, vol. 73, 2008, pp. 73–86.

Reid, J. C. *The Mind and Art of Coventry Patmore*. Routledge, 1957.

Review of *La Vie et les Œuvres de Marie Lataste*. *Dublin Review*, vol. 2, no. 3, 1864, pp. 232–233.

Review of *The Unknown Eros*. *The Athenaeum*, 2578, 1877, p. 377.

Rose, Alan M. "Hopkins' 'Carrion Comfort': The Artful Disorder of Prayer." *Victorian Poetry*, vol. 15, no. 3, 1977, pp. 207–217.

Saville, Julia. *A Queer Chivalry: The Homoerotic Asceticism of Gerard Manley Hopkins*. UP of Virginia, 2000.

Scarry, Elaine. "Consent and the Body: Injury, Departure, and Desire." *New Literary History*, vol. 21, no. 4, 1990, pp. 867–896.

Shanley, Mary Lyndon. *Feminism, Marriage, and the Law in Victorian England, 1850–1895*. Princeton UP, 1989.

Ward, Bernadette Waterman. "Philosophy and Inscape: Hopkins and the Formalitas of Duns Scotus." *Texas Studies in Literature and Language*, vol. 32, no. 2, 1990, pp. 214–239.

———. *World as Word: Philosophical Theology in Gerard Manley Hopkins*. Catholic U of America P, 2002.

West, Robin. "Sex, Law, and Consent." *The Ethics of Consent: Theory and Practice*, edited by Franklin Miller and Alan Wertheimer, Oxford UP, 2009, pp. 221–250.

3 · CONSENSUAL SEX, CONSENSUAL TEXT

Law, Literature, and the Production of the Consenting Subject

JORDANA GREENBLATT

I am the plaited whip that flagellates the skin, *I* am the electric current that blasts and convulses the muscles, I am the gag that gags the mouth, *I* am the bandage that hides the eyes, *I* am the bonds that tie the hands, *I* am the mad tormentor galvanized by torture and your cries intoxicate m/e m/y best beloved the more you restrain them. At this point *I* invoke your help m/y incomparable Sappho, give m/e by thousands the fingers that allay the wounds, give m/e the lips the tongue the saliva which draw one into the slow sweet poisoned country from which one cannot return.

—Monique Wittig, *Le Corps lesbien*[1]

The evidence discloses that the practices of the appellants were unpredictably dangerous and degrading to body and mind and were developed with increasing barbarity and taught to persons whose consents were dubious or worthless.

—Lord Templeman, *Regina v. Brown*

Written against linguistic norms that position the masculine subject as universal, Monique Wittig's *Le Corps lesbien*'s narrative voice is a slashed *I* ("j/e" in the original French, translated as an italicized *I* in English), which both is subject to and enacts ecstatic eroticized violence, identifying itself as a whip, bonds, a gag, and a tormentor, as well as that which "allay[s] the wounds" the

44

tormentor inflicts (14). Wittig's novel places the reader in the position of you (*tu*), dared and seduced to enter "the slow sweet poisoned country" her characters inhabit, one defined by both erotic and textual pleasurable pain (*Lesbian* 14). Meanwhile, many legal decisions that bear on sexual *practice* involving both pleasure and pain categorize such daring as impossible, defining the consent of those who willingly experience eroticized violence as "dubious and worthless" and the experience intrinsically degrading (Regina v. Brown 7). In considering consent; illegal, criminalized, and/or perverse sexualities; and literary and social genre deviance, I bring three works of queer experimental literature—Wittig's *Le Corps lesbien*, Kathy Acker's *Empire of the Senseless*, and David Wojnarowicz's *Close to the Knives*—into conversation with law. Exploring case law pertaining to perverse sexualities and works of literature that represent them, I draw parallels between the pleasures of consent to genre blurring as it takes place in both reading and sexual practice. Similar pleasures and negotiations occur in enacting desires at the borders of the sexual and other social interactions (so anxiously distinguished and codified in legal discourse) and willingly reading texts whose genre deviations defy strict literary categorization. Consent (or not) to these noncanonical modes of literature and eroticism is a necessarily active practice.

Issues of narrative, genre, and sexual perversion come together when we consider textual engagement as an erotically charged act in which consent plays a role. Meanwhile, the law itself functions as a kind of quasi-literary criticism: the arguments implicit in law's taxonomizing function are in many ways commensurate with the laws of literary genre. As Lauren Berlant points out, "The law's typical practice is to recognize kinds of subjects, acts, and identities: it is to taxonomize" (125). In order to include and exclude acts, performances, bodies, and subjectivities from the "consentable," legal texts differentiate elements of the social (the sexual, commerce, violent sport, etc.)—a classificatory and regulatory function whose literary analogue is the codification of genre. Both regimes function to obscure consent, its construction, and how it functions socially. On the one hand, legal and social discourses position marginal sexual activities as something to which no subject capable of consent *would* consent. They thereby tautologically define legitimately granted consent as only belonging to those who only *do* consent to the norm and simultaneously elide processes of implicit consent to the social contract that defines the norm. For example, if anyone would have to be mentally incompetent to want to be whipped, the act of consenting to be whipped would then categorize the consenter as mentally incompetent and thus unable to grant consent to anything, while the implicit belief that we should all want the same things sexually would go unchallenged. The sexual practices we might see as commensurate with Wittig's "slow, sweet poisoned country" (*Lesbian* 14) are represented in legal and social discourses as, in the terms Lord Templeman uses in his British House of Lords Decision for *Regina v. Brown*, manifestations of "barbarity" that stand in opposition to the "civilized" subject capable of consent (7, 9). On the other hand, norms of reading practice and literary genre elide the readerly choices we make when we engage with a given text—our consent to the reading experience—unless those norms are contested.

When it comes to reading, the issue is less the violation of *explicit* agreements as the overturning of genre norms that underlie our assumptions on entering a reading experience. As Linda Zirelli notes regarding Wittig's understanding of language, "The nature of our 'consent' is . . . like the social contract as it was elaborated by Rousseau. . . . This de facto social contract is everywhere and nowhere, for it defines our existence as speaking beings. . . . Language is not something each of us agreed to but a prior agreement in judgments we were born into" (95–96). Like our consent to language in general, our consent to genre is de facto; as Erica Ostrovsky contends, "Both [gender and genre] are such deeply ingrained concepts that any change seems almost inconceivable; as time honored traditions, they are only rarely questioned" (116). In our reading interactions, genre and our consent to it are generally assumed and unquestioned, while in case law pertaining to marginal sexuality, genre is obsessively and explicitly defined.

Drawing from Jacques Derrida's "The Law of Genre," I argue that there are significant congruencies between "The Law of Genre" and the law as arbiter of genre, suggesting that deviant literary genre occupies spaces similar to the socially deviant sexualities upon which the law bears, excluding them from the civil. The ways in which we approach both deviant texts and deviant sex derive from historical and contemporary codification and regulation of social and literary genre—which directs our reading practices with respect not only to text but also to bodies, subjectivities, and acts.

LITERATURE, SEXUALITY, AND "THE LITTLE MAN"

That literary norms have sexual and gendered implications is hardly a new observation. In "Desire in Narrative," Teresa de Lauretis writes, "To say that narrative is the production of Oedipus is to say that each reader—male or female—is constrained and defined within two positions of a sexual difference thus conceived: male-hero-human, on the side of the subject; and female-obstacle-boundary-space, on the other" (121). Elaborating this dynamic, de Lauretis frames existing narrative as sexed and heterosexual; it projects onto audiences figural identification with narrative positions that make sense of the world through a rigidly heterosexist lens. Raising consent and seduction, de Lauretis claims that film "may be said to require women's consent; and we may well suspect that narrative cinema in particular must be aimed, like desire, toward seducing women into femininity," a project that she associates with the incitement to identification implicit in genre (137). De Lauretis, among others,[2] seeks textual and cinematic practices that would allow female desire to avoid co-optation into figuring narrative closure, or the reward for "the little man," to continue de Lauretis's use of Freud's term. However, in such work, antipatriarchal textual and/or narrative erotics are defined primarily as (women's) same-sex desire and/or autoeroticism. De Lauretis's model does not account for the range of erotic deviance and resistance present in the work of writers like those I consider. While Wittig, Acker, and Wojnarowicz all locate moments of textual erotic agency in same-sex encounters, the possibility that each proposes for an actively consensual textual erotics prioritizes perversions that do not rely primarily on sex/gender. As Claire Whatling observes, "Wittig can only be appropriated to a conventional lesbian erotic by a process of assimilation which negates the very impact of her writing" (240). The impact of *Le Corps lesbien* relies far more on the conjunction of eroticism, violence, and pleasure than on the sex of its protagonists in both its vignettes and its use of language.

Le Corps lesbien, Empire of the Senseless, and *Close to the Knives* represent a number of sexual acts—some possible and some fantastically surreal—that are illegal and/or socially defined as perverse. Such acts inherently evoke issues of consent, intersecting with social and legal regulation of which acts can be consented to. All of these texts are also ambiguous in their genre and thus resistant to the heteropatriarchal narrative model de Lauretis critiques. Nominally novels, both *Le Corps lesbien* and *Empire of the Senseless* are sufficiently fragmented and narratively disrupted to make such categorization questionable. Wittig's text is often read as prose poetry rather than a novel and has also been framed as a commentary on anatomical writing.[3] Despite periodic illustrations based on tattooing, Acker's text is in many ways less ambiguously a novel; nevertheless, the terseness of its sentences hyperbolizes prose to an extent that does violence to any "normal" narrative interaction.[4] And as Joseph Conte notes, "Acker's disorientation as a novelist compels the reader to abandon other orderly conventions of reception," as her work is characterized by extreme shifts in register, characterization, and narrative consistency (18).

Billed as autobiography (specifically AIDS memoir), with the subtitle *A Memoir of Disintegration*, Wojnarowicz's text is exceptionally fragmentary and noncohesive, even for contemporary life writing. Exploring sex work and cruising, Wojnarowicz models his violation of genre on casual sexual encounters. Connections between sections (and often sentences) are tenuous—seemingly arbitrary; some approach traditional forms, while others make any sense of event difficult to isolate. Some sentences go on for pages, while others adhere more closely to syntactical and structural norms. In violating genre and style expectations, Wojnarowicz brings us to assess whether we will consent to a reading experience that rejects a narrativizing approach to life writing in favour of more arbitrary experiences of cruising or commercialized sex.

The erotic dynamics of all three texts resist the continuing social and critical reduction of sexuality to object choice, a reduction that affects how sexual subjects and sexual consent are understood. As Eve Kosofsky Sedgwick points out, prioritizing object choice has left "a large family of things *we know* and need to know about ourselves and each other with which we have . . . so far created for ourselves almost no theoretical room to deal" (*Epistemology* 24, emphasis in original). Theoretical interventions into consent are often constrained by the modes of (il)legibility that derive from codification of genres of the social, the sexual, and people themselves according to categories of binary gender and heteronormative sexuality. Purporting to theorize sexual consent in general in *Consent to Sexual Relations*, Alan Wertheimer stipulates that he will assume throughout that the person seeking consent is male and the person from whom he seeks it is female. Wertheimer rationalizes, "First, it makes things simpler. Second, it reflects empirical reality. . . . It is extremely rare for males to claim that they did not consent to sexual relations, whereas the claim is frequently and rightly made by females," and he thereby regulates and rigidifies gender-as-genre and the roles of given "genres" of people within them (8). In so doing, he renders many sexualities and acts illegible and others, such as sex work, peripheral extensions of the necessarily heterosexual, gendered scene of consent, in which men are seekers of sex (and the consent to it) and women providers—a scene that parallels de Lauretis's vision of conventional narrative.

Such restrictive assumptions both elide and coerce consent. They present a transactional (but normatively unpaid) model of sexuality in which there are two options: people will or will not consent to a very narrow range of sexual interactions. This narrowing of legible sex elides the processes by which we are expected and coerced to (at least implicitly) consent to the sexual norm itself (heterosexual, vanilla, amateur, etc.). It simultaneously dismisses the possibility that we might make valid decisions of consent to other practices while coercing us, through various social, institutional, and legal means, not to even consider doing so.

Such elisions and coercions are no less present in textual consent. When we read, we implicitly consent to relationships with text, often without our conscious acknowledgement. Genre is a framework in which we are assumed to participate willingly and in which we make assumptions that allow us to be willing participants. We know ahead of time what we are supposed to be in for and that we are supposed to like it. Despite Derrida's argument that the regulation of genre also contains genre's necessary counterlaw that renders genre itself both possible and impossible, most of the time, we read within a system in which genre, consent, and what consent means are all assumed.

These assumptions derive from a social context in which consent to the elements of the social contract—of which genre is a literary example—is largely occluded. Our quotidian interactions of consent are obscured. Concurrently, our social structures encourage us to assume that we all know what consent *must* mean—and that we know what no one could possibly consent to, because it is beyond the scope of our own imaginable desires. As Elaine Scarry argues with respect to the canonical, frequently cited definition of medical consent in American jurisprudence ("Every human being of adult years and sound mind has a right to determine what shall be done to his own body" [869]), "The canonical . . . *is* the conventional, *is* the consensual even if one day in 1914 it originated in a particular brilliance or elegance of mind. Thus it is a consensual theory of consent" (870, emphasis in original). Scarry extends many of her observations from medical consent to other types of consent, and the issue of canonicity (and consent to the canon) that she raises affects both literary and sexual-legal arenas. Our consent to canonical categories of genre (and to our engagements with the texts that fall within them) is often masked by the very canonicity to which we are consenting. Similarly, our often obscured consent to canonical (here, normative) models of sex, sexuality, and desire serve to position those whose acts and desires lie elsewhere as *not* being "of sound mind" without questioning the consensuality of the canonical grounds for such dismissal.

CONSENT AS REFERENDUM

Failing to actively think through negotiations of consent—sexual, textual, and social—ultimately serves to restrict our possible pleasures and the degree to which we engage creatively and enthusiastically consensually with others. On the textual register, Roland Barthes complains in his foundational distinction between readerly and writerly texts that the readerly text's reader "is . . . plunged into a kind of idleness—he is intransitive; he is, in short, *serious*: instead of functioning himself, instead of gaining access to the magic of the signifier, to the pleasure of writing, he is left with no more than the poor freedom whether to accept or reject the text: reading is nothing more than a *referendum*" (4, emphasis in original). The "poor freedom" of the referendum often also still serves as the central foundation of contemporary theorizations of sexual consent. Pamela Haag represents consent as "a social . . . artifact," which "is always an interpreted idea, not an idealized abstraction" (xv) that functions as "the soul of liberalism's social practices, and figures prominently in the legitimation of its social roles" (xviii); however, many critics simply reiterate the liberal, gendered foundations and functions of (particularly sexual) consent in their critiques, rendering sexual consent as a readerly not writerly act.[5] In *Sexual Consent*, David Archard pays attention to practices such as sex work and sadomasochism, but only because they represent fringe cases for him; he addresses sadomasochism at the outset, but only in order to test his statement that "whatever people do sexually as 'consenting adults' should be allowed, even if the rest of us find a particular practice disgusting or shocking" (1). Archard frames "disgusting" and "shocking" sexual practices as permissible—indeed, consentable—only as extremes that justify the norm. And while Archard does not state his gendered assumptions as overtly as Wertheimer, he primarily uses examples where men seek sexual consent and/or apply coercion and women provide consent and/or are coerced. Women's consent to sex as anything other than, to use Barthes's term, a readerly "referendum" on a predetermined question disappears in this model, and *anyone's* active consent to marginal sexual acts is largely illegible—neither readerly nor writerly but simply unintelligible.

A queer, male sex worker, such as Wojnarowicz in his youth, is incomprehensible within Wertheimer's "simplification" and barely visible in Archard's framework—and so too are the cultural investments that direct certain sex acts to be read into the fringes or completely out of the "consentable." BDSM[6] appears nowhere in Wertheimer's book. It is so illegible in his framework that he contrasts the frequency with which people—or should I say *women*—do consent to sex with a comment that "few people consent to . . . being beaten," listing only boxing as an exception (25). Robin Bauer positions such assumptions that "the ideal sexual interaction [is] devoid of . . . anything that may be thought of as unpleasant emotions or sensations," as a component of heteronormativity (3). The relationship between Bauer's "harmonic sexuality" and heteronormativity is apparent in the most famous legal example criminalizing BDSM, the Spanner Case in the United Kingdom.[7] A number of gay male BDSM tops were successfully prosecuted for assault, against the protests of their willing bottoms,[8] based on films the group made for their private use that fell into the hands of the police. The prosecution's reasoning was that no one can consent to assault—already implicitly an argument of genre, taxonomizing physical violence as unavailable to any grouping with sex. Violence is certainly not always unacceptable—sports and surgery must go on, after all—but it is if its purpose is sexual gratification.

The 1992 decision of the British House of Lords against overturning the Spanner defendants' convictions makes explicit the social motivations to regulate sociosexual genre to remove certain acts (and certain subjects) from the consentable. In the decision, Lord Templeman writes, "Society is entitled and bound to protect itself against a cult of violence. Pleasure derived from the infliction of pain is an evil thing. Cruelty is uncivilized" (Regina v. Brown 9). Earlier, he asserts, "The evidence discloses that the practices of the appellants were unpredictably dangerous and degrading to body and mind and were developed with increasing barbarity and taught to persons whose consents were dubious or worthless" (Regina v. Brown 7).

"Dubious or worthless": this is how the consent of perverse sexual subjects is framed—in this case and elsewhere. In *People v. Samuels*, the 1967 American precedent-setting case regarding BDSM, Justice Shoemaker makes a similar assertion about the consent of masochists—here entirely theoretical and absent masochists since Samuels was arrested for films he had made with men who were never identified by the police.[9] Like Lord Templeman, Justice Shoemaker argues, "It is the rule that the apparent consent of a person without legal capacity to give consent, such as a child or insane person, is ineffective. . . . It is a matter of common knowledge that a person in full possession of his mental faculties does not freely consent to the use, upon himself, of force likely to produce great bodily injury" (People v. Samuels 513–514).

In both *Brown* and *Samuels*, films not meant for public consumption were used to criminalize BDSM *practice*; similar logic is regularly used to regulate obscenity, thus also criminalizing BDSM *representation*. *Regina v. Butler*, the precedent-setting Supreme Court of Canada decision upholding Canada's obscenity legislation and establishing the current test for obscenity, positions representations of acts involving sex and violence as almost always obscene and acts involving sex and degradation or dehumanization as likely obscene. Justice Binnie writes for the majority, "In the appreciation of whether material is degrading or dehumanizing, the appearance of consent is not necessarily determinative. . . . Sometimes the very appearance of consent makes the depicted acts even more degrading or dehumanizing" (Regina v. Butler 479). Both Templeman and Shoemaker are explicit in their determinations that consenting to deviant sex is, itself, *proof* that a given subject does not have the capacity to have given consent in the first place, a perspective echoed in Binnie's assessment of consent in BDSM representation as *increasing* degradation. Elsewhere, this argument is more implicit, though no less insidious.

In 2010, an Ontario Superior Court of Justice (OSCJ) decision struck down three provisions pertaining to sex work, which was not itself illegal, on the grounds that they endangered sex workers. Defending the provisions, the attorney general of Ontario (AGO) claimed that "the physical and psychological harms experienced by prostitutes stem from the inherent inequality that characterizes the prostitute-customer relationship, and not from the *Criminal Code*. . . . The impugned provisions operate to limit the negative effects of prostitution on both the prostitute and the public, as they curtail commercialized institutionalized prostitution and prohibit public prostitution" (Bedford v. Canada 2010, 20). The provisions prevented sex workers from working indoors, hiring help, or communicating effectively with clients. The AGO's defence of the provisions dismisses these pressing material restrictions by rendering the consent of sex workers as, at best, dubious: they cannot truly consent to their profession. Per the AGO, the law exists to protect them (and the "public") from themselves. Yet the attorneys general of Canada (AG) and Ontario argue in their 2012 appeal of the OSCJ decision that "the real cause of any infringement on the respondents' security of person rests in their decision to engage in prostitution. That decision . . . is a matter of personal choice that inevitably places the respondents at risk" (Bedford v. Canada 2012, 122). Ironically, according to the AGO and AG, sex workers are both consenting and unconsenting. The law exists to protect sex workers from their work, to which, per the attorneys general, they cannot truly consent. At the same time, the law has no responsibility to protect them from the risks that they incur while working in a trade that they have chosen at their own peril. Categories shift so as to include certain things (i.e., workplace danger) within the realm of the consentable and make others (i.e., sex work itself) dubious.[10]

At stake in the Spanner decisions, *People v. Samuels*, and *Regina v. Butler* (and implicitly in the sex work example) as the goal of law's taxonomic, genre-regulating function is positioning consent not as that which distinguishes wanted from unwanted interactions but as the dividing line between the civilized and the barbarous. This purpose of "consent" is emphasized by the decision of the prosecutors in the Spanner Case to also criminally charge the masochists for their role in "assaults" upon themselves.[11] Consent is essential to producing and enforcing the civilized subject. Those of us who are uncivil find our consent deemed "dubious and worthless" and, indeed, may be regarded as criminal for trying to give it. Discussing *Regina v. Butler*, Ummni Khan asserts that "censorship policies are also national strategies of identity. . . . Borders . . . are formed not only around geographical lines, but also around sexual normative lines" (202). Indeed, Scarry points to "the kinship between the boundaries of the nation-state and the body in consensual relation" (880). But if the boundaries of the nation, and by extension the civil and the citizen, parallel the boundaries of the body, subjects are no longer recognized as "civil" when they cross those boundaries in the wrong way by practicing willing marginal sex. Crossing the wrong sexual boundaries, they leave behind both "civilization" and accept-able, legible categories of sociality.

Legal rights discourse is itself criticized as relying on the regulation of accept-able social subjects. Though rights discourse can make new categories of person legible, others remain or become illegible, and, indeed, the discourse necessi-tates such an outside. Berlant notes law's taxonomic function in critiquing this dynamic. And as Derrida emphasizes, genre taxonomy itself is multivalent: he refers to "the genre in all genres, be it a question of a generic or a general deter-mination of what one calls nature . . . (for example a biological *genre* in the sense of *gender*, or the human *genre*, a genre of all that is in general)" (56, emphasis in original). He writes that "the law of genre also has a controlling influence and is binding on that which draws the genre into engendering, generations, genealogy, and degenerescence" (74). Thus the regulation of the social, of persons, and of social subjects is already built into Derrida's definition of genre, and these regulatory functions are integral to producing consent to the social contract and keeping it both obscured and assumed. I contend that what the law does is to assert, rigidify, and render legible or illegible social genres in the interest of affirming an idea of the civil and discarding its exteriors, rendering them, in Lord Templeman's terms, no less than barbarous and evil.

How then might we envision a form of sexual and/or textual seduction that refuses to allow the process of consent to be elided or coerced? How might we envision a textual and/or sexual model of consent that goes beyond saying yes or no to the norm and enables active affirmation of desire? Consent as a referendum in which our only power is to give or withhold acquiescence is indeed, as Barthes terms it, "a poor freedom." Even this poor freedom is one we only have if we only consent to acts within the realm of the normatively civil. To approach consent as more than a poor freedom requires that we think about it, what it means, what we want, what we would consider, and what we might want in the future instead of relating to consent solely as the answer to a readerly question. And so we return to the centrality of the sexually perverse and/or illegal in genre-resistant literature. Through raising it on the textual level, such literature poses the question of how to engage in a "writerly" process of consent that evades reduction to a referendum. In contending with writerly consent textually, these texts also extend it to the sexual and the social through the resonances between form and content.

TEXTUAL CONSENT

When we read (or interact with other creative work), we implicitly consent to a textual interaction, often without acknowledging that we do so. When we encounter works that defy our genre expectations, we must engage in more explicit negotiations of consent—decisions about legibility, or openness to the illegible, that bear on our reading practices outside of the literary encounter. As Art Redding notes regarding Acker, "In real terms, it's hard to know what Acker expects or demands of her audience" (297). Facing expectations that are not predetermined or assumed, we must engage in more active negotiations. Indeed, discussing *Le Corps lesbien*, Whatling notes that "consent, of subject, object and reader, is always under negotiation" (243).

Wojnarowicz explicitly meditates on the productivity of defying the categories that cajole us into implicitly consenting to that which is predetermined—from both sexual and artistic perspectives—and on the categories of law that serve to exclude him. "Degenerescence," in Derrida's terms, overlaps with disintegration (and the disintegration of people and categories) as it appears in Wojnorowicz's work. In explaining his rejection of the label "photographer," Wojnarowicz claims that "I have never been comfortable calling myself anything that would label my acts of creativity because I don't ever want to take myself so seriously that others would then pull out their magnifying glasses and hold me or my actions or the artifacts of those actions up to the ART WORLD criteria of any given medium" (138–139). Staking claims to being inside a medium or a genre (barring provocative subtitlings where the point is to disrupt) encourages readers or viewers to embrace a referendum-like state in which they passively, often not consciously, consent to work or reject it as a failure to adhere to predetermined forms rather than engage the possibility of perceiving it as productive deviation, degenerescence, or disintegration. As Derrida writes, "As soon as genre announces itself, one must respect a norm, one must not cross a line of demarcation, one must not risk impurity, anomaly, or monstrosity" (57). But of course, Derrida being Derrida, he also claims that genre fundamentally contains such impurity. For Wojnarowicz, placing himself outside of genre categories encourages his audiences to make more active, hopefully open, decisions of consent to his work, as anomaly becomes the defining trait of encounter rather than failed or successful adherence to genre (and thus subjectivity). In both the work of art and social interactions, such work encourages writers and readers to embrace writerly modes of interaction.

Because all three of the texts I consider are episodic, discontinuous, and often self-contradictory, readers have numerous points of interruption to either withdraw consent or actively reaffirm their consent to the perverse textualities of *Empire of the Senseless*, *Le corps lesbian*, and *Close to the Knives*.[12] Constant interruption dispels the possibility for the gendered and sexualized closure that de Lauretis critiques, bringing together textual and sexual negotiations and removing the option of solely readerly engagement with each. Such interruptions preclude a closed answer to a predetermined question as posed by canonical genre, leaving readers responsible for negotiating their own textual interactions.

WITTIG AND "BRUTAL" INTERRUPTION

In "A Poem Is Being Written," Sedgwick claims, "The two most rhythmic things that happened to me [as a child] were spanking and poetry," relating the tight rhythm of spanking to lyric poetry (182). Later, with a nod to trashy pseudo-scientific paperback porn, Sedgwick draws attention to the greater proliferation of the "perversia" that emerges in longer narrative poetry. But what happens when the rhythms of both lyric and narrative are themselves perverted? The vignettes in *Le Corps lesbien* are interrupted—often midword in the French edition—by lists, primarily of body parts but also of actions such as "THE REACTIONS PLEASURE EMOTION . . . THE CRIES THE WAILINGS THE MURMURS THE HOARSENESS THE SOBS THE SHRIEKS THE VOCIFERATIONS THE WORDS THE SILENCES THE WHISPERINGS THE MODULATIONS THE SONGS THE STRIDENCIES THE LAUGHS" (126). These interruptions enact a perverse textual practice, undermining expected rhythms of narrative, of prose, and of poetry while simultaneously representing a relationship to bodily parts and reactions that refuses to cohere to established sexual genres and narratives.

Both Wittig's word choice and the layout of her text bear on the role of interruption; the way in which both elements are affected by translation illuminates their roles in the original. Wittig's frequent use of the word "brutalement" in *Le Corps lesbien* resists translation, emphasizing its productive polysemy in the French. David Le Vay sometimes translates "brutalement" as "brutally" and sometimes as "suddenly." And, indeed, it means both, but also "roughly," "bluntly," and "plainly." Wittig's interruptions certainly have an element of brutality and of roughness. They come suddenly: the two main styles of her text (lists and vignettes) often interrupt each other midsentence or, in the original, midword, a suddenness that is mellowed by the English translation's refusal to bifurcate words. Yet they are also blunt or plain. They do not conceal themselves. They demand that the reader make an active decision to keep going—or not. They require us to consider and affirm our own desires. As we read in one instance, "*I* touch your skull, *I* grasp it with all m/y fingers, *I* press it, *I* gather the skin over the whole of the cranial vault, *I* tear off the skin brutally beneath the hair, *I* reveal the beauty of the shining bone traversed by blood-vessels" (*Lesbian* 15; *corps* 9). In this passage, brutality but also suddenness, bluntness, and plainness reveal the beauty of what lies beneath the conventionally legible surfaces of the body.

The reaffirmations of consent we must enact at each of Wittig's brutal interruptions are not just those of sexual/textual receptivity. As Lynn Higgins observes, these interruptions are places where "the reader penetrates the text through its holes" (161). Wittig's textual style produces a work full of holes and fissures, which reflect the holes and fissures (or "brutal" making of holes and fissures) in the body that exceed the canonical pantheon of erotic parts. To embrace such holes as readers, we must actively participate in the production of new modes of engagement, with both text and erotic embodiment.

Wittig presents both language/gender and embodied sex/gender as integral to her feminist critique of the social contract. The incessant need to consciously reaffirm consent to Wittig's text works synergistically with her goal of subverting the received social contract. The problem, for Wittig, is that our current contract is fundamentally heterosexual and that "we say yes to the social bond when we conform to the conventions and rules that were never formally enunciated but that nevertheless everybody knows and applies like magic" ("Social Contract" 39). Wittig deems precisely the obscuring of relationships of consent problematic, and so, Wittig's oeuvre implies, to fight problematic structures, we must be blunt and plain. We must consciously and plainly consent, or refuse consent, to contractual rules of our choosing rather than simply inherit a patriarchal contract that precedes us.

According to Wittig, only by escaping the existing contract in favour of voluntary associations that would constitute a new one can we consent in meaningful ways. *Le Corps lesbien* opens with this suggestion, as Wittig writes, "In this dark adored adorned gehenna say your farewells m/y very beautiful one m/y very strong one m/y very indomitable one m/y very learned one m/y very ferocious one m/y very gentle one m/y best beloved to what they . . . call affection tenderness or gracious abandon. There is not one who is unaware of what takes place here, which has no name yet. . . . But you know that not one will be able to bear seeing you with eyes turned up lids cut off your yellow smoking intestines spread in the hollow of your hands"[13] (13). The opening of Wittig's text is both warning and seduction, an incitement to take leave of the norm and enter that perverse thing that is yet unnamed. As Karin Cope observes, Wittig "call[s] for and mak[es] transformative readers" (85), asking, "What will you do? How will you read?" (90). The reader is given the choice to join the ranks of those who cannot bear what Wittig has to offer or to affirm—and reaffirm—her desire to continue, away from the coercions of the default contract or the referendum and toward active, perverse consent.

WOJNAROWICZ AND HUSTLING GENRE

Like Wittig's novel, Wojnarowicz's memoir engages in a deliberate sexual sociopolitical project combining representation of marginal sex with the perversion of genre. Earlier portions of the text are the most decohesive. As Eric Waggoner notes, they "frustrate our reading of Wojnarowicz's text on the level of genre expectation" from the outset (175). Moving in and out of various sexual encounters, fantasies, and moments, these sections contain sentences so lengthy that they are impractical to cite. A sentence in which Wojnarowicz moves from a brief memory of his earlier childhood; to a general recollection of his time as an underfed, underage street hustler; to the description of a specific rubber-fetishist trick exceeds three pages, ending with "when he came into his rubber sneaker he'd roll over all summer sweaty and oh that was a good load musta ate some eggs today and I'm already removing my uniform and he says he loves the way my skeleton moves underneath my skin when I bend over to retrieve one of my socks" (8). The meandering, unpredictable forms of such sentences mirror the meandering, spontaneous encounters and fantasies described throughout the memoir while often also contradicting assumptions that all of Wojnarowicz's underage hustling experiences must be sources of trauma and coercion.

Close to the Knives' explicit statements about the importance of divergent sexual representation are more reproducible. Discussing the manner in which dissident sexualities are excluded from representation, not only by overt censorship but through curatorial practices, Wojnarowicz writes, "It is a standard practice to make invisible any kind of sexual imaging other than white straight male erotic fantasies. Sex in America long ago slid into a small set of generic symbols; mention the word 'sex' and the general public appears to only imagine a couple of heterosexual positions in a bed—there are actual laws in parts of this country forbidding anything else even between consenting adults. So people have found it necessary to define their sexuality in images, in photographs and drawings and movies in order not to disappear" (119). Here, the genres of sex, upheld and regulated by the law, supersede stated consent, and this narrowing of categories so as to exclude dissident acts and subjects from consent (both actual and to representation) is what Wojnarowicz combats. Genre deviation in the realm of art (I would argue this includes text as well as images) is necessary in order to revitalize consent, transforming it from a referendum-like response to symbols of genre into an active relation to both deviant sex and creative production. As Dianne Chisholm notes, in Wojnarowicz's writing, "A radical poetics works with/as a radical erotics works with/as a radical politics" (82). Both sexual and textual production and consent become active and affirmative. As Wojnarowicz elaborates later, "Each and every gesture carries a reverberation that is meaningful in its diversity; bottom line, we have to find our own forms of gesture and communication" (123).

These forms involve consciously both taking leave of and consenting to genres encoded in normative literature, sexuality, and the taxonomies of law. As Wojnarowicz notes, we can never fully exit existing structures, but we can become more consciously aware of our relationships to them, rejecting the slide into implicit consent. He writes that "since my existence is essentially outlawed before I even come into knowledge of what my desires are or what my sensibility is, then I can only step back from the arms of government and organized religion" (59). The law serves to rigidify social genres that both exclude and, like the impugned Canadian sex work provisions, endanger sexual dissidents. Wojnarowicz and his peers experience violence and risk from which the law does nothing to protect them. Yet as he claims, "I'd met guys [including sex-work clients] this society would incarcerate or kill who gave me more than any government official, state agency, or christian outfit . . . ever did or ever could" (233).

Remembering the period after coming off the street, Wojnarowicz recalls that "I crawled through the walls of every social taboo I could come across. I wanted to celebrate everything we are denied through structure of laws or physical force" (171). These boundary crossings, these legally and socially invalidated practices of consent, are far more active and agential than the referendum-like, genre-solidifying functions of the law and of Wertheimer's vision of consent. And this is equally a crossing of more conventionally understood genre boundaries. Wojnarowicz writes that he feels less alone when creating or encountering representations that "disrupt the generic representations that have come to be the norm in the various medias outside my door" (120).

ACKER AND VOICING DESIRE

Like Wojnarowicz's and Wittig's, Acker's text is subject to interruptions. It is episodic, with fragments of (sometimes contradictory) characters' narratives often being designated as "spoken" through other characters. Circuitously, it makes its argument about consent by answering a question about evading coercion posed in its final lines in an interaction that takes place at its centre. In the novel's final pages, Abhor asks her former lover, Thivai, and his male companion "why they kept kicking me. Hadn't imprisoning me been enough?" (Acker, *Empire* 224). Thivai answers, "By enduring and breaking through tribulation, I could become a model and heroine to women" (Acker, *Empire* 224). Abhor's question extends into a hope expressed in the final lines of the novel: "I stood there . . . and thought that I didn't yet know what I wanted. I now fully knew what I didn't want and what and whom I hated. That was something. . . . And then I thought that, one day, maybe, there'ld [sic] be a human society in a world which is beautiful, a society which wasn't just disgust" (Acker, *Empire* 227).

Yet Abhor has already come close to this hope in an earlier episode—a profoundly erotically charged one in which sex is never had, because the answer to her question about evading coercion involves consent that affirms and states perverse desire rather than simply responding yes or no to the desires of others, something Abhor cannot yet do. Wandering around Paris, Abhor decides to cut off her hair. She finds a shop where "inside a pair of grey handcuffs hung from a string from the ceiling. Under no circumstances were the customers allowed to touch their own hair. . . . I felt so comfortable when I was in this operating room, I began to dream. The haircutter . . . was stocky. Her hair was dead, white. I was dreaming. When she asked me what I wanted to look like, I replied, 'Yours.' The truth always surprises me" (Acker, *Empire* 111). In its explicit perversion, the shop allows Abhor to state her own desire: to be "yours." Even so, when the cut is finished, Abhor is unable to extend this frankness, as "[the haircutter] asked me if I wanted anything. *What* is always equal to *who*" (Acker, *Empire* 112, emphasis in original). After failing to answer, Abhor muses, "Because I'm stupid, it's taken me half a lifetime . . . for me to learn that I have to say what I want to get what I want. Who. . . . If I could have spoken at that minute to the haircutter, perhaps I could have been free!" (Acker, *Empire* 112). Acker describes *Empire of the Senseless* as "the beginning of a movement from no to yes," but the movement expressed in this passage goes beyond the framework that would permit simple yes or no answers ("A Few Notes" 36). Here, actively stating and asking for one's desires in a context that will not allow for passive acquiescence presents the possibility to exceed the "poor freedom" of the referendum. And Acker's writing, in its stylistic perversions, similarly refuses passive acquiescence on the part of the reader.

EMBRACING PERVERSION

Ultimately, to the extent to which perversion, sexual and textual, falls sufficiently outside of the norm that its encounters and forms cannot go unspoken or assumed, the perverse both brings into consciousness the ongoing negotiations of consent we ignore in our everyday lives and demands that we make affirmative statements and decisions about our desires that exceed yes and no. In prioritizing perverse pleasures that do not follow goal-oriented narrative trajectories, the perverse evades the problematic position of closure that traditional narrativity coerces women to accept without falling into the passivity that is assumed to go along with voluntarily placing ones hands into the haircutter's cuffs. In choosing and producing generically illegible forms of sexuality, sociality, and creative production, these affirmative practices of consent, of bodily, legal, and social boundary crossing, restructure both legibility and illegibility. They encourage openness to that which normative "generic representations" exclude as illegible. At the same time, their very illegibility makes those who are themselves illegibly dissident, as artists, readers, and sexual subjects, more legible *in their very illegibility* both to themselves and to each other.

NOTES

1. I use David Le Vay's translation, published as *The Lesbian Body*, unless otherwise specified. Page references are to the translation, except where relevant and specifically otherwise noted (cited parenthetically as *corps*).
2. In film studies, Laura Mulvey's foundational work on the male gaze is relevant. On the textual level, *écriture féminine*, most notably associated with Hélène Cixous, is most associated with finding a stylistically antipatriarchal mode of writing.
3. See Ostrovsky, Hélène Vivienne Wenzel, and Diane Griffin Crowder for examples of the former and Kym Martindale the latter.
4. For a discussion of Acker's use of tattoo drawings, see Joseph Conte.

5. While Wertheimer is the most notable of these critics, other book-length studies of sexual consent reproduce similar restrictive assumptions. An exception is Robin Bauer's ethnography of queer women and trans people's BDSM culture; given its specific cultural focus, it necessarily operates around assumptions other than those of most works addressing sexual consent "in general."

6. BDSM stands for bondage and discipline, dominance and submission, and sadism and masochism.

7. Similar reasoning has been used elsewhere. U.S., Canadian, and U.K. legal reasoning regarding consent to BDSM practices are very similar, and the U.S. precedent is also partially motivated by homophobia. Archard explicitly discusses the Spanner Case *as* his example of sadomasochism in his book; however, his analysis goes little beyond establishing that the practices of those involved were very icky but should not have been criminalized.

8. *Top* is a general BDSM term for sadists, dominants, and so on, and *bottom* is a general term for masochists, submissives, and so on.

9. Samuels was turned in by his developing company.

10. While the Supreme Court of Canada ultimately largely rejected the Crown's appeal, striking down the laws that criminalized hiring help and working indoors in the 2013 *Canada v. Bedford* decision, the then conservative Canadian government replaced them with near-identical, and in some ways more restrictive, legislation titled the "Protection of Communities and Exploited Persons Act," whose title (and contents) reproduce the AGO and AG's reasoning. It remains to be seen whether Canada's subsequent Liberal government will rescind the act.

11. According to a 1989 *Herald Scotland* article, which reports on charges faced by fifteen men and a sixteenth who was remanded in absentia, four men were charged with aiding and abetting gross bodily harm on themselves, either alone or in combination with other charges ("15 Charged").

12. Cristina Ionica argues that the discontinuity of Acker's texts alienate the reader in ways that disown female masochism, while Hanjo Berressem suggests that Acker presents sado-masochism as fundamentally Oedipal, contending, "Acker highlights the interrelation of sexuality and culture by identifying the world of the fathers (the world of sado-masochism) with the world of capitalism" (406). I argue (albeit via Wittig) that such textual discontinuity represents, rather, an incitement to perverse readerly agency, one that simultaneously resists Oedipal closure.

13. I deviate from Le Vay's translations here by changing "they, the women" to simply "they," since the class and category of "woman" is explicitly what Wittig strives to evade.

WORKS CITED

Acker, Kathy. *Empire of the Senseless*. Grove, 1988.

———. "A Few Notes on Two of My Books." *Review of Contemporary Fiction*, vol. 9, no. 3, 1989, pp. 31–36.

Archard, David. *Sexual Consent*. Westview, 1998.

Barthes, Roland. *S/Z*. Translated by Richard Miller, Hill and Wang, 1974.

Bauer, Robin. *Queer BDSM Intimacies: Critical Consent and Pushing Boundaries*. Palgrave Macmillan, 2014.

Bedford v. Canada. 102 O.R. (3d) 321. Ontario Superior Court of Justice. 2010. *Superior Court of Justice Decisions.* Canlii.

Bedford v. Canada. 109 O.R. (3d) 1. Court of Appeals for Ontario. 2012. *Court of Appeals for Ontario Decision.* Canlii.

Berlant, Lauren. "The Subject of True Feeling: Pain, Privacy, and Politics." *Left Legalism/Left Critique,* edited by Wendy Brown and Janet Halley, Duke UP, 2002, pp. 105–133.

Berressem, Hanjo. "Body—Wound—Writing." *Amerikastudien,* vol. 44, no. 3, 1999, pp. 393–411.

Chisholm, Dianne. "Outlaw Documentary: David Wojnarowicz's Queer Cinematics, Kinerotics, Autothanatographics." *Canadian Review of Comparative Literature,* vol. 21, nos. 1–2, 1994, pp. 81–102.

Conte, Joseph. "Discipline and Anarchy: Disrupted Codes in Kathy Acker's *Empire of the Senseless.*" *Revista Canaria de Estudios Ingleses,* vol. 39, 1999, pp. 13–31.

Cope, Karin. "Plastic Actions: Linguistic Strategies and *Le Corps lesbien.*" *Hypatia,* vol. 6, no. 3, 1991, pp. 74–96. *JSTOR.*

Crowder, Diane Griffin. "Amazons and Mothers? Monique Wittig, Hélène Cixous and Theories of Women's Writing." *Contemporary Literature,* vol. 24, no. 2, 1983, pp. 117–144.

Derrida, Jacques. "The Law of Genre." Translated by Avital Ronell, *Critical Inquiry,* vol. 7, no. 1, 1980, pp. 55–81.

"15 Charged after Operation Spanner." *Herald Scotland,* 9 Oct. 1989. www.heraldscotland .com/news/11931638.15_charged_after_Operation_Spanner.

Haag, Pamela. *Consent: Sexual Rights and the Transformation of American Liberalism.* Cornell UP, 1999.

Higgins, Lynn. "Nouvelle Nouvelle Autobiographie: Monique Wittig's *Le Corps lesbien.*" *Sub-Stance,* vol. 5, no. 14, 1976, pp. 160–166.

Ionica, Cristina. "Masochism ± Benefits, or Acker with Lacan." *LIT: Literature Interpretation Theory,* vol. 24, no. 4, 2013, pp. 278–298.

Khan, Ummni. *Vicarious Kinks: S/M in the Socio-legal Imaginary.* U of Toronto P, 2014.

Lauretis, Teresa de. "Desire in Narrative." *Alice Doesn't: Feminism Semiotics Cinema,* Indiana UP, 1984, pp. 103–157.

Martindale, Kym. "Author(iz)ing the Body: Monique Wittig, *The Lesbian Body* and the Anatomy Texts of Andreas Vesalius." *European Journal of Women's Studies,* vol. 8, no. 3, 2001, pp. 343–356.

Ostrovsky, Erica. "Transformation of Gender and Genre Paradigms in the Fiction of Monique Wittig." *On Monique Wittig: Theoretical, Political and Literary Essays,* edited by Namascar Shaktini, U of Illinois P, 2005, pp. 115–120.

People v. Samuels. 250 Cal. App. (2d) 501. California Court of Appeals. 1967. *US Law.* Justia.

Redding, Art. "Bruises, Roses: Masochism and the Writing of Kathy Acker." *Contemporary Literature,* vol. 35, no. 2, 1994, pp. 281–304.

Regina v. Brown et al., 1 AC 212. United Kingdom House of Lords. 1992. *United Kingdom House of Lords Decisions.* Bailii.

Regina v. Butler. 1 SCR 452. Supreme Court of Canada. 1992. *Judgments of the Supreme Court of Canada.* Lexum.

Scarry, Elaine. "Consent and the Body: Injury, Departure, and Desire." *New Literary History,* vol. 21, no. 4, 1990, pp. 867–896.

Sedgwick, Eve Kosofsky. *Epistemology of the Closet.* U of California P, 1990.

———. "A Poem Is Being Written." *Tendencies,* Duke UP, 1993, pp. 177–214.

Shaktini, Namascar, editor. *On Monique Wittig: Theoretical, Political, and Literary Essays*. U of Illinois P, 2005.

Silberman, Seth Clark. "'I Have Access to Your Glottis': The Fleshy Syntax, Ethical Irony, and Queer Intimacy of Monique Wittig's *Le Corps lesbien*." *GLQ*, vol. 13, no. 4, 2007, pp. 467–487.

Waggoner, Eric. "'This Killing Machine Called America': Narrative of the Body in David Wojnarowicz's *Close to the Knives*." *a/b: Auto/Biography Studies*, vol. 15, no. 2, 2000, pp. 171–192.

Wenzel, Hélène Vivienne. "The Text as Body/Politics: An Appreciation of Monique Wittig's Writings in Context." *Feminist Studies*, vol. 7, no. 2, 1981, pp. 264–287.

Wertheimer, Alan. *Consent to Sexual Relations*. Cambridge UP, 2003.

Whatling, Claire. "Wittig's Monsters: Stretching the Lesbian Reader." *Textual Practice*, vol. 11, no. 2, 1997, pp. 237–248.

Wittig, Monique. *Le corps lesbian*. Les Éditions de Minuit, 1973.

———. *The Lesbian Body*. Translated by David LeVay, Avon Books, 1976.

———. "On the Social Contract." *The Straight Mind and Other Essays*, Beacon, 1992, pp. 33–45.

Wojnarowicz, David. *Close to the Knives: A Memoir of Disintegration*. Vintage Books, 1991.

Zirelli, Linda M. G. "A New Grammar of Difference: Monique Wittig's Poetic Revolution." *On Monique Wittig: Theoretical, Political and Literary Essays*, edited by Namascar Shaktini, U of Illinois P, 2005, pp. 87–114.

4 · CONSENT AND THE LIMITS OF ABUSE IN *THEIR EYES WERE WATCHING GOD* AND "AIN'T NOBODY'S BUSINESS IF I DO"

KEJA VALENS

In order to posit the ethical importance of using people—that it "allows one to trust, to play, and to experience the reality of both the other and the self" ("Using People" 105)—Barbara Johnson first establishes that it is possible to use people ethically. Immanuel Kant, she points out, has reasoned that the ethical use of people depends on two things: (1) the human being cannot be used merely as a means without being "at the same time a purpose himself" and (2) the human being must consent, "for this moral law is based on the autonomy of his will, as a free will which, according to its universal laws, must necessarily be able at the same time to agree with that to which it is to subject itself" (Kant 167 [132]).[1] Johnson focuses on the first of Kant's conditions to show how using people requires seeing others as separate from ourselves and independent of our desires and vice versa. Kant's second condition, which he actually sets out as a basis for the first, explains that we must see people as purposes in themselves because they are "the subject of the moral law" that is based on the free will (167 [132]). Possessing a free will allows a person to consent—to use or deny consent—to abuse.

I began to wonder about the mutually constitutive limits of consent and abuse in being struck by two powerful moments in the depiction of African American women: when Janie in Zora Neale Hurston's *Their Eyes Were Watching*

God and the singing subject in Billie Holiday's "Ain't Nobody's Business If I Do" consent to being hit by "their man."[2] I am not arguing that Hurston's Janie and Holiday's singing subject are actually consenting to abuse. But I *am* arguing that if we consider the possibility that they might exercise their free will to consent to something that would otherwise be abuse, we gain the opportunity to consider what "abuse" is exactly, how consent interacts with it, and how, as Johnson says, ethics might function as something other than "only a form of restraint" (94).

Abuse is bad. It belongs to the field of what Johnson calls violence and appropriation. The fact that domestic abuse is a leading cause of emergency room visits by women in the United States indicates the danger of suggesting that women can consent to what would be abuse.[3] Women and African Americans, among others, have been subjected to abuse based on the assumption, which it also promotes, that they belong to a group of beings that are not deserving or able to be ends in themselves, to exercise free will, to be persons. Ensuring for every human being the ability to be seen always as a purpose in himself or herself and respecting his or her ability to grant or refuse consent might eliminate abuse. For postcolonial and feminist criticism, the task of exposing the structures, the ideological forces and individual foibles, that allow and even promote the abuse of women and "minorities" are key to this process of emancipation.

Nonetheless, I wonder if literary and critical analyses that target exposing and eliminating the abuse of women and "minorities" do not at the same time disempower and oversimplify the subjectivity of the very people they claim to shield from abuse by disallowing that they might consent to it. To simply and prima facie exclude certain acts (including being hit by one's partner) from the possibility of being consented to or certain individuals (such as women who are in relationship with men who hit them) from the possibility of granting consent in my view only introduces another level of disempowerment or even subjugation without consent. If we make blanket exclusions, do we not cross the fine line between pointing out the denial of subjectivity and denying a means for the acquisition or expression of subjectivity? Where exactly is the line between using the idea of consent to critique its inaccessibility to certain subjects at certain times and reinforcing limiting determinations of what a subject can and cannot consent to, of which subjects can and cannot grant consent? It seems to me that acknowledging the potential as well as the danger of allowing consent to violence can serve as a timely reminder and requirement that we focus not on promoting the act of consent but on understanding how abuse happens, securing the conditions for consent, and respecting the free will and agency of even those who grant consent to things that we condemn.[4]

Arguing that "the black performative is inextricably linked with the specter of contented subjection," Saidiya Hartman seems to pose rhetorical questions when she asks, "Is it possible to consider, let alone imagine, the agency of the performative?" (52) and "Do points of resistance inhabit the enactment of willed surrender?" (103). Enslaved black women, Hartman claims, cannot obtain the conditions for granting consent, and so their claims of "willed surrender" to the sexual demands of white men can only reinscribe their subjection. Similarly, the transformation of pain into pleasure through performance can only reinscribe the black body as the body in pain. Although the legacy of slavery cannot be underestimated, I believe that it has become possible, indeed necessary, to ask as open questions: Can consent turn subjection into subjectivity? Abuse into use? Can Hurston and Holiday perform contented subjection as scenes of objection?[5] If withdrawing consent can transform something from use to abuse and vice versa, then there is a possibility of empowerment at the mutual limit of consent and abuse. For as much as it derives from the ability to determine what is abuse and what is not, consent creates that capacity—and perhaps also the opportunity to contend with ways that use and abuse may be less distinct than we would like.

In the rest of this chapter, I explore Hurston's *Their Eyes Were Watching God* and, more briefly, Holiday's "Ain't Nobody's Business if I Do" as exemplifying the performance and analysis of transformative consent that not only result *from* but that also resulted *in* the acquisition and expression of a new black American subjectivity that began to emerge in the Harlem Renaissance and that remains both tangible and elusive.

EMPOWERING CONSENT

Their Eyes Were Watching God offers a powerful tale of black female empowerment, exposing the particular struggles, strategies, and achievements of black women in the face of abuses from white society and from black men. At the time of its publication, 1937, the setting of *Their Eyes Were Watching God* (all-black communities in Florida in the 1930s) was judged impossible by white critics while the novel's focus (Janie Crawford's complicated relationships with men) was judged politically unengaged and even retrograde by black critics, most famously Richard Wright. In the 1980s, *Their Eyes Were Watching God* was so successfully rescued and rehabilitated by black women scholars that it is now considered a classic text in American and African American literature.[6] How deserving it is of this place is perhaps best evidenced by its ability to continue to move readers and critics to keep reconsidering its many valences.

Their Eyes Were Watching God opens with Janie returning home alone, at the end of her third marriage, to Tea Cake. Janie ignores all the questions her neighbors have about what happened but undertakes to tell her friend Phoeby. Janie starts her story not where she last left Phoeby, about a year previously, but back around when she was six years old and includes the series of abuses to which she did not consent and which she struggled to escape throughout her early life. When Janie hits puberty and recognizes the possibility of her own sexual desire and pleasure, her grandmother arranges and enforces her first marriage with Logan Killiks. Although Killiks only threatens violence toward Janie, the marriage itself constitutes an abuse. Janie's grandmother has arranged a marriage for the purpose of protecting Janie financially and physically. Janie wants a marriage to someone she loves. "Naw, Nanny, no ma'am!" Janie says when her grandmother tells her she is set to marry Killiks (13). Janie's grandmother responds by hitting Janie, recounting the stories of the brutal work and violent rapes that she and Janie's mother suffered and alternately deriding Janie's desire for love in marriage and telling Janie she will come to love Killiks with time (13–20). Three months after the wedding, Janie's grandmother dies. Freed from Nanny's coercive force, Janie comes into her own womanhood: "She knew now that marriage did not make love. Janie's first dream was dead, so she became a woman" (24), able to leave Killiks. Janie chooses her next husband herself: Joe Starks, with his talk of "change and chance" and his promises that, if she comes with him, "den all de rest of yo' natural life you kin live lak you oughta" (28), but the marriage ends up holding Janie fixed in *Joe's* design for how she ought to live. This might itself constitute a certain abuse, even if only of her expectations. And after a while, Joe begins to hit Janie, another abuse to which she does not consent. Janie eventually ends the marriage to Joe as well. Finally, Janie meets Tea Cake.

Although their marriage is significantly different from the first two—as Janie says, "Dis ain't no business proposition, and no race after property and titles. Dis is uh love game" (108), full of play and pleasure—Tea Cake also hits Janie:

> When Mrs. Turner's brother came and brought him over to be introduced, Tea Cake had a brainstorm. Before the week was over, he had whipped Janie. Not because her behavior justified his jealousy, but it relieved that awful fear inside him. Being able to whip her reassured him in possession. No brutal beating at all. He just slapped her around a bit to show he was boss. Everybody talked about it next day in the fields. It aroused a sort of envy in both men and women. The way he petted and pampered her as if those two or three face slaps nearly killed her made the women see visions and the helpless way she clung to him made men dream dreams. (140)

This element of Janie and Tea Cake's relationship leads Mary Helen Washington, among others, to "questions about [*Their Eyes Were Watching God's*] uncritical depiction of violence toward women" (xiv). To argue that Janie consents to Tea Cake might raise even more such questions, or it might reveal that rather than an uncritical depiction of violence toward women, *Their Eyes Were Watching God* offers a deeply complex consideration of women's options, of their empowerment, and perhaps also of their pleasures.

It is important to pause here to consider what exactly constitutes abuse. By speaking of the use and abuse of people and by locating abuse in the realm of "violence and appropriation," I have been focusing on one aspect of abuse: that covered under the fourth definition in current use (of five) in the *Oxford English Dictionary* (*OED*) and the second (of three) in *Merriam-Webster's Dictionary of Law* (*MWL*)—for there is certainly a legal element underlying questions of the abuse of people, which appears explicitly in the trial at the end of *Their Eyes Were Watching God*. The *OED* definition reads, "a. Sexual violation, esp. rape; sexual assault or maltreatment (esp. of a woman or child). In later use freq. including also physical or emotional ill-treatment. b. Physical or mental maltreatment; the inflicting of physical or emotional harm or damage." The *MWL* definition is "to inflict physical or emotional mistreatment or injury on (as one's child) purposely or through negligence or neglect and often on a regular basis b: to engage in sexual activity with (a child under an age specified by statute)." This kind of abuse is the subject of legal intervention. But while there are some actions that are both illegal in and of themselves and that often fall under the definition of abuse, such as sex with a minor, in most cases the place of the will (and often most importantly its expression) in the experience is the key determining factor for a finding of abuse.[7]

The definitions of abuse as it relates to persons are certainly related to the other definitions of abuse in the same dictionaries, but the specificity of physical, and often sexual, harm is unique. In part, the specificity relates directly to the abuse of people, for, as Kant makes clear, to use a person involves the recognition and respect of the other, absent of which physical as well as moral harm occurs. In as much as consent is an expression of will, the issue of consent may only be relevant in regards to the abuse of persons (which still leaves questions of what constitutes a person). But I also want to invoke other understandings and objects of abuse because they require consideration of the tenuous distinction between use and abuse and of a much less clear judgment as to the badness of abuse.

The first definitions of abuse in the *OED* and *MWL* relate to misuse.[8] When one abuses language or other nonhuman things, one makes words or things serve a purpose other than the expected or regular one. This kind of abuse can be not only relatively harmless but perhaps also inevitable and even desirable. Most swears involve making words serve a purpose other than the expected or regular one, but so do most metaphors. Many drug addictions involve making a substance serve a purpose other than the expected or regular one, but so do many major advances in medicine (think penicillin).

The role of "expected or regular use" attests that it is not only the individual will that matters in the determination of abuse but also the social will. Indeed, while competency and autonomy are conditions for the ability to grant consent, it turns out that they are often also determined on the basis of what is consented to. The prohibition on consenting to certain kinds of harm goes something like this: no one in their right mind would freely consent to this; if someone consents to it, they are not in their right mind or they are being coerced. Or, in Kantian terms, one is an end in oneself in as much as one consents to things that one wants freely and that any rational being could want freely (42–45).[9] As brilliant as his moral reasoning may be, Kant's list of harms that cannot be consented to reveal the profound influence of dominant ideology in the determination of the grounds for valid, morally transformative consent. For Kant, no dignified and self-respecting human could want freely to sell body parts or sexual services, use sexual organs outside of the context of heterosexual marriage, commit suicide, self-mutilate, or use stupefying liquors or drugs.[10] The restriction to consent to certain kinds of harm is regularly codified with the justification that, in as much as it accomplishes something that no rational being could freely want, it harms not only the individual but also the society in which it occurs.[11] At the time Hurston was writing, interracial marriage, among other things, was illegal on the basis of its supposed harm not only to individuals but also to the social body, the person of the state that is harmed when its moral and its legal rules are broken. And Pamela Haag reminds, "Seduction, abduction, white slavery, arranged marriage, interracial sexuality, and interracial rape . . . were understood as acts of 'violence' or 'choice' in revealingly distinct, yet sometimes contradictory, ways at different times" (xvii).

How then might we read Tea Cake's hitting Janie? Is it "violence against women"? Is it abuse? When he hits Janie, does Tea Cake use her merely as a means "without [her] also being a purpose [her]self"? Can Janie, if she acts with free will, consent to it in such a way as to render it use rather than abuse?

Just because the "whipping" happened and Janie the following day clung to Tea Cake does not necessarily mean that she consented to it. Indeed, this might rather exemplify why we should be wary of unproblematic qualifications of consent. Janie never says any version of "I consent to your whipping me." Rather, we read her consent after the fact through her actions, which we take as signs of her will, before and after the event.

Where explicit consent is not given but is assumed through the repeated action of noncomplaint, we are either in the realm of something like Stockholm syndrome or else we are in the realm of what John Locke calls "tacit consent through residence" (*Second Treatise* 8.119–122), derived from the Platonic argument in the *Crito* that if someone is free to leave (Athens) and does not, he has agreed, by remaining, to the laws of the land. If you are free to leave a situation to which you do not consent and you stay, you have consented. Now what constitutes the ability to leave certainly requires some investigation.

When Elaine Scarry studies consent in warfare, she deems the soldier who is drafted as consenting if he has the ability to flee or go to jail or file for some exemption (*Body in Pain* 153). The options that Janie's grandmother offers prior to her first wedding—Janie can marry Logan or "maybe de menfolks white or black is makin' a spit cup outa you" (19)—show that the conditions, or expected conditions, that one might meet upon exercising the freedom to leave can render that freedom unreal. Such considerations lead Heidi Hurd to conclude that "actus reus," which is at the basis of "tacit consent through residence," is not a good measure of consent. Hurd prefers "mens rea" or the "subjective mental state" of the person as a measure of consent (135–137). I believe, however, that by thinking through "tacit consent through residence," we can see how both measures need to be considered. If Janie's actions, such as staying in a situation, suggest consent, then we should consider that consent *may* be present and go on to investigate what we can know of her "subjective mental state."

In the first year of Janie's first marriage, she believes that the conditions outside of that marriage would be even worse than those in it, and so she is not free to leave. But as soon as Joe comes along and tells Janie about "dis place dat colored folks was buildin' theirselves" where "he meant to buy in big" (27), Janie learns of different possible conditions. She takes her chances and leaves Killiks, seizing on the idea that "even if Joe was not there waiting for her, the change was bound to do her good" (31). Although she is able to walk into the marriage with Joe, quickly cut off from those around her by Joe's great success in setting himself up as mayor and her as the wife of the mayor, she is much less able to walk out. Indeed, when Joes takes to hitting her, Janie goes about her business as if nothing happened; "she bathed and put on a fresh dress and head kerchief and went on to the store before Jody had time to send for her. That was a bow to the outside of things" (68). But in the cultivation of an interior life that is distinct from her exterior life—one that Johnson examines in her "Metaphor, Metonymy and Voice in *Their Eyes Were Watching God*"—Janie shows how the outward appearance of tacit consent can coexist with an interior leaving that refuses consent.

By the time she gets to the marriage with Tea Cake, Janie has acquired the real ability to voice her refusal of consent—as evidenced both in the verbal showdown she eventually has with Joe and in an ultimatum that she issues early in her relationship with Tea Cake: "If you ever go off from me and have a good time lak dat and then come back heah tellin' me how nice Ah is, Ah specks tuh kill yuh dead. You heah me?" (119). Janie also ensures her ability to exercise her freedom of movement in her marriage with Tea Cake, retaining nine hundred dollars and a house of her own. Subsequent events, in which Janie forces a rabid Tea Cake to head north in search of medicine and then shoots him dead when he points a gun at her, prove her possession of the conditions for granting consent and her ability to deny consent when her remaining a "purpose in herself" is threatened.[12] And Janie is not an exception among the women around her in this respect. Indeed, what is exceptional about Janie is that she does not stop Tea Cake when he hits her: "Take some uh dese ol' rusty black women and dey would fight yuh all night long," Sop-de-Bottom knows from personal experience, for his "woman would spread her lungs all over Palm Beach County, let alone knock out [his] jaw teeth" if he ever hit her (141). When Janie instead "hung on him" the morning after, she shows that she has consented to Tea Cake's hitting her. Or more radically, Janie's consent itself transformed it from abuse to use. The hitting became "not-abuse"—nonabusive—in the moment when Janie, operating from a position where she was able to give consent, consented.

EMPOWERING CONSENT AS SOCIAL PROTEST

But what about Kant's condition: consent is possible, and abuse is transformed, only when the person is taken not merely as a means but "at the same time a purpose himself"? When Tea Cake hits Janie, he clearly has an end: "to show he was boss" (140). Read this way, Janie seems not to serve as a purpose in herself, and we can say that Tea Cake abuses Janie. But Tea Cake's end is not to show *Janie* that he is boss, nor is he necessarily laying claim or demonstrating to those present to being the boss of Janie. Rather, if Tea Cake's hitting is meant to show that he is boss, he is demonstrating this power to the Turners, who are trying to enforce a color code that says whiter is better. Just before the hitting incident, Mrs. Turner shares her analysis of the "race problem" with Janie: "[Black folks] makes me tired. Always laughin'! Dem laughs too much and dey laughs too loud. Always singin' ol' nigger songs! Always cuttin' de monkey for white folks. If it wuzn't for so many black folks it wouldn't be no race problem. De white folks would take us in wid dem. De black ones is holdin' us back" (135). Janie, says Mrs. Turner, should join with her to "lighten up de race" by leaving Tea Cake and marrying her brother—who is light skinned like herself and Janie. Janie questions Mrs. Turner's position and makes clear that she likes Tea Cake and his blackness, but she does not directly tell Mrs. Turner off. Then Mrs. Turner brings her brother over, and the hitting scene follows. It is not, then, jealousy over some feared relationship between Janie and Mrs. Turner's brother that motivates Tea Cake but Mrs. Turner's insistence that whiter is better. The possession, in which "being able to whip her reassured him" (140), is not of Janie but of the terms of desirability. So by accepting his blows, Janie consents neither to Tea Cake being her boss nor to his possessing her. Rather, Janie's consent to the hitting is a way of aligning herself with Tea Cake. When she goes about the next day such that "uh person can see every place you hit her" (140), Janie shows off her bruises as a way of showing to the Turners that she agrees with Tea Cake's idea of the color line, not theirs. If Janie is just the means for Tea Cake to assert his possession over the right point of view, then she could still be a means without being an end in herself; however, in as much as the point of refusing the Turners' view is to assure that every black person, light or dark, is a purpose unto themselves, not just a means for lightening (or failing to lighten) the race, Janie is both a means and an end in herself.

My reading here shares Shawn Miller's argument that the key difference between Janie's first two marriages and her third lies less is the ways that Tea Cake is different from Killiks and Joe and more in the ways that Janie changes over the course of the novel (83). However, while Miller takes Janie's primary goal to be "love" in "her ideal marriage" (84) and reads her as developing, over the course of the novel, a changed sense of what that means and how that is to be achieved (83), I find rather that Janie moves over the course of the novel from taking "her ideal marriage" as the end to taking herself to be an end-in-herself. The marriage with Tea Cake turns out to be a key turning point because in it Janie is able to effect the transformation from marriage as an end with herself and her husband as the means to herself as an end with consent as the means. I agree with Miller that she "uses submission as a strategy of resistance," but I believe that she uses it not to achieve "mastery of [the] form" of marriage or "love" but rather to achieve autonomy (83, 93). Janie uses consent as a mode of empowerment that allows her, and the novel, to achieve not social mastery but "social protest."

Janie consents to being hit because, all things considered, it is the best option; although being hit is not desired in itself, consenting to it achieves something beyond the experience of being hit that is more important than the undesirableness of being hit. Even though her own person suffers a certain degree of harm, Janie chooses to align with Tea Cake; she performs subjection to Tea Cake as a scene of objection to racist economic, legal, and moral orders.

I want to highlight this aspect of my reading with a detour to Billie Holiday's "Ain't Nobody's Business If I Do." Like Janie's relationship with Tea Cake, this song is often read as representing the problem of black women's abuse and their apparent acceptance of it.[13] And I contend that, like Janie with Tea Cake, Holiday's singing subject consents to (here, potentially) being hit by "her man," turning what would be abuse into use. How exactly Holiday's singing subject does that—in distinction to the singing subjects in the performances of other singers doing the same song—and what that shows about jazz, the performative, consent, and black women will have to be developed elsewhere. What I am interested in here is how, like for Janie, the consent serves not so much to allow the man to hit her because she desires to be hit (although, as with Janie, I also want to maintain that as a possibility) but more to form an alliance with the man against the dominant racist society.

As recorded in the Commodore and Decca Masters single, Holiday sings,

There ain't nothin' I ever do or nothin' I ever say
That folks don't criticize me, but I'm going to do
Just as I want to anyway
(And don't care just) what people say.

If I should take a notion, to jump (right) into the ocean,
Ain't nobody's business if I do.

If I go to church on Sunday, then cabaret all day Monday,
Ain't nobody's business if I do.

If my man ain't got no money, and I say, "Take all of mine, honey,"
Ain't nobody's business if I do.

If I give him my last nickel, and it leaves me in a pickle,
Ain't nobody's business if I do.

I'd rather my man would hit me
Than for him to jump up and quit me,
Ain't nobody's business if I do.

I swear I won't call no copper, if I'm beat up by my poppa,
Ain't nobody's business if I do,
Ain't nobody's business, nobody's business, nobody's business if I do.

Holiday's singing subject leverages the transformative power of consent to challenge dominant ideological forces that construct black women as incompetent or incapable to consent *and* to challenge the dominant construction of what can be consented to. This two-pronged critique occurs at the two levels of the song: the frame of the title and refrain and the possibility that frame allows in the verses.

The title and refrain of "Ain't Nobody's Business If I Do" defy "folks" who think it is their place to determine when consent can be or has been granted, claiming that what the singing subject might consent to in the verses of the song is "nobody's business." "Ain't Nobody's Business If I Do" addresses the problem of a disjunction between the views of those who seem to occupy the position of the arbiter of what ought to be consented to and the views of the singing subject. In the position of the arbiter are the "folks" who criticize. Unlike "poppa" and "copper," which appear later in the song and which are clearly racialized in Holiday's lexicon and in that of the Harlem Renaissance, "folks" refers both to blacks, as in W. E. B. Du Bois's *The Souls of Black Folk* (1903), and to whites, as in Langston Hughes's *The Ways of White Folks* (1934). The singing subject's insistence on it being "NOOOBody's business" suggests a double address, to both white and black folks, to both the broad regulatory structures of the state and the small regulatory structures of the community. This singing subject refuses all judgments other than her own as to what she can and does consent to. It is a radical position, one that pushes against foundational concepts of liberal democracy but that does so by asserting the singing subject's ability to stand in one of its most powerful positions, that of arbiter of what can be consented to, and to wield one of its most powerful tools, the moral transformation of consent.

Holiday's performance is striking in its assertion of control and power for the singing subject. The refrain becomes jaunty when Holiday exerts her characteristic control of timing—stretching the notes over the beats, lagging over folks' criticism and then easily catching up, almost skipping ahead—at "I'm going to do just what I want to." The improvisation in the melody line as Holiday emphasizes various words and parts of words highlights the role of the singer in determining the tone. Holiday lilts over "ain't nobody's business" creating a playful and carefree rhythm. When she almost stops singing to speak "honey," that "honey" falls below her, spoken down to. The emphasis that she puts on rhyming words—nickel-pickle, hit me-quit me, poppa-coppa—renders them poetic elements, tools not only for conveying meaning but for making and remaking it.

As Holiday's singing subject claims a preference—rather than a need or even an acceptance, she would "*rather* my man would hit me / than for him to jump up and quit me"—she points to how we might think about her choice in terms of a critique of the conditions in which she lives. Pointing out that her will is likely to be exerted in less-than-ideal circumstances highlights that she consents to things that any rational being might not wish they *would* consent to but understands they *could* consent to. The singing subject in Holiday's "Ain't Nobody's Business If I Do" is like those of other black women singers who, as Nghana Lewis argues, are "self-conscious characters who examine their options and then choose to act in ways that facilitate their interests, whether or not observers/readers/listeners believe that they (re)act appropriately" (605).

So why would Holiday's singing subject consent to being hit? If we read the line "I'd rather my man would hit me / than for him to jump up and quit me" along with the previous and especially the following lines, we see that the singing subject aligns herself with a black man in opposition to a white police force and to the economic pressure that black women and men both face. The singing subject connects her potential consent to being hit to her poppa's potential arrest, noting the possibility that she could in the moment of being beat up by her poppa turn to a "copper," the necessarily white representative of American law, and shift her alliance. But she will not do this. And that she announces as much *prior* to the occurrence of any violence, faced only with its imagination, renders her refusal of police help *not* as the recognition that black women are between a rock and a hard place but as an assertion of the depth to which she refuses white law. Even should her own person suffer a certain degree of harm, she will choose to align with the black man, for she is performing subjection to the black man as a scene of objection to the white economic, legal, and perhaps also moral and pleasure-desire orders.[14]

The frame in which Hurston has Janie repeat her story back to Phoeby in defiance of the folks from her home town who would judge her choices with Tea Cake to be improper expressions of black womanhood is like Holiday's refrain, rendering Janie's an objection not only to the Turners' racism but also to the limits that anyone would place on how she can object to any of the social conditions that she finds problematic.

THE USE AND ABUSE OF CONSENT

It remains that Janie is "whipped." Does this act, which technically is violence against a woman, constitute the kind of abuse generally understood by "violence against women," whatever its end and whatever consent Janie may give? If it is not abuse because it has Janie as an end as well as a means and because Janie consents to it, what about what happens to Janie's body in the process?

Unlike the detailed description, two chapters previously, of Janie's blow to Tea Cake and the ensuing fight-becoming-sex (131–132), the actual whipping that Tea Cake delivers is not described. We see only its effects, briefly in the voice of the narrator and in scant more detail in a conversation between Tea Cake and Sop-de-Bottom. It would seem, from those passages as well as from her subsequent interactions with Tea Cake, that Janie experiences some kind of pleasure either in the act of being hit or in the effect it produces. Janie shows off her bruises not only to the Turners but to "everybody," and they both demonstrate "next day in the fields" increased signs of affection: "he petted and pampered her," "she hung on him" (140). Similarly, Holiday's singing subject can be read to consent to being hit not only because it is a harm that through consent can be transformed from abuse to use but because she takes some kind of pleasure in it, because she derives something that is like—though different enough to get its own line—the pleasure of jumping into the ocean or dancing Monday after having gone to church on Sunday.

The danger of using the experience of pleasure as a definition that excludes abuse is that in abusive situations there can be what seems to be the experience of pleasure: people orgasm during rape; repeated abuse can lead to a misplaced sympathy with the abuser that can manifest as a mistaken pleasure in the abuse. But to deny the possibility that acts or experiences that look like violence or abuse might bring real pleasure, might be sought after for pleasure, is to participate in the kind of logic that treats as either criminal or sick—for example, onanists, sodomites, and masochists.

The possibility that acts that are by some classified as abusive and doing violence can be occasions for pleasure has been played out in BDSM and queer theory, perhaps best summarized in Michel Foucault's remark that "the idea that S&M is related to a deep violence . . . is stupid. We know very well what all those people are doing is not aggressive; they are inventing new possibilities of pleasure with strange parts of their body—through the eroticization of the body" (165). That the end is pleasure rather than pain, even if it is pleasure through pain, renders the act useful rather than abusive. The means may be rather unusual, may even look like violence, but the end is the granting of pleasure to a person, and what could better recognize a person as a purpose in him or herself?

If we listen to Augustine, the granting or finding of pleasure in a person is precisely what turns the use of them into the abuse of them. For finding pleasure in a person is finding pleasure in a means, in something on our path to divine pleasure. That Augustine makes these remarks early in his discussion of signs and figures in *On Christian Teaching* is not accidental, for the problem of finding pleasure in the means and thus never getting to the end is precisely the problem of figurative language. Augustine advocates for the importance of figurative language so long as it is recognized as such and then deciphered and understood as part of an end, indeed the specific end of divine love. The danger of finding pleasure in a means is the danger that lurks behind all figurative language: that we might get stuck in the means, the figure, the embodiment, and never reach the proper end; we might treat the means as the end rather than seeing in the means (pleasure in things of this world) that which is also the end (pleasure in the divine). This same possibility of the ways that figurative language can get us stuck in appearances rather than convey substance is what concerns Locke in *An Essay Concerning Human Understanding*. But as he reads Locke's "Epistemology of Metaphor," Paul DeMan returns us to the point I also find in Foucault: use and abuse of language—and, I would add, use and abuse of people—might be inseparable (15–21). Indeed, use and abuse are so commonly paired that it is neither revolutionary nor extreme when Marjorie Garber writes, in *The Use and Abuse of Literature*, that "use and abuse are versions of the same" (33) and, after surveying an impressive series of writings about the use and abuse of literature from Plato to Harold Brooks, concludes that "it would be possible to reclassify the abuses as uses, and the uses as abuses, and to emerge with an equally viable and persuasive argument" (45).

Now perhaps I should return to my consideration that using language and using people are different. If we think of language and literature as operating in the realm of ideas and perspectives, it may seem not only easy but natural and right to use a simple shift in perspective or reclassification to transform abuse into use or vice versa, while there seems to be a material reality to the abuse of a person that cannot just be thought out of. But if W. E. B. DuBois and Louis Althusser and Frantz Fanon and Foucault have taught us anything, it is that ideas have material impact on people, and while the actual steps to thinking oneself out of physical and psychological abuse may be impossible to outline, let alone take, it happens. And Garber defends the uses and abuses of literature for life, pointing out that the problem with the abuse of language, if it is a problem, is that by extension, it abuses people—Plato wanted poetry excluded from his Republic not because it hurts language but because it "deforms its audience's minds" with its ability to (ab)use rhetoric to do such things as elicit emotion (*Republic* X). Nonetheless, the limitations on choice, on empowerment, and on people who are abused are such that the transformation from abuse to use often takes much more than a shift in perspective. The conditions for transforming use and abuse of language from one to the other may, in other words, be quite different from the conditions for granting consent (to abuse to anything else). And it may be that once the conditions for granting consent are secured, that alone makes whatever would be consented to use rather than abuse, while so long as the conditions for granting consent are not present, consent to abuse is impossible. And yet, *Their Eyes Were Watching God* opens with a reflection on women's ability to reconfigure their experience even after it has occurred through the creative practice of using memory to create a dream—in other words, through representation and figuration. The first two paragraphs of the novel read,

> Ships at a distance have every man's wish on board. For some they come in with the tide. For others they sail forever on the horizon, never out of sight, never landing until the Watcher turns his eyes away in resignation, his dreams mocked to death by Time. That is the life of men.
>
> Now, women forget all those things they don't want to remember, and remember everything they don't want to forget. The dream is the truth. Then they act and do things accordingly. (1)

This ability to exchange dream, or rememory, for "all those things they don't want to remember" and to render the dream the truth, provides for a tremendous amount of empowerment. And it is an empowerment found in the ability to effect material change through perspective change rather than vice versa. The danger here, of course, is once again to suggest that a perspective change is a sufficient response to abuse; that after experiencing "all those things they don't want to remember," women are still in a position to claim and to act on their dreams; and that "all those things they don't want to remember" need not be combatted in any way other than forgetting. But the former, at least, is precisely the empowering resilience that I find Hurston positing in *Their Eyes Were Watching God*. And it is not that women simply shift perspective, deciding to consent to abuse and keep on being abused; rather, that moment when the dream becomes the truth is the moment after which she becomes able to "act and do things accordingly."

In speech acts, and in speech act theory, the use and abuse of language is similarly inseparable from, and of a same order with, the use and abuse of people. When I promise—the speech act par excellence, as Shoshana Felman points out in *The Scandal of the Speaking Body*—I use people and words. When I promise without sincerity or without the ability to deliver on the promise and yet "the [speech] act is achieved," J. L. Austin says, it is a particular kind of infelicity that we can call abuse (16).

It might not, then, be so incidental that Tea Cake's hitting Janie is introduced with a complicated bit of figurative language: "Tea Cake had a brainstorm." Originally, "brainstorm" referred, according the *OED*, to "a fit of rage, melancholy, etc.; a sudden change of mood or behaviour; (also) a sudden and severe attack of mental illness; an epileptic seizure. In later use also *fig.* or hyperbolically: a temporary loss of reason, a serious error of judgment." This meaning persists, but by 1925 in U.S. usage, it has also come to mean "a sudden and usually fortunate thought," and by 1948 it refers to "a concerted attempt to solve a problem, usually by a group discussion of spontaneously arising ideas." *Their Eyes Were Watching God* was published in 1937. Hurston was a student of language, paying careful attention in her field studies to local usages and making a concerted effort to render those in her fiction, but it is impossible to determine from context which meaning is correct here. This is precisely one of the ways that figurative language might be abusive to the reader: it leaves the reader unsure of how to determine meaning. Does the narrator condemn or laud Tea Cake's idea? Should we like or dislike Tea Cake? Or, perhaps more to the point, how is it that the reader ends up liking Tea Cake, hitting Janie and all? It is perhaps to answer this question for myself that I have undertaken this investigation. *Their Eyes Were Watching God*, like Holiday's "Ain't Nobody's Business," begins and ends on questions of the judging audience, the ability of storytelling to convey an experience that is not shared, and the qualities that might allow a friend, a judge, a reader, and the subject herself to "come and see" a variety of perspectives on Tea Cake, love, and "her horizon" (184). Perhaps what is at stake is a certain kind of communal blindness that fixes consent and abuse, to which the community holds in order to protect itself and which grand theories of use or consent or ethics try to stake out and shore up—even at the price of a blindness to the truth of a dream where the remembering or imagining woman is empowered to grant consent as she sees fit.

NOTES

1. Bracketed numbers refer to the page numbers of the standard edition of Kant's works, *Kants gesammelte Schriften, Königlich Preußische Akademie der Wissenschaften*, vol. 5. Edited by Paul Natorp. G. Reimer, 1908.

2. The original music and lyrics were written in 1922 by Porter Grainger and Everett Robbins. The song has been performed by countless singers. The collaborative nature of musical performance combined with the distinct process of making songs her own for which Billie Holiday is famous render Holliday's "Ain't Nobody's Business If I Do" a distinct song with a distinct meaning and figuration of consent and abuse. I distinguish between the singing subject in this performance and Billie Holiday. At the same time, Holiday created a persona that begged to be taken as the singing subject not only throughout her performances but also, in the tradition of Hurston's *Dust Tracks on the Road*, in her autobiography *Lady Sings the Blues*.

3. For documentation of the prevalence of domestic abuse, see the End Abuse "Fact Sheet."

4. Personhood and autonomy are of course unstable, narratively constructed, and embedded in the questionable reification of liberal subjectivity; however, their at least temporary acquisition is, I believe, essential for any project aiming even partially at liberation and/or equal rights within the frame of eighteenth–twenty-first century U.S. political and social relations.

5. Thanks to Stacie McCormick for the formulation "scenes of objection."

6. King traces the ascension of *Their Eyes Were Watching God* to canonical status.

7. Similarly, "assault" and "battery" are crimes only if they are "offensive" to the potentially assaulted or battered person (*Merriam-Webster's Dictionary of Law*).

8. The *Oxford English Dictionary*'s first definitions are "1. Improper usage; a corrupt practice or custom; *esp.* one that has become chronic. 2. a. Wrong or improper use (*of* something), misuse; misapplication; perversion. [3 and 4 are obsolete] 5. Contemptuous or insulting language; reviling, scurrility. Formerly also: a verbal insult." *Merriam-Webster's Dictionary of Law*'s first definition is "to put to a use other than the one intended."

9. Sara Ahmed takes on this question as she examines how "willful subjects" are pathologized or demonized for exercising their will to consent to things that do not conform with the dominant social or moral order.

10. Green offers a longer argument for how "there is good reason to believe that most of Kant's arguments around these first and second interpretations of the 'end in itself' formula are little more than refined prejudices" (250).

11. For a full discussion of consent to harm, see Vera Bergelson.

12. In this I respectfully disagree with Miller and others who find that "Tea Cake, after all, mistreats her in the same ways that her first two husbands did" (Miller 84). My reading is more in line with Dale Pattison's.

13. Angela Davis notes in her analysis of Bessie Smith's performance of "Taint Nobody's Bizness," "The song's seeming acquiescence to battering occurs within a larger affirmation of

women's right as individuals to conduct themselves however they wish—however idiosyn-cratic their behavior might seem and regardless of the possible consequences." Davis, however, continues, "Violence against women remains pandemic. Almost equally pandemic—although fortunately less so today than during previous eras—is women's inability to extricate them-selves from the web of violence. The conduct defended by the woman in this male-authored song is not so unconventional after all" (31).

14. While my position here is different from Hartman's, so is my context. Hartman is con-cerned with the impossibility of interracial consent, and the ways that even where the perfor-mance of consent is intraracial, its effect is to replay and to reify the subjection of the black American to the white American. Holiday's travels through the South certainly alerted her to the problems Hartman identifies, but Harlem also offered a different context for a black com-munity in which every act was not necessarily also about the white community—like that at Café Society, where Holiday frequently performed.

WORKS CITED

"Abuse, n." *Merriam-Webster's Dictionary of Law*, 1996.

"Abuse, n." *OED Online*, Oxford University Press, January 2018, www.oed.com/view/Entry/821.

Augustine of Hippo. *On Christian Teaching*. Translated by R. P. H Green, Oxford World's Clas-sics, 2008.

Austin, J. L. *How to Do Things with Words*. 2nd ed., Harvard UP, 1975.

Bergelson, Vera. "Consent to Harm." *Ethics of Consent: Theory and Practice*, edited by Franklin Miller and Allan Wertheimer, Oxford UP, 2010.

Davis, Angela. *Blues Legacies and Black Feminism: Gertrude "Ma" Rainey, Bessie Smith, and Bil-lie Holiday*. Vintage, 1999.

DeMan, Paul. "Epistemology of Metaphor." *Critical Inquiry*, vol. 5, no. 1, 1978, pp. 13–30.

End Abuse. "Fact Sheet." 21 March, 2015, www.tncoalition.org/getattachment/Resources/ipv.pdf.

Felman, Shoshana. *The Scandal of the Speaking Body*. Stanford UP, 2003.

Foucault, Michel. "Sex, Power, and the Politics of Identity," interview with Bob Gallagher and Alexander Wilson. *Ethics: Subjectivity and Truth*, by Michel Foucault, edited by Paul Rabi-now, New Press, 1997, pp. 163–175.

Garber, Marjorie. *The Use and Abuse of Literature*. Anchor Books, 2011.

Green, Ronald Michael. "What Does It Mean to Use Someone as 'A Means Only'? Rereading Kant." *Kennedy Institute of Ethics Journal*, vol. 11, no. 3, 2001, pp. 247–261.

Haag, Pamela. *Consent: Sexual Rights and the Transformation of American Liberalism*. Cornell UP, 1999.

Hartman, Saidiya. *Scenes of Subjection*. Oxford UP, 1997.

Hurd, Heidi. "The Moral Magic of Consent." *Legal Theory*, vol. 2, 1996, pp. 121–146.

Hurston, Zora Neale. *Their Eyes Were Watching God*. Harper Perennial, 1990.

Johnson, Barbara. "Metaphor, Metonymy and Voice in *Their Eyes Were Watching God*." *Zora Neale Hurston's Their Eyes Were Watching God*, edited by Harold Bloom, Chelsea House, 1987, pp. 41–57.

———. "Using People." *Persons and Things*, by Barbara Johnson, Harvard UP, 2008, pp. 94–105.

Kant, Immanuel. *Critique of Practical Reason*. Translated by Werner S. Pluhar, Hackett, 2002.

Locke, John. *An Essay Concerning Human Understanding*. J. M. Dent, 1961.

———. *Second Treatise of Government*. Edited and introduction by C. B. McPherson, Hackett, 1980.

Miller, Shawn E. "'Some Other Way to Try': From Defiance to Creative Submission in *Their Eyes Were Watching God.*" *Southern Literary Journal*, vol. 37, no. 1, 2004, pp. 74–95.

Pattison, Dale. "Sites of Resistance: The Subversive Spaces of *Their Eyes Were Watching God.*" *MELUS*, vol. 38, no. 4, winter 2013, pp. 9–31.

Plato. *Plato I: Euthyphro, Apology, Crito, Phaedo, Phaedrus.* Translated by Harold North Fowler, Harvard UP, 2001.

———. *The Republic.* Translated by Robin Waterfield, Oxford UP, 1993.

Scarry, Elaine. *The Body in Pain: The Making and Unmaking of the World.* Oxford UP, 1987.

———. "Consent and the Body: Injury, Departure, and Desire." *New Literary History*, vol. 21, no. 4, 1990, pp. 867–896.

Washington, Mary Helen. Introduction. *Their Eyes Were Watching God*, by Zora Neale Hurston, Harper Perennial, 1990, pp. vii–xiv.

Wright, Richard. "Between Laughter and Tears," October 1937, rpt. *Critical Essays on Zora Neale Hurston*, edited by Gloria L. Cronin, G. K. Hall, 1998, p. 778.

PART 2 CONSENT, VIOLENCE, AND REFUSAL

5 · THE SEDUCTION OF RAPE AS ALLEGORY IN POSTCOLONIAL LITERATURE

JUSTINE LEACH

> In over simplified form, allegory can be understood as a mode of repre-
> sentation that proceeds by forging an identity between things, and it reads
> present events, whatever the signifying system in which they are found, as
> terms within some already given system of textualised identification or codi-
> fied knowledge. As Paul de Man points out, allegory consists of semantic
> *repetition* in a rhetoric of temporality, and within this rhetoric the sign is
> always grounded to *another* sign which is by definition anterior to it. . . . In
> allegory, signs are interpreted as modalities of preceeding signs which are
> already deeply embedded in a specific cultural thematics, and they work to
> transform free-floating objects into positively identified and "known" units
> of knowledge.
>
> —Stephen Slemon, "Monuments of Empire"

At the interstices where national metaphors that allegorize rape
meet depictions of sexual violence between characters, the ambiguation of
nonconsent in postcolonial novels challenges our understanding at both levels
of representation. This chapter explores the unusual treatment of rape tropes in
Tayeb Salih's *Season of Migration to the North*. Over a decade after Sudanese
independence, this novel was published in Arabic as *Mawsim al-Hijra ilā al-
Shamāl* in 1966 and translated into English in 1969.[1] It portrays sexual consent in
ambiguous, disjunctive, and unsettling ways to reveal the twisted trajectories of
desire and power involved in both colonial and heterosexual relationships. And
it questions whether the individual, pulled to the extremes of rapacity or purity

by colonial and patriarchal discourses, can experience and express desire in a way that is not harmful to self and other. The ambiguation of rape in the novel reveals not just the contradictions of colonial discourse but also the problematic ground that supports such discourse—the normalization of violent heterosexuality through the disregard for the female subject's consent.

Season of Migration to the North is structurally complex.[2] The dual perspectives of the unnamed narrator and his interlocutor (and doppelgänger), Mustafa Sa'eed, disrupts the perception of time in the novel. Mustafa Sa'eed's recursive and invasive narration of his experiences throws into confusion the present moment of the narrator's chronological account of the events that follow his return to his village in Sudan after an interim of several years in England while he pursued a doctorate in English literature. This narrator expects all to be the same upon his return, but he soon feels disturbed by the presence of the stranger, Mustafa Sa'eed, who has married Hosna Bint Mahmoud, a local woman, and settled in the village. Mustafa Sa'eed's account of his own time in England, where he too studied and worked, forms much of the novel's narrative, and his story and person continue to haunt the narrator well after Mustafa Sa'eed's death in the Nile: as the narrator says, "Mustafa Sa'eed has, against my will, become a part of my world, a thought in my brain, a phantom that does not want to take itself off" (42). In his often elliptical narrative, Mustafa Sa'eed describes the events that culminate in his murder of his English wife, Jean Morris, by stabbing her through the heart during sexual intercourse. This sexualized murder is preceded by his colonial education in Sudan, Egypt, and England, where he becomes the toast of the wealthy bohemian London society in the 1920s and where his cruel seduction of several English women—Ann Hammond, Sheila Greenwood, Isabella Seymour—takes place, for whose suicides, the novel implies, he bears at least partial responsibility. Though the novel does not suggest that these women are raped, these sexual conquests are represented through the rhetoric of sexual violence and violation as acts that literalize the trope of colonialism as an act of rape.[3] As Africa was raped—the title of one of Mustafa Sa'eed's books is *The Rape of Africa* (114)—so, Mustafa Sa'eed jokes, "I'll liberate Africa with my penis" (100).

By acting out the trope of rape, Mustafa Sa'eed becomes complicit in a colonial discourse that sexually oppresses both Sudanese men and women. As Stephen Slemon writes, "If allegory literally means 'other speaking', it has historically served as a way of representing, of speaking *for*, the 'other', especially in the enterprise of imperialism" ("Post-colonial Allegory" 161). In rape tropes, the Other is discursively constructed by the European colonizer as female and therefore sexually available, but this tells only part of the story, for such discourse also assumes the inevitability of female desire in response to sexual force.

Imperialist language casts European colonialists in a romance plot in which the colonial man acts out the heroic penetration of either a virgin land or a sexually lascivious and secretly consenting Other. When Sir Walter Raleigh claims that "Guiana is a country that hath yet her maidenhead, never sacked, turned, nor wrought" (142), he figures colonialism as a romantic endeavor, in which Guiana is a woman whose anticipated rape is justified through her desirability as a virgin. The virgin's desire for penetration is not a question that requires inquiry. It is either irrelevant or assumed. In the colonial metaphor, rape is never quite rape. European assertions of proprietary rights to the colonial body through the language of gender violence largely rely on the trope's evocation of rape myths that deny the validity of female nonconsent.[4]

Monique Y. Tschofen argues that the use of rape tropes in postcolonial discourse remains oppressive even if they serve to denounce colonialism, for postcolonial allegories of rape do nothing to challenge the "master code"[5] that subordinates women through a discourse of sexual violence and violation. She critiques Salih's novel, arguing that by representing Mustafa Sa'eed's resistance to British colonization in Sudan through sexual violence, Salih condemns one form of exploitation (colonial) by uncritically reproducing another (patriarchal). Taking Slemon's insights into allegory, Tschofen makes the case that the "colonialism-is-rape" equation should be criticized for leaving unchallenged the violent imposition of gender hierarchies.

While I find Tschofen's general point insightful, the ambiguation of female sexual consent in *Season of Migration to the North* renders Salih's depiction of sexual violence complex. Not only is the novel implicitly critical of Mustafa Sa'eed's disinterest in his lovers' experiences of either pleasure or violation as he embarks upon his undertaking to reverse British colonialism in Sudan, but it also reveals that the female rape victim as metaphor for land or nation is paradoxically an unstable fantasy of women so suffused with sexuality and desire that their consent is presupposed. Although it is possible to read the novel as unwittingly replicating rape myths, such an interpretation does not account for Salih's careful paralleling of ambiguously consensual sexual violence with unambiguously nonconsensual sexual violence. At times, the representation of female ambiguous consent and complicity to sexual violation appears to stand as a trope for the complicity of some Sudanese to the colonial administration of their land and peoples. However, drawing an analogy to the ambivalent desires of some Sudanese elites only partially accounts for the novel's ambiguation of the trope of rape. This analogy is troubled by the parallel drawn in the text between Mustafa Sa'eed's first wife, Jean Morris, and her apparent consent to her sexualized murder and the rape and murder/suicide of his second wife, Hosna Bint Mahmoud, who is forced into an unwanted marriage to Wad Rayyes after Mustafa

Sa'eed's death. Indeed, the rape of Hosna Bint Mahmoud at the end of the novel exposes the lie at the heart of rape/seduction tropes: the lie that the female subject, like the racial Other, is in a perpetual state of consent.

RAPE AS SEDUCTION IN *SEASON OF MIGRATION TO THE NORTH*

A link between sexual violence and sexual desire is figured in both interpersonal relationships and geosociopolitical metaphors throughout *Season of Migration to the North*. Both national and city spaces are personified and sexualized. In parallels with Joseph Conrad's *Heart of Darkness*, Mustafa Sa'eed describes his life as the penetration of a foreign land, but rather than an African nation standing for the Other, it is England that is the unknown land to which the Sudanese man Mustafa Sa'eed comes "as a conqueror" (50). Reversing European orientalism, Mustafa Sa'eed directs a desirous gaze back at Europe and at European women. This first occurs before Mustafa Sa'eed has even left the African continent when he meets Mrs. Robinson upon arriving in Cairo to pursue his secondary education. Her embrace triggers sexual desire that mingles with his experience of Cairo, a city that, foreign to him in this moment, appears not as an African but as a European woman (22–23). Mustafa Sa'eed's sexual arousal returns upon his arrival in England, where "the smell of the place is strange, like that of Mrs. Robinson's body" (24).

Once in London, Mustafa Sa'eed personifies the city as the exotic and passive female Other that he has come to debauch. His language is territorial as he lays claim not merely to English women but, through the possession of their bodies, to London and by extension the British Empire. In a paragraph describing his pursuit of his wife Jean Morris and his seduction of Sheila Greenwood, Mustafa Sa'eed describes how "the city was transformed into an extraordinary woman, with her symbols and her mysterious calls, towards whom I drove my camels till their entrails ached and I myself almost died of yearning for her" (30). Then a few pages later, upon describing his first encounter with Isabella Seymour, he uses the image again: "The city has changed into a woman. It would be but a day or a week before I would pitch tent, driving my tent peg into the mountain summit" (34). Here Isabella Seymour becomes a geographical abstraction; she symbolizes London, where Mustafa Sa'eed will "pitch tent" (34), a potent symbol for sexual intercourse as well as for the declaration of territorial dominion. Mustafa Sa'eed's sexualized imagery of the tent peg driven into the mountain summit or body of the woman recalls the beginning of his narrative when he describes his experience of freedom from affective relationships: "I used to have—you may be surprised—a warm feeling of being free, that there was not a human being, by father or mother, to tie me down as a tent peg to a particular spot, a particular domain" (18). As an agent free from emotional connection to person or to place, Mustafa Sa'eed feels no compunction in asserting his ownership of England through his possession of women.

This rhetoric mimics even as it inverts colonial discourses that vindicate colonial violence as the rational exercise of the male liberal individual's power, as Anne McClintock suggests when she argues that European explorers and colonialists charted the world that was unknown to them through "a metaphysics of gender violence" (23). Through imperial rhetoric, the supposedly inherent male and female characteristics of dominance and subordination are transfigured onto the colonial realm, while indigenous resistance is figuratively morphed into a seduction script. Not only does consent transform rape into seduction at the last moment, the desire of the seduced is imagined in, not despite, the act of resistance. The representation of consent in rape tropes delegitimizes all forms of resistance whether to sexual violence or to colonial domination by intimating the desire for, and so ultimate necessity of, European rule. The intimation of desire does imperialism's ideological work by allegorizing the history of actual violence and violation as an act of mutually desired seduction.

In his analysis of *Season of Migration to the North*, Wail S. Hassan argues that Mustafa Sa'eed treats the women he seduces as though they are abstractions in a discursive war, literalizing the trope of rape in order to condemn European colonialism: "Mustafa fails to grasp the metaphoricity of 'the rape' of Africa, or the difference between the discursive trope (the speaking) and its reality (the doing)" (Hassan 312). Mustafa Sa'eed collapses the distinctions between the abstract metaphor of rape and the sexual use of women, just as the trope of rape collapses the distinction between the bodies of women and geosociopolitical space.

Northrop Frye writes that "the metaphor, in its radical form, is a statement of identity: 'this is that.' In all our ordinary experience the metaphor is non-literal: nobody but a savage or a lunatic can take metaphor literally" (151). Using Frye, Paul Huebener implies that Mustafa Sa'eed is mad, for "madness, in this sense, is metaphor taken to the extreme; if metaphor is the process of experiencing one kind of thing in terms of another, madness is what happens when the boundary between things disappears altogether, leaving no coherent 'essences' in place" (21). And yet, even as he acknowledges getting caught up in the madness of his fantasies, Mustafa Sa'eed rejects madness as an excuse for his violence against women. When his lawyer at his trial attempts to attribute his murder of Jean Morris to a crime of passion provoked by an emotional breakdown in response to the clash of civilizations, Mustafa Sa'eed rejects this interpretation (29). All the same, in the next breath, he attributes his destruction of white women to his coming from the South through the geospatial metaphor of the desert, a metaphor that folds the discursive into the concrete: "I am the desert of thirst"

(29). In fantasy, Mustafa Sa'eed loses touch with the symbolic—the implied *as if*—and so the symbol becomes concrete.

Mustafa Sa'eed implies that his lawyer sought to locate the blame for the deaths of his lovers not in his own person but elsewhere, in "a conflict between two worlds, a struggle of which I was one of the victims" (29). Indeed, the lawyer attributes culpability not to Mustafa Sa'eed but to a disease—"These girls were not killed by Mustafa Sa'eed but by the germ of a deadly disease that assailed them a thousand years ago" (29)—an image that becomes a trope for colonial desire and colonial violence throughout the novel. Later, the narrator remembers Mustafa Sa'eed drawing together the colonization of Sudan, the indoctrination of Sudanese children through their colonial education, the loss of life in the First World War, and Mustafa Sa'eed's own enterprise of reverse colonization through disease as a metaphor: "The ships at first sailed down the Nile carrying guns not bread, and the railways were originally set up to transport troops; the schools were started so as to teach us to say 'Yes' in their language. They imported to us the germ of the greatest European violence, as seen on the Somme and at Verdun, the like of which the world has never previously known, the germ of a deadly disease that struck them more than a thousand years ago. Yes, my dear sirs, I came as an invader into your very homes: a drop of poison which you have injected into the veins of history" (79). Here Salih critiques both the violent and nonviolent coercive tactics of British colonialism that produced Sudanese submission to and complicity with the colonial administration: railways are built to transport troops, while schools are built to produce "consent"—that is, "to teach us to say 'Yes' in their language" (79).

The metaphor of disease also takes on sexual and gendered connotations. Despite rejecting his lawyer's account of his actions, Mustafa Sa'eed uses the extended metaphor of disease to describe what transpires between himself and the women he seduces. He describes, "My bedroom was a spring-well of sorrow, the germ of a fatal disease. The infection had stricken these women a thousand years ago, but I had stirred up the latent depths of the disease until it had got out of control and had killed" (30). Through contact with Mustafa Sa'eed, Sheila Greenwood becomes sexually infected: "She entered my room a chaste virgin and when she left it she was carrying the germs of self-destruction within her" (30). The temporality of this infection is complex—time collapses as infection occurs both at the moment of contact with Mustafa Sa'eed and a thousand years prior. Mustafa Sa'eed links this metaphor to sexual desire for the gendered and racialized Other and suggests that by arousing this desire in white women, he is able to control them. Speaking of Isabella Seymour, he says, "You, my lady, may not know, but you . . . have been infected with a deadly disease which has come from you know not where and which will bring about your destruction, be it sooner or later. . . . I felt the flow of conversation firmly in my hands, like the reins of an obedient mare: I pull at them and she stops, I shake them and she advances; I move them and she moves subject to my will, to left or to right" (34). Mustafa Sa'eed's imagery transfigures Isabella Seymour into a female horse, whom he rides in a sexually suggestive image, and their conversation into reins that enable Mustafa Sa'eed to fully control her. Infected with the desire for Mustafa Sa'eed as the racialized and gendered Other, Isabella Seymour is at his mercy.

At his trial for murder, Mustafa Sa'eed sees himself as having reversed the relation of power between colonizer and colonized through his sexual relationships. He asserts that he is not so much subject to the decision of a court of law but architect of that court's presence before him: "I had a sort of feeling of superiority towards them, for the ritual was being held primarily because of me; and I, over and above everything else, am a colonizer, I am the intruder whose fate must be decided" (79). Yet as Huebener points out, "While Mustafa's deadly seductions of white women are a form of revenge for the European colonization of Africa, a pointed reversal of power relationships, they also represent a decision to perpetuate acts of violence and domination" (25), making Mustafa Sa'eed "both perpetrator and victim of imperial conquest" (25).

Mustafa Sa'eed's reverse colonialism by sexual conquest fails to transform relations of power in part because he continues to collude with European orientalist fantasies about himself. While it is true that Mustafa Sa'eed's lovers eroticize his racial difference, Mustafa Sa'eed encourages and returns their objectifying and dehumanizing gazes. He transforms his room into an oriental cliché, "heavy with the smell of burning sandalwood and incense" (27). For Isabella Seymour, he produces, it seems, almost every stereotype about Africa and African men: "I related to her fabricated stories about deserts of golden sands and jungles where non-existent animals called out to one another. I told her that the streets of my country teemed with elephants and lions and that during siesta time crocodiles crawled through it.... Then came a moment when I felt I have been transformed in her eyes into a naked, primitive creature, a spear in one hand and arrows in the other, hunting elephants and lions in the jungles. This was fine" (32–33). Thus "by perpetuating colonial binaries and stereotypes both in his characterization of the women he seduces and in his means of seduction, which entail his inhabiting the colonial image of the African" (17), as Byron Caminero-Santangelo argues, Sa'eed fortifies the very imperialist epistemic structures he fights against and reproduces without thought gender hierarchies that oppress women. By so doing, he also perpetuates a colonial "discourse of power capable of coding anticolonial struggle as the violation of white women" (130), as Jenny Sharpe writes in her analysis of E. M. Forster's *A Passage to India*.[6]

Mustafa Sa'eed seems to have internalized the racist logic of European colonialism that identifies the black male body with impurity, primitivism, degeneracy, and hypersexuality. As explored by Fanon in *Black Skin, White Masks*, the white gaze transforms the black man into an object, imprisoning him in his sexual body and causing a disturbance in the black man's body image, a process he names as the "epidermalization of . . . inferiority" (xv). In the white imagination, black men are reduced not only to nonrational bodies but also to a sexualized synecdoche: "He has been turned into a penis. He *is* a penis" (147). Meanwhile, white women become the symbolic markers of purity and chasteness, and thus the desire to sexual possess white women arises from a desire to possess the aspects of the self that have been denied to black men by the racist imperial hegemony: as Fanon explains, "Between these white breasts that my wandering hands fondle, white civilization and worthiness become mine" (45). By seeking mastery over "white civilization" (45) through the sexual possession of women, Mustafa Sa'eed colludes with "the very principles of the Eurocentric desire to conquer, control, and civilize other nations and cultures," as R. S. Krishnan writes (11).

The relationship between Mustafa Sa'eed and the women he seduces is erotically charged with binaries: master/slave, hunter/prey, white/black, god/devotee, civilized/savage, violator/violated. The women ascribe to the kind of orientalizing fantasies that involve their own violation. Anne Hammond, for example, plays the part of the slave and Mustafa Sa'eed the master in a fantasy that leaves the relation of power between the two unchanged: "'Come here,' I said to her imperiously. 'To hear is to obey, O master!' she answered me in a subdued voice. While still in the throes of fantasy, intoxication and madness, I took her and she accepted, for what happened had already happened between us a thousand years ago" (121). Still in the throes of colonial and masochistic fantasy, Anne Hammond can do nothing but accept. Playacting her part, to hear is to obey; her acceptance of violation is dictated by a historical fantasy that the two of them are compelled to repeat. While Ann Hammond only playacts the part of a slave, the fantasy is described as though it in fact determines her submission—and yet, the fantasy remains pleasurable only in so far as Ann Hammond maintains her racially privileged position as a white woman.

By participating in orientalist fantasies that require their submission to Mustafa Sa'eed, figured as master, savage, or god, the English women negate their ability to give or withhold their consent. Even the word *no* in the novel does not represent an unambiguous articulation of refusal. According to Mustafa Sa'eed, when, during intercourse, Isabella Seymour calls out, "No. No" (37), the time for a refusal has passed: "The critical moment when it was in your power to refrain from taking the first step has been lost. I caught you unawares; at that time it was in your power to say 'No.' As for now the flood of events has swept you along, as it does every person, and you are no longer capable of doing anything" (43). Isabella Seymour is figured as swept along by a flood that enforces her passivity; her will is immaterial. The moment that voided her ability to say no is the moment she accepted Mustafa Sa'eed's oriental illusion and thus, like Anne Hammond, was infected with a disease that binds fantasy and desire. However, the temporality of this disease, the fact that it infected colonizer and colonized alike a thousand years ago, implies that it has never been in Isabella Seymour's power to say no.

Mustafa Sa'eed's disregard for what appears to be a moment of nonconsent in this scene is immediately complicated when he describes her relaxation and surrender to intercourse with the words "I love you" (37), at which point, it is not Isabella's voice that rises up in protest but Mustafa Sa'eed's—there is "a weak cry from the depths of my consciousness calling on me to desist" (37). Later, Isabella Seymour appears to articulate a rape fantasy when she says, "Ravish me, you African demon. Burn me in the fire of your temple, you black god. Let me twist and turn in your wild and impassioned rites" (88).[7] According to Fanon, the racist fear of black men, experienced by both white men and women but mainly analyzed by Fanon in terms of white women, is the fear of rape: "Whoever says rape says black man" (143). This fear of rape he suggests represents an unconscious desire for rape, which arises from the fact that black men, reduced to pure sexuality, become the repository of fantasies and desires that white women in particular, reduced to pure chasteness, are required to disavow (156).[8] The appearance of rape fantasy ambiguates the representation of Isabella Seymour's consent. Rape fantasy suggests erotic role-play rather than undesired violation, and yet, for the fantasy to be acted out, consent must be withheld at least in performance. During the fantasy's enactment, saying no becomes meaningless playacting, obscuring both consent and nonconsent alike.

In *Season of Migration to the North*, love, like desire, is something over which the individual has no control. Indeed, after Mustafa Sa'eed falls in love with Jean Morris "against [his] will" (129), he, like Isabella Seymour, could no longer "control the course of events" (129). Throughout their relationship, Jean Morris and Mustafa Sa'eed do not come together as two equals, nor do they seek to do so, as what they appear to desire is dominance over the other. Incommensurate, both Mustafa Sa'eed and Jean Morris engage in a mutually destructive battle in which love and hate are hardly distinguishable. For the first two months of their marriage, Jean Morris withholds her consent to sexual intercourse, triggering her husband's first murderous rage and her first response of desire to his threat to kill her: "'I'll kill you,' I told her. She glanced at the knife in my hand with what seemed like longing. 'Here's my breast bared to you,' she said. 'Plunge the knife in.' I looked at her naked body, which though within my grasp, I could not possess" (131). Were he to rape or murder his wife at this moment, these acts of violence would not give Mustafa Sa'eed what he desires—complete power over his wife. Even when she does agree, consent to intercourse has little power to make things right between them. Indeed, their relationship is premised upon a struggle for mastery, and consent has little power to reconcile as it is used as a weapon to taunt and torment. Their "murderous war" (131) continues, and though he does not rape his wife, Mustafa Sa'eed's relationship with Jean Morris allegorizes the colonial encounter as sexual violence.

Mustafa Sa'eed's story culminates in Jean Morris's ambiguously consensual death as she is penetrated by a knife during intercourse.[9] Sexual violence and murder are conflated in this act. During this scene, Jean Morris is depicted as both volitionless and as desiring her death by kissing the knife and inviting her husband to penetrate her. On the one hand, Jean Morris's will appears absent; even her gaze is completely controlled by Mustafa Sa'eed: "I looked at her breast and she too looked at where my glance had fallen, as though she too had been robbed of her own volition and was moving in accordance with my will" (135). And on the other hand, his desire to kill appears to be orchestrated and invited by her: "She continued to look at the blade-edge with a mixture of astonishment, fear, and lust. Then she took hold of the dagger and kissed it fervently. Suddenly she closed her eyes and stretched out in the bed, raising her middle slightly, opening her thighs wider. 'Please, my sweet,' she said, moaning: 'Come—I'm ready now'" (135–136). Though violent, the murder is erotic, weirdly consensual, and sexually arousing for both Mustafa Sa'eed and Jean Morris. The penetration of the knife mimics the penetration of the penis—it is as though they are the same weapon: "I put the blade-edge between her breasts and she twined her legs round my back. Slowly I pressed down" (136). As he drives the knife in, again time collapses: "The universe, with its past, present and future, was gathered together into a single point before and after which nothing existed" (136). In its collapse, the entire history of colonial and gender oppression is concentrated into a perverse single act of violence and violation—a condensation that blurs the boundaries between victim and persecutor, murder and suicide, desire and hate, sex and rape.

SUBVERTING THE "CODE OF RECOGNITION": MARITAL RAPE AND ITS DISAVOWAL

Further complicating Jean Morris's consent to her sexualized death is the death of Mustafa Sa'eed's second wife, Hosna Bint Mahmoud, who after Mustafa Sa'eed's apparent suicide, is forced into marriage with Wad Rayyes, a man several years older than her and to whom she has refused her consent. Wad Rayyes is revealed to be a philanderer and rapist, who jovially recalls sexually assaulting women in his youth. He becomes fixated upon possessing Hosna Bint Mahmoud after she is widowed. He states in response to the narrator's objection, "She'll marry me whatever you or she says or does. Her father's agreed and so have her brothers. . . . In this village the men are guardians of the women" (82).

Indeed, because of the patriarchal rural culture in which "women belong to men, and a man's a man even if he's decrepit" (83), Hosna Bint Mahmoud's refusal to marry Wad Rayyes is never taken seriously—she has no right to refuse her consent because she belongs to men who have the right to use and exchange her body as they see fit.

Upon hearing Wad Rayyes's plans, the narrator conflates Hosna Bint Mahmoud with Jean Morris in a disturbing sexual fantasy: "The obscene pictures sprang simultaneously to my mind, and, to my extreme astonishment, the two pictures merged: I imagined Hosna Bint Mahmoud, Mustafa Sa'eed's widow, as being the same woman in both instances: two white, wide open thighs in London, and a woman groaning before dawn in an obscure village on a bend of the Nile under the weight of the aged Wad Rayyes. If that other thing was evil, this too was evil, and if this was like death and birth, the Nile flood and the wheat harvest, a part of the system of the universe, so too was that" (72). The narrator resists calls, including Hosna Bint Mahmoud's, to take her as his second wife and so save her from an unwanted marriage to Wad Rayyes. He rejects this solution partly because he is uncomfortable with the idea of polygamy but also because he is uncomfortable with his own desire for her—desire he describes using the motif of the fatal disease: "I—like [Mustafa Sa'eed] and Wad Rayyes and millions of others—was not immune from the germ of contagion that oozes from the body of the universe" (86).

After being forced to marry Wad Rayyes, Hosna Bint Mahmoud, like Jean Morris, maintains her nonconsent, refusing him entry to the marriage bed and into her—a right Wad Rayyes believes to be his. When Wad Rayyes decides to force her, Hosna Bint Mahmoud kills him and herself in a repetition and an inversion of Mustafa Sa'eed's murder of Jean Morris. The novel links Hosna Bint Mahmoud's unambiguously nonconsensual experience of sexual violence with Jean Morris's ambiguously consensual experience of sexual violence, forcing the reader to evaluate one in light of the other. In a breakdown of chronological time, the two events are synchronically brought together by the contagion of sexual and colonial desire that operates like a curse throughout the novel. Jean Morris's consent, like Hosna Bint Mahmoud's, is revealed to be meaningless in a system, whether colonial or patriarchal, that does not recognize the female subject's right to refuse intercourse after marriage and which justifies violence to bring about her submission.[10]

In *Season of Migration to the North*, the villagers do not have a way of understanding both the violence inflicted upon Hosna Bint Mahmoud and the violence she returns: "It was all without rhyme or reason. She accepted the stranger—why didn't she accept Wad Rayyes?" (106). It becomes a thing "that shouldn't be spoken about" (108), a crime that is hushed up, buried along with the bodies. Rather than understood, it is regarded as something that "wasn't the act of a human being" (109). Meanwhile, consent becomes a problematic frame for understanding either Jean Morris's or Hosna Bint Mahmoud's deaths. Indeed, while I classify Hosna Bint Mahmoud's experience as rape, the novel suggests that such a conceptualization is not available to those who witness the violence inflicted upon her.

POSTCOLONIAL ALLEGORY AND THE PROBLEM OF CONSENT

Gender oppression intersects but is not necessarily coterminous with other forms oppression, such as those founded on race and class. As a result, when violence against women is used as a trope for violence against the nation, the differential positions of gender are asymmetrically and imperfectly mapped onto systems of racial and political inequality that affect both men and women. As Hassan writes, "The convergence of colonial and racial stereotypes, therefore, produces a troubled gender configuration in which an African man occupies masculine and feminine subject positions and in which, conversely, a European woman occupies the equally uncertain positions of masculinity and femininity" (309). Rape tropes operate as though at the place where race and gender intersect, one sign can be exchanged for the other. Postcolonial theory often attempts to be sensitive to hierarchies and prejudice that subordinate categories of difference. However, as Clare Counihan points out, "Despite this aspiration to accommodate all versions of (racial, sexual and gender) difference as irreducible to each other, in practice postcolonial theory loses differences along the way: either racial difference *or* sexual difference *or* gender difference—usually racial difference—functions as the primary and paradigmatic difference while all other forms of difference become additive or tropologically related" (162). Counihan argues that once "postcolonial theory translates sexual difference into racial difference" (162), the figure of woman becomes a ghostly apparition, who "in her oscillating presence *and* absence, functions within postcolonial theories of difference as the moment at which these translations become visible and haunting" (Counihan 162). This haunting body, transposed into allegory, is crisscrossed and overdetermined by the discourses, institutions, and practices that buttress colonial and patriarchal power, facilitating the continued denial of the position of the subject to actual women.

In colonial discourse, rape can act, in Sharpe's words, "as a concept-metaphor for imperialism" (137), especially in "representations that authorize a European claim of ownership through a feminization of the colonial body" (137). As McClintock writes, "In these fantasies, the world is feminized and spatially spread for male exploration, then reassembled and deployed in the interests of massive imperial power" (23). Colonial discourse transfixes its subject through symbols that tie the colonization of peoples and lands to the already fixed significations of the female subject as a body that is desiring, that consents, and/or that is will-less. It, therefore, obscures and abstracts concrete experiences of rape, denying the violence and violation of both rape and colonialism.

In contrast, postcolonial discourse has tended to emphasize the violence of rape and the victims' lack of consent. When British imperialism in India is characterized through personification as an act in which the British "seized her body and possessed her, but it was a possession of violence" (qtd. in Kolsky 109) by the first prime minister of India Jawaharlal Nehru, the second clause makes clear that the seizure and possession of India's personified body should not be confused as a seduction. Desire, where signified, is shown to have belonged to the colonizer alone. By allegorically substituting colonial violence with sexual violence, postcolonial discourse can efficiently figure concepts of violent penetration, possession, and loss of autonomy. However, as Lydia Liu writes, "In such a signifying practice, the female body is ultimately displaced by nationalism, whose discourse denies the specificity of female experience by giving larger symbolic meanings to the signifier of rape" (44). It is all too easy for the allegory to use "gender difference between women and men" (McClintock 354) to symbolically establish "the limits of national difference and power between men" (354) and so for the story of a violated woman, in Harveen Sachdeva Mann's words, to be "exploited so that the story of the nation can be enunciated" (131).[11] Likewise, Gunne and Brigley Thompson express concern with the deployment of rape tropes in postcolonial discourse. They point to feminist analysis that suggests it is potentially "exploitative" (2) and dehumanizing for a writer to substitute rape for colonialism. Allegorically replacing the land with the female body maintains "the view of women's bodies as a resource, property or guarded secret belonging to men" (2). As the vehicle of the metaphor, the female gender as a subjugated class is maintained.

Thus the trope of rape can be dangerous because "to read post-colonial allegories of rape as resistance against racial or cultural systems, one must recognize a hierarchy in which women are always already subordinate" (Tschofen 509). Moreover, for some (often male) authors, it can be tempting to fall back on the rusty metaphors of female complicity and desire and so unwittingly replicate colonial use of patriarchal logic that rape is always a seduction or uncritically parrot rape myths. In particular, anticolonial discourse does not always do away with the imagery of seduction when deploying the trope of rape. In David LaChapelle's anticolonial photograph "The Rape of Africa" (2009), LaChapelle makes Africa legible to his Western audience as a desirable object of possession whose very desirability, both sexually and economically, accounts for her victimization.[12] In the photograph, Africa is reduced to the trite signs offered by the long history of orientalist representation: primitive, natural, exotic, sexual, static, and female, though the extent to which LaChapelle is aware of this reproduction is unclear. Naomi Campbell's torn dress completely exposing one breast and riding high on her thighs acts as a metonym for the rape alluded to in the title, yet the exposure of her body at the same time invites the viewer to take sexual pleasure at the beauty of the supermodel.

However, there is also the possibility that the rhetoric of seduction that ambiguates rape in postcolonial allegory can be used to undermine the "code of recognition" (Tschofen 509) upon which the analogy that justifies colonialism as rape/seduction relies. Certainly, *Season of Migration to the North* ambiguates rape tropes by deploying the rhetoric of seduction at the level of national allegory and obscuring female sexual consent and nonconsent at the level of event. In this regard, Salih's work appears to align with colonial discourse, which deemphasizes the violence and trauma of colonialism by intimating that rape is really only ever a seduction. And yet, at the same time that he ambiguates rape tropes through the rhetoric of seduction, he reinstates sexual violence as the "code of recognition" (Tschofen 509) in allegories of colonialism by drawing an analogy to marital rape. Thus the text reveals that seduction belongs to the same discourses, practices, and institutions that deny the female subject the power of her nonconsent and so disregard her sexual desire and facilitate her sexual violation. Consent to intercourse after marriage is represented in *Season of Migration to the North* as ambiguous at best and meaningless at worst. Within the patriarchal society depicted in the text, in which men administer women's sexuality through marriage, female sexual nonconsent has no force because it has no meaning. Consent is irrelevant if legitimate sex is defined as that which occurs within marriage and illegitimate sex is everything that falls out with the bounds of marriage.

Ultimately, the novel reveals women may actually be positioned as always consenting, making nonconsent unintelligible. In *Season of Migration to the North*, Hosna Bint Mahmoud's forced marriage makes her nonsubmission to intercourse incomprehensible to the villagers who answer her murder/ suicide with silence. Thus Salih blurs boundaries sexual consent is supposed to police, exposing borders of sexual freedom to be constrained, not by individual choice, but by orientalist and patriarchal responses to desire. By offering marital rape as the anterior "code of recognition" (Tschofen 509) upon which allegories of colonialism as rape/seduction depend, Salih critiques patriarchal and colonial power that deny the female subject her sexual autonomy by positioning her as a person whose consent is always already presumed or entirely moot. Meanwhile, metaphors that link women to land and thus to nation are exposed as a language of dispossession—a reclamation of both the female body and voice is revealed to be inherently ambiguous, its authority suspect, and its language permeated by the very discourses it resists.

NOTES

1. *Season of Migration to the North* was serialized in *Hiwar*, a Lebanese magazine, and then published as a book in 1967 (Lalami ix). Salih had significant impact on the English translation, working intimately with the novel's translator Johnson-Davis (Lalami ix, xviii). South Sudan separated from Sudan in 2011; when I refer to Sudan in this chapter, I am referring to the political and geographical region that existed prior to this change.

2. For an analysis of the complex structure of *Season of Migration to the North*, see Joseph E. Lowry.

3. Fredrick Jameson has famously argued that "all third-world texts are necessarily . . . allegorical, and in a very specific way: they are to be read as what I will call *national allegories*" (69). For a rebuttal of Jameson's totalizing position, see Aijaz Ahmad.

4. Another permutation of rape tropes in colonial discourse, white women under threat from dark men, is analyzed at length by Jenny Sharpe in *Allegories of Empire*.

5. See Jameson, *Political Unconscious* 25–33; Slemon, "Post-colonial Allegory" 161.

6. Sharpe notes that the myths of the black rapist and the oriental male are different: "The myth of the black rapist presupposes even as it reproduces the Negro's lustful bestiality; the Oriental male, by contrast, is constructed as licentious rather than lustful, duplicitous instead of bestial" (128). Mustafa Sa'eed purposely inhabits both figures.

7. It is implied that Isabella Seymour says these words to Mustafa Sa'eed, but her desire to be violated is ambiguously located in the narrator's musings and not in Mustafa Sa'eed's reported speech.

8. While there are parallels to the representation of white women's desire in *Season of Migration to the North* here, Fanon is perpetuating rape myths. He implies not only that white women desire rape but also that some ask for it: "Basically, isn't this *fear* of rape precisely a call for rape? Just as there are faces that just ask to be slapped, couldn't we speak of women who just ask to be raped?" (134). Such a position may be contextualized by Fanon's concern with the lynching of black men for false accusations of sexual transgression; nonetheless, his use of psychoanalytic theory denies both black and white women their capacity to give or withhold consent and their experiences of violation. He extends the desire to be raped to black women of whom he famously admits he knows nothing about (157) and of whose experiences he shows little interest in exploring beyond what he has to say about their supposed desire to whiten the race.

9. For an analysis of the associations among the "images of ritualized sex" (Quayson 765), Othello's murder of Desdemona, and the ambiguation of consent in this scene, see Quayson 764–776.

10. In both England and Sudan at the time *Season of Migration to the North* was written, marital rape was not considered a crime. In jurisdictions where rape is defined as a form of adultery, marital rape is oxymoronic, but it should be noted that marital rape remains difficult to conceptualize and prosecute even where there are explicit prohibitions against it.

11. Thus, literary critics often praise authors who represent the "real" suffering of rape victims rather than transforming that suffering into national allegory. Lucy Valerie Graham appears to praise Coetzee in "Reading the Unspeakable" (442), and Kerry L. Johnson argues, after citing Liu, that Wilson Harris "retains the specificity of the woman's experience of rape" (83).

12. For a critique of LaChapelle's image, see Inna Arzumanova.

WORKS CITED

Ahmad, Aijaz. "Jameson's Rhetoric of Otherness and the 'National Allegory.'" *Social Text*, vol. 17, 1987, pp. 3–25.

Arzumanova, Inna. "Politics of Outrage: David LaChapelle's 'The Rape of Africa.'" *American Quarterly*, vol. 63, no. 2, 2011, pp. 367–374.

Caminero-Santangelo, Byron. "Legacies of Darkness: Neocolonialism, Joseph Conrad, and Tayeb Salih's 'Season of Migration to the North.'" *ARIEL*, vol. 30, no. 4, 1999, pp. 7–33.

Conrad, Joseph. *Heart of Darkness*. Edited by Paul B. Armstrong, Norton Critical Edition, 4th ed., Norton, 2006.

Counihan, Clare. "Reading the Figure of Woman in African Literature: Psychoanalysis, Difference, and Desire." *Research in African Literatures*, vol. 38, no. 2, 2007, pp. 161–180.

Fanon, Frantz. *Black Skin, White Masks*. Translated by Richard Philocox, Grove, 2008.

Frye, Northrop. "Towards Defining an Age of Sensibility." *ELH*, vol. 23, no. 2, 1956, pp. 144–152.

Graham, Lucy Valerie. "Reading the Unspeakable: Rape in JM Coetzee's Disgrace." *Journal of Southern African Studies*, vol. 29, no. 2, 2003, pp. 433–444.

Gunne, Sorcha, and Zoë Brigley Thompson. *Feminism, Literature and Rape Narratives: Violence and Violation*. Routledge, 2010.

Hassan, Wail S. "Gender (and) Imperialism: Structures of Masculinity in Tayeb Salih's *Season of Migration to the North*." *Men and Masculinities*, vol. 5, no. 3, 2003, pp. 309–324. SAGE.

Heaney, Seamus. "Act of Union." *North: Poems*, Faber and Faber, 1975.

Huebener, Paul. "Metaphor and Madness." *Mosaic*, vol. 43, no. 4, 2010, pp. 1–17.

Jameson, Frederick. *The Political Unconscious: Narrative as a Socially Symbolic Act*. Methuen, 1983.

———. "Third World Literature in the Era of Multinational Capitalism." *Social Text*, vol. 15, 1986, pp. 65–88.

Johnson, Kerry L. "From Muse to Majesty: Rape, Landscape and Agency in the Early Novels of Wilson Harris." *Journal of Postcolonial Writing*, vol. 35, no. 2, 1996, pp. 71–89.

Kolsky, Elizabeth. "'The Body Evidencing the Crime': Rape on Trial in Colonial India, 1860–1947." *Gender & History*, vol. 22, no. 1, 2010, pp. 109–130.

Krishnan, R. S. "Reinscribing Conrad: Tayeb Salih's Season of Migration to the North." *International Fiction Review*, vol. 23, 1996, pp. 7–15.

LaChapelle, David. *The Rape of Africa*. 2009. Photograph. Davidlachapelle.com.

Lalami, Laila. Introduction. *Season of Migration to the North*, by Tayeb Salih, translated by Denys Johnson-Davies, New York Review of Books, 2009.

Liu, Lydia. "The Female Body and Nationalist Discourse." *Scattered Hegemonies: Postmodernity and Transnational Feminist Practices*, edited by Inderpal Grewal and Caren Kaplan, U of Minnesota P, 1994, pp. 37–62.

Lowry, Joseph E. "Histories and Polyphonies: Deep Structures in Al-Tayyib Sālih's *Mawsim al-hijra ilā al-shamāl* (*Season of Migration to the North*)." *Edebiyât*, vol. 12, 2001, pp. 161–193.

Mann, Harveen Sachdeva. "Woman in Decolonization: The National and Textual Politics of Rape in Saadat Hasan Manto and Mahasweta Devi." *Journal of Commonwealth Literature*, vol. 33, no. 2, 1998, pp. 127–141.

McClintock, Anne. *Imperial Leather: Race, Gender, and Sexuality in the Colonial Contest*. Routledge, 1995.

Quayson, Ato. "Symbolization Compulsion: Testing a Psychoanalytical Category on Postcolonial African Literature." *University of Toronto Quarterly*, vol. 73, no. 2, 2004, pp. 754–772.

Raleigh, Walter. *The Discovery of Guiana: And the Journal of the Second Voyage Thereto*. Cassell, 1887.

Said, Edward W. *Orientalism*. Random House, 1978.

Salih, Tayeb. *Season of Migration to the North*. Translated by Denys Johnson-Davies, New York Review of Books, 2009 [1969].

Sharpe, Jenny. *Allegories of Empire: The Figure of Woman in the Colonial Text*. U of Minnesota P, 1993.

Slemon, Stephen. "Monuments of Empire: Allegory/Counter-discourse/Post-colonial Writing." *Kunapipi*, vol. 9, no. 3, 1987, pp. 1–16.

———. "Post-colonial Allegory and the Transformation of History." *Journal of Commonwealth Literature*, 1988, pp. 157–168.

Tschofen, Monique Y. "Post-colonial Allegory and the Empire of Rape." *Canadian Review of Comparative Literature/Revue Canadienne de Littérature Comparée*, vol. 22, nos. 3–4, 1995, pp. 501–515.

6 · WILLFUL CREATURES

Consent, Discord, Animal Will, and Thomas Hardy's *Tess of the d'Urbervilles*

KIMBERLY O'DONNELL

For at least the last forty years, philosophers and theorists have turned to what Jacques Derrida has famously called the question of the animal and, for a large subfield, the question of animal ethics.[1] As Kelly Oliver notes, their inquiries have focused largely on two overlapping areas: "the ways in which animals are—or are not—like us and therefore should—or should not—be treated like us" (25). For example, if animals and humans share common traits, behaviours, or adaptations, then we ought to be similarly moral beings and be worthy of similar rights. Meanwhile, some scholars have argued that the difference between humans and animals guarantees humans more power, and they therefore have obligations relative to their intervention in animal worlds. However, both these approaches to ethics continue to be rooted in humanism—in a system of rights and obligations based on human capacities, powers, behaviours, and structures. Nevertheless, Elisabeth Arnould-Bloomfield has noticed a recent rejection of the "justice-and-rights tradition" in favour of affect (1467). In many ways, this turn to the ethical significance of feeling coincides and overlaps with a turn to the ethics of response. "Response ethics," as Cynthia Willett points out, have their roots in Continental philosophy and proceed on the principle that ethics begin with "an appeal from the vulnerable stranger—the Other whose singular identity exposes the epistemic poverty of language and concepts" (9). This shift away from humanism has made response ethics fruitful ground for animal philosophers committed to demanding a nonanthropocentric ethical framework, like Willett, Derrida, Oliver, and Donna Haraway.[2] Response implies interspecies communication, in which humans receive a "call" from an animal and must respond or in which humans pay attention to the ways animals are responding to them or each other. Because this communication is nonhumanist, it is, as Willett points out, not necessarily about human language but about something located within or between bodies.

Consent is generally seen as an issue of humanist ethics because consent is usually understood as linguistic, cognitive, rational, and individual. However, the turn by some nonanthropocentric animal philosophers to the ethical significance of embodied response gives us insight into consent's relevance there. As feminist philosopher Sara Ahmed's recent work, *Willful Subjects*, suggests, a nonanthropocentric ethics would be one that embraced the possibility of negative response. Extending Ahmed's insight, I take seriously here the significance of animal objection or dissent in the framework of animal response ethics. If we are committed to addressing the ethics of uneven human-animal power relations, we must attend to discord—states of negative, disruptive, or illegible affect apart from the category of suffering. As Ahmed reminds us, resistant objects can be "checking powers, reminders that the world is not waiting to receive our shape" (189); Oliver agrees, asserting that "mastering the animal, animality, and animals is an illusion," and that philosophical animals who "bite back" can help us "reconceiv[e] our relationships to the earth, the environment, animals, and 'ourselves'" (22). After a brief sketch of the relationship between consent and animal objection, I engage with their significance through animal philosophies that emphasize positive affective interspecies response, particularly Haraway's notion of companion species. I then turn to other animal response ethics that emphasize discord and offer a model of animal response ethics that has the potential to disrupt humanist and capitalist power via a reading of Thomas Hardy's *Tess of the d'Urbervilles*.

THE QUESTION OF ANIMAL DISSENT

In approaching the notion of consent in relation to animals, we would do well to turn to the framework that rejects it.[3] Carol Adams insists that the notion of consent cannot be ethically applied to animal-human relationships because "consent is when one can say no, and that no is accepted. Clearly animals cannot do that" (in Steeves 153). H. Peter Steeves examines this claim by suggesting that consent "must not be reduced to the linguistic matter of talking," arguing that the real philosophical questions are raised by Adams's earlier claim that human-animal relationships "leave animals unempowered" (153). This dyad of nonlinguistic response and unequal power appears again in other philosopher's discussions of animal consent and can help us to think about the importance of dissent in animal response ethics. Palmer, for example, gestures to a model of consent in contractual ethics called tacit consent, and although it is not the basis for her own ethics, the example she gives is illustrative: "We could say that the cat 'consented' to have its fur brushed," Palmer writes, "meaning that if an animal does not display behavioral objections to a particular human practice when it is free to do so (by struggling, scratching, etc.) it is consenting to the practices" (59). Like Adams, Oliver hesitates over consent's ethical potential when the consenting party enjoys an unequal share of power and provides insight into why we must take care in assuming nonlinguistic consent. She notes that "feminist criticisms of liberal theories that assume the Cartesian autonomous individual challenge the notion that 'free' participation necessarily means consent. . . . Women have been expected to perform certain functions and to behave in self-sacrificing ways for so long that they often 'freely consent' to their own subordinations. . . . If women consent to social subordination by occupying traditional roles, do domestic animals?" (38). When consenting to certain circumstances may be necessary for survival, both social and otherwise, Oliver suggests that it is impossible to tell what "consent" really means.

Ahmed echoes Oliver's argument that valorizing the freedom of consent obscures social forces that prevent resistance. Ahmed turns away from humanism both in her work broadly by drawing on animals and objects and in her discussion of consent by problematizing its linguistic basis: it is "all-too-human," she writes, "to assume a yes as a sign of being willing, a sign that is taken up as the giving of permission to proceed" (189). Ahmed turns instead to willfulness, an assertion of the will that any material form might display, "a potential that matters to all matter" (12). Like Oliver, she argues that it is insufficient to pay attention to nonlinguistic signs of willingness, because being willing can sometimes be the only way to avoid force, oppression, marginalization, or even outright violence (55).[4] Shifting from defining consent linguistically to recognizing consent in the affective state of willingness is a nonanthropocentric move because it reformulates ethical relations to include nonlinguistic bodies, objects, or parts. However, when we read those bodies and forms as "willing," Ahmed suggests, we must also recognize the cultural and political contexts that work to suppress resistance.

Instead, Ahmed sees potential in willfulness—disagreement, disobedience, refusal, and the bad feelings they produce. If willfulness, as in Ahmed's theory, reveals nonanthropocentric agency and disrupts power relations, then I argue it is a crucial aspect of thinking through the ethics of animal response. Where animal response ethics tends to highlight the significance of attunement—what Ahmed calls "a harmonious or *responsive* relationship"—willfulness reveals a "queer ethics": "an ethics that registers those who are not attuned as keeping open the possibility of going another way" (50–51, emphasis mine). The negative response of willful animals, then, can help reveal the embodied heterogeneity of creaturely life—what Cary Wolfe calls "the specific materiality and multiplicity of the subject" (9). I argue that affective discord thus extends an ethics of response to those animals who are unruly, stubborn, disobedient, intractable, or just uncommunicative—troublemakers and killjoys in interspecies relatings.[5]

THE TROUBLE WITH WILLING ANIMALS
AND THE IMPORTANCE OF ANIMAL TROUBLE

Animal philosophers that focus on training, like Haraway, Vicki Hearne, and Paul Patton, recognize the communicative and emotional equality of animals, and, I argue, raise questions about consent in their focus on animal willingness *within* unequal relations of power. The ethics of such training lie in the attention of the trainers toward states of willing cooperation and joyful participation between animals and humans. In *Adam's Task*, Hearne insists trainers should remember that "the ability to exact obedience doesn't give you the right to do so—it is the willingness to obey that confers the right to command" (66). If an animal refuses to obey its trainer, the trainer has the responsibility to adjust her methods to produce willingness on the animal's part; moreover, it is the trainer's responsibility to provide the conditions to which the animal will happily consent. Like Hearne, Haraway affirms the ethical significance of attending to animal willingness, communicated through, or understood as, positive affect. Haraway asks, "What if work and play, and not just pity, open up when the possibility of mutual response . . . is taken seriously as an everyday practice available to philosophy and to science? What if a usable word for this is *joy*?" (*When Species Meet* 22). For Haraway, good feelings signal responsiveness, allowing her to theorize the response ethics of animal training as a mutually beneficial activity for both human and animal. She claims that "the experience of sensual joy in the nonliteral open of play might underlie the possibility of morality and responsibility for and to one another" (*When Species Meet* 242). By her paradigm, an animal's willingness, registered as joy, is more than just obedience and thus more than just one side of an unequal power relationship in which the animal is compelled to consent to what the human asks. Joy appears in *When Species Meet*, for example, in both the accomplishment of skilled behaviour and the excessive feeling of undirected play; what connects those types of joy to responsiveness is what Haraway calls "skilled inventiveness" or "'getting it' together in action" (220, 241).[6] Her use of the term "joy," then, refers to bodies responding positively in mutual understanding, an embodied communication that implies willingness.

In her descriptions of mutual response and the mutual influence or "nonmimetic attunement" of animal and human bodies that produce real and material changes (229), Haraway acknowledges human openness and vulnerability to animals and listens carefully for what I argue is the consent implied by an animal's enthusiastic willingness. These are surely an important part of the "ethics and politics committed to the flourishing of significant otherness" that characterize Haraway's companion species philosophy (*Companion* 3). However, an attunement valued in Haraway's work occurs when the animal is responding positively to human direction, as in the "positive bondage" of Susan Garrett's dog-training philosophy, where the goal is "non-optional, spontaneous, oriented enthusiasm" (*Companion* 43). The dog in this case must respond positively and, moreover, must do so spontaneously, without hesitation, and without the need for force. Haraway claims that the benefit for the dog in such a training philosophy is precisely the possibility of a responsiveness that is "eagerly offer[ing]" rather than "morosely complying" (45), that not despite but *because of* its "near total control in the interests of fulfilling human intentions," Garrett's training insists on paying attention to "what the dog actually likes; . . . to play . . . in a way *the dogs* enjoy" (*Companion* 44, 45). While the move to canine-centric play is an ethical response, training still implies a mode of weeding out willfulness to replace it with mutual happiness—a will alignment, to use Ahmed's term. There seems to be not much space in this ethical paradigm for dissent, for bad feelings; as Ahmed points out, Haraway's concept of companion species is a "helpful expression for describing helpful encounters" but is less so when accounting for willful ones (44, 178).[7] Haraway and other animal trainer-philosophers do not ignore the possibility of willfulness, dissent, or discord; as horse trainer Monty Roberts acknowledges, animals "can either accept or refuse to cooperate in the training process" (in Patton 85). However, while Haraway notes that the dance of embodied communication can sometimes be discordant (*When Species Meet* 26), her companion species model writ large responds to unwillingness by finding ways to encourage willingness.[8] I want to flesh out the response ethics of those "out of synch" bodies (*When Species Meet* 26).

When Species Meet includes both an appreciation for and a critique of Derrida's treatment of response in *The Animal That Therefore I Am (More to Follow)*, a text that shows us the potential of discord in animal response ethics. On the one hand, Derrida performs a crucial intervention in Western philosophy in this text by deconstructing the difference between animal reaction and human response and proposing an ethics based on the possibility that agential communication can occur on the part of either the human or the animal.[9] On the other, Haraway laments Derrida's material failure to communicate with his cat one morning as she watches him and suggests that in doing so, Derrida stops short of respect (*When Species Meet* 20).[10] However, Derrida's feeling of shame in this interaction also reveals a mode of cross-species communication that marks cooperative difficulty and underlines both the respect and undecidability that characterize Derrida's nonanthropocentric response ethics.[11] In Derrida's description of his cat's demands and his suggestion that his cat looks at him "just to *see*," we can read a recognition of creaturely willfulness and a respect for the alterity that this willfulness implies (4). This is further emphasized in Derrida's citation of Michel de Montaigne, who writes, "When I play with my cat (*ma chatte*), who knows if I am not a pastime to her more than she is to me?" and in another edition of this text adds, "If I have my time to begin or to *refuse*, so has she hers" (in Derrida 7, emphasis mine). In these representations of feline refusal and discord, we can recognize the cat's ability to enact her will outside of human desire and acknowledge that interspecies communication may not always be pleasurable. Further, Derrida's reaction of shame shifts the animal-human power relations implied by response because it suggests that, at times, humans are no more capable of measured, attentive, and enthusiastic response than animals. As Arnould-Bloomfield suggests, Derrida and Haraway "need each other" (1474). Reading them together here suggests that the disruption of human expectations by an animal's will prompts the practical necessity of deciding how to proceed (ethically).

Willett notes that a recent turn toward conceiving of animals as labourers and as anticapitalists can give us insight into the companion species model of response ethics through resistance (57). Work is a key framework for Haraway's paradigmatic companions, and her attention to labour calls for attention to the difference between forms of animal and human labour (*When Species Meet* 67). The "tough love" of animal training, however, reproduces the terms of management and productivity under capitalism, those of "high-pressure, success-oriented, individualist America" (*Companion* 46). In this particular formulation of dogs as labourers, trainers occupy positions akin to capitalist employers rather than coworkers. For both working animals and humans, then, the performance of willing participation does not necessarily mean that consent was theirs to freely give. As Jonathan L. Clark points out, both humans and animals are coerced into certain kinds of labour, even if the means of coercion are different—financial necessity for the former and physical force for the latter (140). Moreover, where consent was supposed to ensure the difference between humans and animals, exposing the social forces that make free consent a fiction works to expose humans and animals as coworkers and labour as nonanthropocentric (139). Agnieszka Kowalczyk takes the idea of human and animal solidarity in labour one step further and, as I do, turns to the significance of animal resistance. In Kowalczyk's analysis, animal resistance in labour functions in the same way that human worker resistance traditionally has, creating solidarity by blurring the hierarchical divisions of labour structured by capital. Kowalczyk reinforces the nonanthropocentric agency of animal resistance precisely by refusing to divide response from reaction or place them in a hierarchical relation: "Acts of resisting exploitation performed by non-human bodies do not necessarily have to be thoughtful ... to be recognized as significant. ... Whether or not a response or a reaction of the exploited to exercised power is planned or intentional, it is within this realm of the body that the individual non-human animal becomes a part of the political collectivity" (194–195). These philosophers show how labour can give us another way to see the ethical significance of animal discord.

ANIMAL WILL IN THE NINETEENTH CENTURY

Thomas Hardy's *Tess of the d'Urbervilles* (1891) offers a model of animal response ethics that engages questions of consent and dissent through willing and willful animals, including those that labour with humans. In emphasizing the importance of creaturely response, *Tess* represents agency as the willfulness of humans and nonhumans alike in their refusal to "agree" or consent to submission. It does so particularly with respect to those animals that labour with and for humans. Reading Hardy's work in the company of these philosophers can, I hope, illuminate and texture the ethical stakes of each. In *Tess*, Hardy tells the story of the eldest daughter of the Durbeyfield family, who goes to work for Alec d'Urberville (whom they believe is a relative) when her family loses their source of income following the tragic death of the Durbeyfield's workhorse. Alec pursues a resistant Tess, and he eventually rapes her, an act that results in a pregnancy. In scholarly work on the novel, some writers also use the language of rape to refer to Tess's assault, but others reflect on an uncertainty in the text regarding Tess's consent, because the moment is not explicitly narrated. In response to this scholarly debate, Sarah E. Maier insists that whatever consent looks like explicitly, Tess's will is ignored, and "it is made painfully clear that her experience was neither a pleasant one, nor one which she chose to endure *willingly*" (21, emphasis mine). Maier recognizes that questioning whether a yes or no response was heard obscures the question of coercion, and the version of agency Maier offers for Tess turns largely on refusal, as she "adamantly and repeatedly refuses to be a kept woman" and "refuses to be appropriated by Alec, or later, by Angel" (22). In the willful "spirit and individuality" that Maier attributes to Tess (22), we can recognize Hardy's insistence that will *itself* is individuating and that discord is enough to mark agency and demand respect. For example, in describing his mistaken inability to forgive Tess for not being a virgin at marriage, her husband, Angel, "asked himself why he had not judged Tess constructively rather than biographically, by the *will* rather than by the *deed*" (Hardy 371, emphasis mine). "Constructively" here captures the individuality wrought by willful desire.

Rebecca Mitchell argues for an ethics of alterity in *Tess*, reading Tess's individuality and Angel's inability to recognize that he cannot ever really know it as the ethical crux of the novel because "recognizing that limitation [of knowing the other] is necessary to positive affective relationships" (73).[12] Elisha Cohn also turns to alterity in *Tess*'s human-animal ethics, drawing on Derrida to argue that Hardy emphasizes human agency and represents sympathy as the compassionate response of humans to animal suffering ("Creature" 499-500). Cohn claims that *Tess* represents a transition in Hardy's work away from a conception of "biological determination"—represented by Charles Darwin's evolutionary thinking—that "negated autonomous human agency and . . . threatened notions of responsibility" ("Creature" 496).[13] The materialism that threatened human agency is repeated in the realm of Victorian psychology, where the presence of a volitional and agential will was being debated.[14] Hardy's evolutionary thinking was influenced by Victorian materialist and Darwinian Thomas Huxley, whose controversial essay "On the Hypothesis That Animals Are Automata, and Its History" suggests that it would be impossible to distinguish between animal reaction and human response.[15] Huxley's theory, that humans and animals were both a kind of conscious machine and that consciousness was a physiological effect produced by the nervous system and the brain, was seen by many to suggest that humans lacked souls and thus had no real volitional power for direction, control, and responsibility. Automatism can be interpreted as making questions of consent irrelevant, as it seems to do with questions of choice.[16] However, we can also read Huxley's theory as an extension of the capacity for willfulness to other forms of life, since he does not deny that animals have free will—he just reconceives what free will might mean, claiming that "an agent is free when there is nothing to prevent him from doing that which he desires to do" (575). Huxley's influence on Hardy's work suggests that Hardy may have understood animal reaction as willfully agential and perhaps, by extension, as responsive and ethically meaningful.

Cohn's and Elsie B. Michie's readings support the possibility that Hardy saw animal will in *Tess* as ethically meaningful by claiming Hardy's representations of animals are "linked to the novel's ongoing critique of sexual coercion" (*Still* 168) and, I would add, as actors in their discord. As Michie describes, nineteenth-century equine knowledge and symbolism affirmed the value of both the horse's "ability to accept discipline" and its "aggression"—we might say its willingness and its willfulness (146). Following the publication of Darwin's *Origin of the Species* in 1859, the pressing question around equestrian relationships became whether "the rider [was] controlling the horse, or the horse the rider" (146), and certainly, as Michie makes clear, Alec d'Urberville's horse, Tib, has a willfulness and agency that are recognized by him as a power to be mastered. Alec claims that Tib "has a very queer temper," describing his training of Tib as a murderous battle: "Just after I bought her she nearly killed me. And then, take my word for it, I nearly killed her" (Hardy 83). Michie ties this management to the labouring classes, characterizing Alec as part of the "new managerial business class" of the late nineteenth century (147). Although she highlights Alec's mastery of Tib more than his management, this context underscores the importance of discord, since the *Oxford English Dictionary's* (*OED*) definitions of "manage" include attaining consent as well as training (in Michie 147). In this depiction of horse and driver, Alec wants Tib's obedience; there is no depiction here of a mutually beneficial or even companionable relationship. Tib, importantly, keeps a measure of her own will in Alec's description of her as "touchy still, very touchy" (Hardy 83), which also serves as a reminder that this training relationship is a struggle of wills. Tib's objections mean that she has been either coerced into submission or trained into performance. When she races down a hill, "it was evident that the horse, whether of her own will or of [Alec's] (the latter being the more likely), knew so well the reckless performance expected of her that she hardly required a hint from behind" (83). Alec's training succeeds in producing a will alignment, but that does not mean Tib is completely, and certainly not joyously, willing. Brief though the scene may be, the ethical import of recognizing animal discord or dissent lies in the rendering of Alec's management, exposing the performance of power, and in the appearance of Tib's will as both connected and individuating.

The treatment of another horse, the Durbeyfields' Prince, complicates the ethics of training and willingness as a willingness to labour. When Prince is harnessed in the middle of the night to cart beehives to Casterbridge for the next day's market, he makes no outward protest to the arrangement. He nevertheless "looked wonderingly round at the night . . . as if he could not believe that at that hour, when every living thing was intended to be in shelter and at rest, he was called upon to go out and labour" (Hardy 62). Here, Hardy represents Prince's point of view as individual and in discord with the demands of labour to which he is subject. Cohn notes that this representation of Prince connects animals and humans in the novel as both "suffering under exploitative labor" and that "the horse's own attitude to work prefigures the novel's interrogation of labor practices" ("Creature" 510). When Tess falls asleep at the reins and her poor management of the obedient Prince leads to his death, his willingness is fatal. Cohn makes the insightful point that when Tess "regard[s] herself in the light of a murderess" over Prince's death (Hardy 66), she takes "responsibility to the laboring animals who make up a part of her family" (*Still* 163), but response ethics are also significant here because, as she has also pointed out, Tess and Prince are both vulnerable labourers. I would extend Cohn's insight by pointing out that while Tess takes responsibility for Prince's death, she only risks driving Prince and the beehives to the market because the alternative is the loss of her family's precarious livelihood. Later, Tess's feelings of responsibility and her family's need for subsistence compel her to work at the d'Urbervilles, despite her considerable discomfort in doing so; in this switch, Tess and Prince are interchangeable forms of labour for the working class.

LABOUR AND DISCORDANT ETHICS

Hardy's novel offers another version of response ethics that recognizes and respects animal alterity in the discordant willfulness of animals. During the time when Tess works at Talbothay's dairy, we find a model of how respect for discord and alterity might occur between animal and human labourers. Livestock provide fruitful cases for thinking through response ethics because cows are both labouring partners and resources in agriculture, as they do not fit neatly into paradigms of companionship, training, or wildness;[17] Harriet Ritvo notes that cattle were considered good domestic animals, but as a model for "the relations between human superiors and inferiors," they were not "the most appreciated" (18–19). In the sociality of Talbothay's dairy, the animal and human labourers may affect and respond to one another, but neither is jockeying for a position of mastery, and the willfulness of the cows both reveals and creates disruptions in capitalist power structures.

When Tess first sees the dairy cows, their wills are described in relation to the needs of a profitable farm, with "the less restful cows . . . stalled," while "those that would stand still of their own will were milked in the middle of the yard, where many of such better behaved ones stood waiting now" (133). This referral to the will of the well-behaved cows implies the expression of a kind of tacit consent, or will alignment, that allows them a certain amount of freedom. Almost immediately, though, another kind of will is introduced as the milkers describe a slackening of production, with Dairyman Crick claiming that "the cows don't gie [sic] down their milk to-day as usual" and accusing one of them of "keeping back" her milk (136). This language can be taken to suggest the refusal of the cows to be willing or generous. In response, the milkers decide to sing, because "songs were often resorted to in dairies hereabout as an enticement to the cows when they showed signs of *withholding* their usual yield" (136, emphasis mine). The music is intended to move the cows in a beautiful confusion of reaction and response wherein both the withholding of milk and the enticement to yield it are affective states: the first is seen to be caused by the arrival of a new maid and the second by the emotional and physiological response to music. As the willfulness of the resistant dairy cows and the singing of the milkers demonstrate, Hardy's model focuses on the body and its instinctual reactivity, evoking a responsive relationship between species while at the same time maintaining the alterity of the animal. If music brings the milkers and cows into affective attunement, it is first with the acknowledgement that animal lives and worlds exist beyond the demands of humans and second as an alternative model to exploited labour.[18]

I argue that ethics emerge as humans respond to the will of these animals. The partnerships between species are unequal because each embodied creature has different capacities and is subjected to labour structures in different ways, but the animals and humans are willful partners because, in the enterprise of modernity, neither the labouring humans nor animals are in real positions of capitalist control. The cows are giving milk because their calves have been taken from them after birth; they are not equal or willing participants in that arrangement. Crick, running the farm, must subdue the willfulness of the cows in order to ensure the profitability of his endeavor. But the livestock have their desires too, and

> certain cows will show a fondness for a particular pair of hands, sometimes carrying this predilection so far as to *refuse* to stand at all except to their favourite, the pail of a stranger being unceremoniously kicked over. It was Dairyman Crick's rule to insist on breaking down these partialities and aversions by constant interchange, since otherwise, in the event of a milkman or maid going away from the dairy, he was placed in a difficulty. The maids' private aims, however, were the reverse of dairyman's rule, the daily selection by each damsel of the eight or ten cows to which she had grown accustomed rendering the operation on their willing udders surprising easy and effortless. (147, emphasis mine)

The willfulness of the cows in this case and the respect of the milkers' hands to the cows' desires mean that the labour is also easier for the milkers, and so the maids choose those cows that have also chosen them. It is telling in the context of affective labour, and the elision of reproductive labour in the history of capitalism, that it is the female milkers who are mentioned here choosing to resist the demands of capital and instead engaging in what Haraway calls "emergent practices": "Vulnerable, on-the-ground work that cobbles together *non-harmonious* agencies and ways of living that are accountable to their disparate inherited histories and to their barely possible but absolutely necessary joint futures" (*Companion* 7, emphasis mine). This labour together is not really based on love or sympathy but rather on a shared discord—unwilling, both cow and milkmaid, to care too much about Crick or to make their labour any harder than necessary. Together they assert their unwillingness to submit—to management, to capitalism, to agricultural control—and when they do, their labour is easier with each other.

The pails that have been kicked over are evidence of a resistance to being broken, of a creaturely world that refuses to align itself with the will of the farm or the will of the market. The ease of labour that emerges from the practice of responding to creaturely will again blurs the lines of reaction and response. For example, when the milkers move their labour outside in the heat of the summer to milk in the fields, "for coolness and convenience, without driving in the cows," Tess milks Old Pretty, "who loved Tess's hands above those of any other maid" (Hardy 172). With her face sideways against the cow's flank, Tess "might have been in a trance, her eyes open, yet unseeing. Nothing in the picture moved but Old Pretty's tail and Tess's pink hands, the latter so gently as to be a rhythmic pulsation only, as if they were obeying a reflex stimulus, like a beating heart" (173). In its embodied automaticity, we might think of the alignment or agreement of embodied will here as perhaps related to a more obscure physiological definition of consent as "a relation of sympathy between one organ or part of the body and another, whereby when the one is affected the other is affected correspondingly" (OED). If Tess's hands obey a reflex stimulus, it might very well be from the other's body, as she reaches across otherness, unseeing and reactive but nevertheless responsive. This moment arises only after Tess adjusts her body to the desire of the cow, bringing her world and the cow's as comfortably close together as possible.

Hardy suggests that physiological consent, a mutual automatic willingness between body parts, is only possible *as* consent if it includes the possibility of discord. The cow's willful udders are parts whose will is figured on behalf of the whole and, at the same time, distinct physiological parts of assemblages that interrupt organic wholeness. The connection between Tess's hands and Pretty's udder does not obscure the position of the cows as resource, and neither does it guarantee consent, despite its embodied automatism. If the willfulness of the animal is also a glimpse of alterity, it is made manifest at the dairy in the possibility that relating does not proceed through the ability of the cows to understand what the milkers want. When Angel finally demonstrates his feelings for Tess, he does so beside the flank of Old Pretty, interrupting the consensuality of the maid and the cow with his embodied desire, one that created "an *aura* over his flesh, a breeze through his nerves . . . and actually produced, by some mysterious physiological process, a prosaic sneeze" (173, emphasis in original).[19] While Tess's desire matches Angel's in its material reaction as the two impulsively embrace, the gaze of the cow intrudes into the scene, as "Old Pretty by this time had looked round, puzzled; and seeing two people crouching under her where, by immemorial custom, there should have been only one, lifted her hind left crossly. 'She is angry—she doesn't know what we mean—she'll kick over the milk!' exclaimed Tess, gently striving to free herself" (174). The willfulness of the cow, appearing as Tess tries to remove herself from Angel's embrace, reminds us that, even as embodied agreement, consent is conditional and not free from questions of power and force.

In fact, Angel "checked himself" from kissing Tess, despite the "inevitableness" of the moment, and he apologizes for not having asked first (174). In this moment, Pretty is both an individual creature and a helpful companion to manifest Tess's will, as Tess becomes increasingly concerned over how her past will complicate or prevent her relationship with Angel. As Angel reads her embodied distress, he asks her not to think he has "presumed upon [her] defencelessness—been too quick and unreflecting . . . ?" (174). Tess, in this case, holds her reassurance of willingness in reserve, saying only "N'—I can't tell," as Angel "allowed her to free herself" (174). As Hardy shows, it is in attending to affective discord and making room for dissent that we constitute nonanthropocentric response ethics. Following Ahmed again, we could call the threat of Pretty's kick "a willful gift" from one part to another (176), from Pretty's will to Tess's, but we must keep in mind that Pretty's will is also her own. If Tess's heart is "more deeply concerned with herself and Clare," her eyes still need to be "concerned with the quadruped's actions" (Hardy 174). Pretty's will makes her an individual, and while her consensuality connects her world to Tess's, her discord reminds us of her alterity.

CONCLUSION

In my discussion of Hardy's response ethics, I do not mean to suggest abstracted analogies between kinds of consent or willingness, between sex and labour, or between women and animals. Hardy does, however, make clear the ways in which we can draw connections between creatures who are accustomed to having their willingness coerced or their willfulness suppressed. Dissent and discord, not volition, characterizes a mode of individuation and contingent relating in his novel, and so it can help us to see willfulness as the embodiment of differentiated, vulnerable, and feeling creatures and to respond and define a model of individuality that does not fall prey to humanism. Attending to the good feelings of companions in their specificity and materiality is an ethical task, but discord too opens the possibility of ethical relating, where we might begin to understand how "the capacity not to be compelled by others is made into the promise of a queer thing" (Ahmed 192).

NOTES

1. Thank you to Margaret Linley, Carolyn Lesjak, Jennifer Scott, Sarah Creel, Sarah Bull, and Marc Acherman for generously reading and rereading this chapter and offering their invaluable responses.
2. See Arnould-Bloomfield for a discussion of affect in Derrida and Haraway.
3. The field of animal ethics is very broad, as Oliver notes, and many thinkers working in it take up the question of consent. This selection is meant only to provide a nonanthropocentric framework for thinking about consent.
4. For example, Ahmed points out the history of women's consent to marriage as the path of least resistance in a position of little to no power. She paraphrases the marriage contract as "*if not willing then forced, if not consent then war*" (233n21, emphasis in original).
5. Ahmed has developed the concept of the feminist killjoy in *Willful Subjects* and elsewhere to describe someone who disrupts compulsory positive feelings as she draws attention to the oppression or marginalization that produces or accompanies them (2).

6. For examples of joy in skilled behaviour in *When Species Meet*, see pages 183 and 220; for joy in undirected play, see 228, 229, 232, and 240.

7. For an overview of critique and defense of *The Companion Species Manifesto*, see Chris Vanderwees.

8. The quotation from Haraway reads, "The flow of entangled meaningful bodies in time— whether jerky and nervous or flaming and flowing, whether both partners move in harmony or painfully out of synch or something else altogether—is communication about relationship, the relationship itself, and the means of reshaping relationship and so its enacters" (*When Species Meet* 26).

9. See Oliver.

10. Haraway is disappointed that Derrida "did not become curious about what the cat might actually be doing, feeling, thinking, or perhaps making available to him in looking back at him that morning," and in doing so, he ignored embodied "practices of communication" (20, 21). Willett offers a similar critique, claiming that "Derrida . . . aims to stay clear of any seeming illusion of animal communication or mutual understanding" (42).

11. See Bloomfield-Arnould. On shame as an individuating affect, see Eve Sedgwick and Adam Frank. Thank you to Lindsay Reeve for first pointing me toward the significance of reaction as affect in Derrida's essay.

12. Rachel Hollander has also recently noted the relationship between another of Hardy's novels and a Derridean ethics of "unconditional hospitality" and "openness to the absolutely other" (89-90).

13. See also Ivan Kreilkamp on pastoral care and animal agency in another of Hardy's novels. See Gillian Beer and John Glendening on the significance of the human for Hardy within the evolutionary order; see Donald R. Wehrs for the ethics of self-preservation in *Tess* in the context of cognitive science and evolutionary theory.

14. Ahmed notes this and draws examples from the nineteenth century. See also Adam Crabtree.

15. Both Suzy Anger and Suzanne Keen note the same reference to automatism in Hardy's notebook: "Action mostly automatic, reflex movement, etc. Not the result of what is called *motive*, though always ostensibly so, even to the actors' own consciousness" (Anger 51–52; Keen 98). See Keen also for Hardy's turn to empathy as a response to materialist psychology.

16. This is the conclusion William James draws in his response to Huxley in 1879, in which he emphasizes the importance of conscious, agential choice (13). James nevertheless also refuses any hard and fast distinction between animals and humans based on their capacity for response; rather, he notes only that the more complex a nervous system, the greater the "incalculableness" of the reaction (4) and grants even a frog the unpredictability of "ideas, emotions or caprices" (4). James claims that the body responds to the world it "picks out" via the senses (9), and a human's world "is but one in a million alike embedded, alike real to those who may abstract them. Some, such other worlds may exist in the consciousness of ant, crab and cuttle-fish" (14).

17. Thank you to Scott Mackenzie for this insight.

18. Michael Hardt notes that "affective labor produces . . . social networks, forms of communities, biopower" (96). While he sees this as a result of the current valorization of affective labour, we can nonetheless see in *Tess* how the response ethics that work via affect for the resistance, dissent, or discord of animals subverts capitalist structures, as human labourers adjust their behaviour in order to accommodate the will of the livestock. Trish Ferguson

notes that work at Talbothays is "dictated by the needs of the animals," that there is "harmony of work with nature," and that the labourers enjoy "freedom from the pressures of industrial capitalism"(64–65).

19. See Keen for another physiological reading of this moment.

WORKS CITED

Ahmed, Sara. *Willful Subjects*. Duke UP, 2014.

Anger, Suzy. Review of "On the Hypothesis That Animals Are Automata" (1874), by Thomas Huxley. *Victorian Review*, vol. 39, no. 1, 2009, pp. 50–52. *JSTOR*, www.jstor.org.proxy.lib .sfu.ca/stable/27793698.

Arnould-Bloomfield, Elisabeth. "Posthuman Compassions." *PMLA*, vol. 130, no. 5, 2015, pp. 1467–1475.

Beer, Gillian. *Darwin's Plots: Evolutionary Narrative in Darwin, George Eliot and Nineteenth-Century Fiction*. 2nd ed., Cambridge UP, 2000.

Clark, Jonathan L. "Labourers or Lab Tools? Rethinking the Role of Lab Animals in Clinical Trials." *The Rise of Critical Animal Studies: From the Margins to the Centre*, edited by Nik Taylor and Richard Twine, Routledge, 2014, pp. 139–164.

Cohn, Elisha. "'No Insignificant Creature': Thomas Hardy's Ethical Turn." *Nineteenth-Century Literature*, vol. 64, no. 4, 2010, pp. 494–520. *JSTOR*, www.jstor.org.proxy.lib.sfu.ca/stable/10.1525/ncl.2010.64.4.494.

———. *Still Life: Suspended Development in the Victorian Novel*. Oxford UP, 2016.

"Consent." *Oxford English Dictionary*. 2015.

Crabtree, Adam. "'Automatism' and the Emergence of Dynamic Psychiatry." *Journal of History of the Behavioural Sciences*, vol. 39, no. 1, 2003, pp. 51–70. Wiley, doi:10:1002/jhbs.10089.

Derrida, Jacques. *The Animal That Therefore I Am*. Edited by Marie-Louise Mallet, translated by David Wills, Fordham UP, 2008.

Ferguson, Trish. "Hardy's Wessex and the Birth of Industrial Subjectivity." *Victorian Time: Technologies, Standardizations, Catastrophes*, edited by Trish Ferguson, Palgrave Macmillan, 2013, pp. 57–76.

Glendening, John. "The Entangled Heroine of Hardy's *Tess of the d'Urbervilles*." *The Evolutionary Imagination in Late-Victorian Novels: An Entangled Bank*, Ashgate, 2007, pp. 69–106.

Haraway, Donna. *The Companion Species Manifesto: Dogs, People, and Significant Otherness*. Prickly Paradigm, 2003.

———. *When Species Meet*. U of Minnesota P, 2008.

Hardt, Michael. "Affective Labor." *boundary*, vol. 26, no. 2, 1999, pp. 89–100. *JSTOR*, www .jstor.org.proxy.lib.sfu.ca/stable/303793.

Hardy, Thomas. *Tess of the d'Urbervilles* [1891]. 2nd ed., edited by Sarah E. Maier, Broadview, 2007.

Hearne, Vicki. *Adam's Task: Calling Animals by Name*. Skyhorse, 2007.

Hollander, Rachel. *Narrative Hospitality in Late Victorian Fiction: Novel Ethics*. Routledge, 2013.

Huxley, Thomas. "On the Hypothesis That Animals Are Automata, and Its History." *Fortnightly Review*, vol. 16, no. 95, 1874, pp. 555–580. *ProQuest*, proxy.lib.sfu.ca/login?url=http://search.proquest.com.proxy.lib.sfu.ca/docview/2464973?accountid=13800.

James, William. "Are We Automata?" *Mind*, vol. 4, no. 13, 1879, pp. 1–22. *JSTOR*, www.jstor .org.proxy.lib.sfu.ca/stable/2246561.

Keen, Suzanne. *Thomas Hardy's Brains: Psychology, Neurology, and Hardy's Imagination*. Ohio State UP, 2014.

Kowalczyk, Agnieszka. "Mapping Non-human Resistance in the Age of Biocapital." *The Rise of Critical Animal Studies: From the Margins to the Centre*, edited by Nik Taylor and Richard Twine, Routledge, 2014, pp. 183–200.

Kreilkamp, Ivan. "Pitying the Sheep in *Far from the Madding Crowd*." *Novel: A Forum on Fiction*, vol. 42, no. 3, 2009, pp. 474–481. *Academic Search Complete*, doi:10.1215/00295132-2009-044.

Maier, Sarah E, editor. Introduction. *Tess of the d'Urbervilles*, 2nd ed., Broadview, 2007.

Michie, Elsie B. "Horses and Sexual/Social Dominance." *Victorian Animal Dreams: Representations of Animals in Victorian Literature and Culture*, edited by Deborah Denenholz Morse and Martin A. Danahay, Ashgate, 2007, pp. 145–166.

Mitchell, Rebecca N. *Victorian Lessons in Empathy and Difference*. Ohio State UP, 2011.

Oliver, Kelly. *Animal Lessons: How They Teach Us to Be Human*. Columbia UP, 2009.

Palmer, Clare. *Animal Ethics in Context*. Columbia UP, 2010.

Patton, Paul. "Language, Power, and the Training of Horses." *Zoontologies: The Question of the Animal*, edited by Cary Wolfe, U of Minnesota P, 2003, pp. 83–99.

Ritvo, Harriet. *The Animal Estate: The English and Other Creatures in the Victorian Age*. Harvard UP, 1987.

Sedgwick, Eve Kosofsky, and Adam Frank. "Shame in the Cybernetic Fold." *Critical Inquiry*, vol. 21, no. 2, 1995, pp. 496–522. *JSTOR*, www.jstor.org/stable/1343932.

Steeves, H. Peter, editor. "They Say Animals Can Smell Fear." *Animal Others: On Ethics, Ontology, and Animal Life*, edited by H. Peter Steeves, SUNY, 1999, pp. 133–178.

Vanderwees, Chris. "Companion Species under Fire: A Defense of Donna Haraway's *The Companion Species Manifesto*." *Nebula*, vol. 6, no. 2, 2009, pp. 73–81. *Humanities Source*, proxy.lib.sfu.ca/login?url=http://search.ebscohost.com/login.aspx?direct=true&db=hus&AN=43373423&site=ehost-live.

Wehrs, Donald R. "Levinas, Cognitive Science, and Post-Darwinian Fiction: The Conundrum of *Conatus* in Hardy's *Tess of the d'Urbervilles*." *Nineteenth-Century Studies*, vol. 22, 2008, pp. 57–74.

Willett, Cynthia. *Interspecies Ethics*. Columbia UP, 2014.

Wolfe, Cary. *Animal Rites: American Culture, the Discourse of the Species, and Posthumanist Theory*. U of Chicago P, 2003.

7 · CONSENTING TO READ
Trigger Warnings and Textual Violence

BRIAN MARTIN

In May 2014, two of my students—who volunteer as peer counselors with our campus's Rape and Sexual Assault Network (RASAN)—asked if I could add "trigger warnings" to my syllabi for courses that include texts on sexual violence. Amid a national campus culture in which as many as one in four women has been sexually assaulted during her undergraduate career, the activist work of these two students reflects the efforts on many campuses nationwide to urge American colleges and universities to more effectively investigate, prosecute, and prevent campus rape and sexual assault (Pérez-Peña).

In April 2014, the first report of President Barack Obama and Vice President Joe Biden's White House Task Force to Protect Students from Sexual Assault confirmed that "one in five women is sexually assaulted in college" and launched policy initiatives and an education campaign to combat sexual assault on campus (White House Task Force; Kessler). Vice President Biden later wrote an open letter of support in June 2016 to a sexual assault survivor at Stanford University, when her assailant was given a lenient sentence following his conviction (Kessler; Namako).[1]

Amid these wide-ranging efforts—from my home campus to the White House and from my own students to the president and vice president—to educate and to combat sexual violence, I found my students' requests for trigger warnings entirely reasonable and was pleased to make my classroom and courses safer (if not always comfortable) places for discussion and debate on gender and sexuality. That said, I also empathize with many of my colleagues nationwide and abroad who feel that trigger warnings represent a form of censorship and an unwillingness to engage in difficult but necessary discussions on sexuality and sexual violence. During the past few years (2013–2017), these two positions on trigger warnings have been largely articulated (by a broad range of teachers, students, scholars, administrators, and journalists) as being in stark opposition. In this chapter, I argue that such opposition has in some ways created a false dichotomy that can be better understood by both a careful review of some of the major voices in these trigger warning debates and a thoughtful discussion of some of the pedagogical techniques that many of us already use in our courses and teaching.

Many of my courses in French and comparative literature include texts that denounce misogyny, homophobia, and sexual exploitation, coercion, and assault. Despite the way some of these texts offer a social critique of sexual violence, their inclusion in course syllabi presents a challenge to what one might call *pedagogical consent*, or students' (un)willingness to read. Even as we continue to include such texts in our courses (as means of educating students about misogyny and sexual assault), how should we frame their sexual and textual violence? In what ways might trigger warnings protect vulnerable students and faculty but also discourage enrollment and engagement? What mechanisms and strategies might we explore in order for our students to *consent to read*?

I. TRIGGER WARNING DEBATES (2014–2017)

Before discussing the use of trigger warnings in my own courses, it's important to understand the broader history of their controversial use and abuse on university campuses. This controversy became heated in the spring and summer of 2014, when action on several American campuses (including the University of California at Santa Barbara as well as Oberlin, Rutgers, and Wellesley) both in favor of and in opposition to trigger warnings unleashed a wave of responses from students, professors, and journalists in global media (from the *New York Times* to the *Guardian*) and in academic conferences and professional organizations (from the Modern Language Association [MLA] to the American Association of University Professors [AAUP]).[2]

Trigger warnings find their origins in feminist websites and blogs from the 1990s and 2000s that attempted to warn readers of troubling content, particularly on rape and sexual violence (but also other forms of physical and social trauma linked to misogyny and racism), in the hopes that such content might not "trigger" post-traumatic stress and suffering. As university students began to ask their instructors to add trigger warnings to syllabi, there was criticism that this represented a new kind of censorship at odds with the goals of academic freedom, inquiry, and debate. For some faculty, this kind of censorship echoed the McCarthyism and communist witch hunts of the 1950s, the feminist pornography debates or "sex wars" (between antipornography and sex-positive feminists) of the 1970s, and the political correctness debates of the 1980s and 1990s.

While some students and administrators at Columbia, Oberlin, and Rutgers have called for warnings and even the exclusion of such texts as Ovid's *Metamorphosis*, F. Scott Fitzgerald's *The Great Gatsby*, and Chinua Achebe's *Things Fall Apart* (for their content on sexual violence, misogyny, racism, and colonialism), many have speculated on how this leaves other texts such as William Shakespeare's *Merchant of Venice*, Mark Twain's *Huckleberry Finn*, Virginia Woolf's *Mrs. Dalloway*, Williams Butler Yeats's *Leda and the Swan*, and Vladimir Nabokov's *Lolita* equally vulnerable to calls for trigger warnings, censorship, and omission (for their own content on racism, anti-Semitism, sexual assault, and suicide).[3] At Duke University, several conservative students refused to read Alison Bechdel's *Fun Home*, arguing that this lesbian graphic novel offended their religious values. As one student explained, "I am a Christian, and the nature of *Fun Home* means that content that I might have consented to read in print now violates my conscience due to its pornographic nature" (Flaherty, "Not So Fun Home"). At Harvard Law School, Professor Jeannie Suk Gersen reports that some students have asked law faculty "not to use the word 'violate' in class—as in 'Does this conduct violate the law?'—because the word was triggering. Some students have even suggested that rape law should not be taught because of its potential to cause distress" (Suk Gersen). Lamenting that colleagues at numerous law schools have begun "dropping rape law and other topics related to sex and gender violence" from their courses, she concludes that "if the topic of sexual assault were to leave the law-school classroom, it would be a tremendous loss—above all to victims of sexual assault" (Suk Gersen).

As these examples from Duke and Harvard make clear, calls for trigger warnings and for censorship of controversial texts and material have come from both conservative and progressive groups across a broad range of social, political, and religious points of view. For instructors, such controversies have led to fears of a wide range of pedagogical challenges and professional exclusions: from textual censorship, student absences, and lower enrollments; to protests, boycotts, and physical threats; to loss of funding and promotion, disciplinary action and dismissal, and even legal action and prosecution.

The controversy on trigger warnings has extended beyond teachers, students, and classrooms to university administrators and national organizations for higher education. While Oberlin advised its faculty to issue trigger warnings in 2014, explaining that "triggers are not only relevant to sexual misconduct, but to anything that might cause harm [such as] racism, classism, sexism, heterosexism, cissexism, ableism, and other issues of privilege and oppression," the AAUP argued the same year that "the presumption that students need to be protected rather than challenged in a classroom is at once infantilizing and anti-intellectual.

It makes comfort a higher priority than intellectual engagement" (Flaherty, "Trigger Unhappy"; AAUP). In a 2014 report written for its Committee on Academic Freedom and Tenure, the AAUP further argued that "trigger warnings suggest that classrooms should offer protection and comfort rather than an intellectually challenging education. They reduce students to vulnerable victims rather than full participants in the intellectual process of education" (AAUP). The AAUP report goes on to cite the American Library Association (ALA) and its position that "prejudicial labels are designed to restrict access" and that "labeling as an attempt to prejudice attitudes is a censor's tool" (ALA; AAUP).

While there has been some support for trigger warnings among college instructors, large numbers of faculty members from the United States and beyond have voiced their opposition and concern (Hanlon; Nadeau). In 2015, the College Art Association (CAA) and the MLA surveyed its members on trigger warnings and reported that "45 percent of respondents who have had first-hand experience with trigger warnings see it as a real threat to academic freedom" (Downs). And in her September 2015 report from the MLA Committee on Academic Freedom and Professional Rights and Responsibilities, Judith Butler writes, "The debates about trigger warnings raise the question of whether controversial topics are being purposefully or inadvertently banned from the classroom. It would, in my view, be important for the MLA to develop a nuanced and thoughtful position on how the commitment to opposing all forms of bigotry and prejudice can be understood in the light of controversial curbs on academic freedom" (Butler).

Still others argue that the debate on trigger warnings grossly misrepresents the psychological mechanisms and complexities of trauma, resilience, recovery, and consent. In their September 2015 cover story for the *Atlantic*, "The Coddling of the American Mind," Jonathan Haidt (a social psychologist) and Greg Lukianoff (a constitutional lawyer) express their concern with both the harm done by students who use emotional reasoning to attack others and the harm done to students who are overprotected from uncomfortable but necessary debate. Arguing that the trigger warning debates demonstrate a lack of understanding for the psychological mechanisms and treatments for post-traumatic stress disorder (PTSD), Haidt and Lukianoff write, "According to the most-basic tenets of psychology, the very idea of helping people with anxiety disorders avoid the things they fear is misguided" (Haidt and Lukianoff).[4] Having asked, "What are we doing to our students if we encourage them to develop extra-thin skin in the years just before they leave the cocoon of adult protection?" they insist that "attempts to shield students from words, ideas, and people that might cause them emotional discomfort are bad for the students" and that "colleges should do all they can to equip students to thrive in a world full of words and ideas that they cannot control" (Haidt and Lukianoff). In other words, students who offer their pedagogical consent or demonstrate a willingness to read may be better equipped to face the challenges of life after college.

In her 2015 book *How to Raise an Adult*, Julie Lythcott-Haims argues that this culture of overprotection may be linked to the historical context in which today's generations of college students came of age. The rise in child abductions during the 1980s, school shootings in the 1990s, and terrorist violence in the 2000s (combined with the financial instability created by the global economic crisis of 2008 and following) all led to a new culture of supervised playdates, helicopter moms, and overprotective parents, as well as increased fear, anxiety, and need for safety (Lythcott-Haims 1–28). As the social psychologist Sherry Turkle has written in *Alone Together* (2011), this coincided with the advent of personal computing, the internet, smartphones, and social media, where interpersonal communication and social interaction (including texting and Facebook) are mediated through screens that isolate individuals who are attempting to connect with others. All this has combined to create a new generation of students who are less comfortable with face-to-face discussion, disagreement, and debate and who are (according to Lythcott-Haims) emotionally unprepared for college, coping, and independence. During her ten years as freshman dean at Stanford, Lythcott-Haims discovered that many eighteen-year-olds cannot effectively "handle interpersonal problems," "cope with ups and downs," and "take risks" (82–83). Because of the "misguided attempt to protect kids from hurt feelings," she writes, many of today's college students "have real difficulty knowing how to handle the disagreement, the uncertainty, the hurt feelings" because of their "inability to cope" (91).[5] This has in turn contributed to the debates over controversial course material, trigger warnings, and pedagogical consent.

Perhaps the most famous response to the trigger warning debate is Jack Halberstam's July 2014 article "You Are Triggering Me! The Neo-liberal Rhetoric of Harm, Danger, and Trauma" in which the celebrated queer scholar criticizes "the re-emergence of a rhetoric of harm and trauma that casts all social differences in terms of hurt feelings, and that divides up politically-allied subjects into hierarchies of woundedness" (Halberstam). In this article, Halberstam argues that "as people 'call each other out' to a chorus of finger-snapping, we seem to be rapidly losing all sense of perspective, and instead of building alliances, we are dismantling hard fought for coalitions" (Halberstam). Underscoring the generational differences between today's students and older LGBT people who faced queer bashing, pervasive misogyny, massive discrimination (in housing, employment, marriage, and other legal protections), staggering suicide rates, and gross indifference to HIV/AIDS, Halberstam asks, "What does it mean when younger people who are benefitting from several generations now of queer social activism by people in their 40s and 50s (who in their childhoods had no recourse to anti-bullying campaigns or social services or multiple representations of other queer people . . .) feel abused, traumatized, abandoned, misrecognized, beaten, bashed, and damaged?" (Halberstam).

Halberstam further suggests that the overwhelming focus on microaggressions has distracted queer communities from the even more threatening macroaggressions of the past and the present. In this way, he argues, student demands for safe spaces and trigger warnings (or what I more broadly call *pedagogical consent*) take disproportionate priority over more insidious forms of homophobia, misogyny, racism, exploitation, and violence: "As LGBT communities make 'safety' into a top priority . . . the fight against aggressive new forms of exploitation, global capitalism, and corrupt political systems falls by the wayside" (Halberstam). Halberstam thus calls for "an end to the finger snapping moralism," arguing, "Let's not fiddle while Rome (or Paris) burns, trigger while the water rises, weep while trash piles up; let's recognize these internal wars for the distraction they have become" (Halberstam).

As the positions of the AAUP, ALA, CAA, and MLA and the arguments of Suk Gersen, Butler, Haidt, Lukianoff, Lythcott-Haims, and Halberstam all make clear, the 2014–2017 debates on safe spaces, microaggressions, and trigger warnings demonstrate the significant challenges to pedagogical consent and to students' willingness or unwillingness to read. Before I speak about my own teaching and offer some suggestions for addressing the challenges of pedagogical consent, I want to discuss five issues that are central to these trigger warning controversies but have had less attention in the many published texts on this contentious debate: student-faculty relations, humanities challenges, course descriptions, campus resources, and macroaggressions. These five issues collectively demonstrate some of the larger stakes of the trigger warning debates, from institutional dangers to potential solutions.

1. Student-Faculty Relations

Between student requests for greater safety and faculty fears of censorship, the trigger warning debates have created new tensions between students (who often do not understand the potential consequences of such demands on their instructors) and faculty (who are sometimes impatient with the generational differences between their students and themselves). Students need to understand that their demands for trigger warnings and their harsh criticism of instructors who are uncomfortable with such warnings have in many cases placed an undue burden on the very faculty who are most passionate about combatting racism, classism, misogyny, homophobia, and other forms of social injustice. Even as they denounce privilege and demand safe spaces, some students misuse their own privilege to create unsafe spaces for faculty, especially those whose courses on gender, sexuality, race, ethnicity, and class are most harshly scrutinized. As Halberstam suggests, the very faculty who have dedicated their careers, scholarship, and lives to educating others about gender, sexual, and racial difference are those whose jobs may be placed in jeopardy by claims that their courses are unsafe. This has created new inequalities that single out women faculty, queer faculty, faculty of color, and nontenured adjunct faculty who disproportionally teach courses in which controversial content leaves them vulnerable to negative student evaluations, disciplinary action, and dismissal. For such faculty, the demands for trigger warnings have triggered fear and created an unsafe professional environment.

At the same time, many students whom we should applaud for their activism and engagement against sexual assault and violence, racism, homophobia, misogyny, and discrimination have often felt embattled by professors who are unwilling to see their desire for trigger warnings as part of a socially engaged movement.[6] Such tensions between faculty and students with similar goals but differing approaches have left many disheartened and less willing to engage with one another, in the classroom and beyond.

2. Humanities Challenges

These tensions are enormously dangerous for liberal arts education, which has seen declines in both majors and course enrollments in the Humanities, as students flock in greater numbers to fields such as economics and computer science. Concomitant with the trigger warning debates (2014–2017), journalists, statisticians, writers, and academics—from David Brooks and Nate Silver to Verlyn Klinkenborg and Michael Bérubé—have debated in recent years (2013–2017) the fears and realities of what has been ubiquitously called an ongoing "crisis in the Humanities."[7] Such fears have led some to worry about a dystopian future like the one in Jules Verne's *Paris in the Twentieth Century* (1863), where universities become engines for global capital and libraries are repositories for forgotten literature.

In this futurist novel, the University of Paris becomes a vast centralized institution called the Academic Credit Union, where the Humanities have been eliminated in favor of multidisciplinary programs in engineering and finance.

> The Academic Credit Union included no fewer than 157,342 students, to whom knowledge was imparted by mechanical means. . . . The study of *belles lettres* and of ancient languages (including French) was at this time virtually obsolete; Latin and Greek were not only dead languages but buried as well; for form's sake, some classes in literature were still taught, though these were sparsely attended. . . . Classical authors and the entire book trade . . . peacefully crumbled to dust on the shelves . . . but introductions to mathematics, textbooks on civil engineering, mechanics, physics, chemistry, astronomy, courses in commerce, finance, industrial arts—whatever concerned the market tendencies of the day—sold by the millions. . . . Few among those young people whose vocation inclined them

toward a literary career sought instruction . . . [and] the last pedagogues of Greek and Latin where vanishing from their deserted classrooms. (Verne 6–8)

Some, like Bérubé, might find Verne's dystopian vision of a future without Humanities an exaggeration. However, several universities have in recent years consolidated Humanities programs into monolithic departments of "Languages, Literatures, and Cultures" or "Languages, Literatures, and Linguistics." Other institutions have eliminated entire Humanities departments altogether.

In 2010, the State University of New York at Albany cut its programs of Theater, Classics, Russian, Italian, and French, despite global outcry from New York to Paris.[8] Citing economic factors, the university eliminated Theater and French, even though SUNY Albany is the flagship campus of a major public university whose state is home to the billion-dollar theater industry of Broadway and shares a vast border with French-speaking Québec, with whom New York state did more than fourteen billion dollars of trade in 2011.[9] As these few examples demonstrate so dramatically, economic factors alone cannot either explain or protect Humanities programs under institutional, ideological, and cultural siege. The trigger warning debates have contributed to new cuts in texts, participation, and enrollments in Humanities courses. At a time when the Humanities themselves are denied safe spaces and secure futures, we should be wary of alienating new generations of students or creating disincentives from enrollment in our courses.

3. Course Descriptions

One simple solution to the call for trigger warnings would be to encourage institutions and instructors to create better course descriptions in their online catalogs. While many colleges and universities already offer detailed descriptions in their course catalogs, many others provide only a title, a one-line description, or practical information on class hours, location, and credits. Such listings do not provide enough information for students to assess their interest or for faculty to encourage enrollments and may lead to the kinds of criticism that those asking for trigger warnings have expressed.

Rather than listing a course as simply English 120: Introduction to the Novel or Spanish 200: Twentieth-Century Literature, one might provide a longer description that would both inform and potentially attract students. Here is an example from my course French 224: Sexuality and Seduction in Nineteenth- and Twentieth-Century France:

In 1857, both Flaubert's *Madame Bovary* and Baudelaire's *Les Fleurs du mal* were put on trial for sexual indecency and "crimes against public morality." In 1868, *Le Figaro* attacked Zola's novel *Thérèse Raquin* as "putrid literature" for its depiction of adultery, murder, and scandalous sexuality in nineteenth-century Paris. A century later, Gide, Colette, and Duras continued to shock French readers with their extraordinary novels on male and female homosexuality, inter-generational lovers, and bi-racial relationships. In this course, we will examine a wide range of issues on eroticism and sexuality in nineteenth- and twentieth-century France, including marriage and adultery, seduction and desire, love and betrayal, prostitution and fetishism, gay and lesbian identity, cross-dressing and gender representation, exoticism and colonial (s)exploitation. Readings to include texts by Chateaubriand, Balzac, Flaubert, Zola, Maupassant, Barbey d'Aurevilly, Gide, Proust, Colette, Duras, and Guibert.

While there is no trigger warning in this course description, it explains the course's goals of examining a broad range of issues on sexuality, gender, race, and even violence. Long before attending the first class or reading the syllabus, students can already see that this course will examine sexuality in ways that might be challenging. For students who fear that such material might trigger memories of sexual assault, they can make an informed decision from this course description whether this is an appropriate course for them. Course descriptions thus serve as preliminary syllabi, in which course content can be announced and considered before the course begins. If the syllabus is a contract to which students consent, the course description is a helpful preview of that contract and allows students the opportunity to decide on both enrollment and pedagogical consent.

The added advantage of detailed course descriptions is that they may also attract larger numbers of students with an interest in the stated material. Before the advent of online catalogs, some institutions might have been concerned that long course descriptions would increase the cost of printing voluminous catalogs. But since most course catalogs are now online, such cost considerations are no longer an obstacle to providing informative and enticing course descriptions that might go a long way to addressing students' concerns and encouraging their enrollment and enthusiasm.

4. Campus Resources

For faculty who are not averse to offering some kind of acknowledgment that their courses or some of their assigned material may be emotionally and psychologically challenging, the syllabus and the first day of class are opportunities to inform students about the resources at many colleges, universities, and local communities that can provide help and support beyond the classroom. Either as part or in lieu of a trigger warning, it can be quite helpful to both students and instructors to learn about (and list in the syllabus) campus resources that can help students with physical and mental health, personal and professional counseling, academic support and tutoring, and both financial and material support. While students get such information at orientations, they may appreciate that instructors care about their well-being and are eager to connect them to other available resources. It is also helpful for instructors to know that they are not alone in managing the complexities of students' individual needs. Amid the many demands of academic careers and schedules, instructors who are fully aware of campus support services (including health centers, psychological services, deans' offices, peer tutors, academic advisors, residential staff, chaplains' offices, and campus security) can better help students in distress and more effectively find collegial support for themselves.

5. Macroaggressions

As we move into an era of even greater threats to our students and colleagues from presidential policies and decrees, these earlier preoccupations with trigger warnings and microaggressions may unfortunately give way to the more frightening realities of macroaggressions. Citing the generational tensions between students who denounce microaggressions and faculty who've lived through macroaggressions (including gay bashing, military expulsion, marriage inequality, and HIV/AIDS), Halberstam argues that students' focus on "distraction[s]" eclipses the need to "fight against aggressive new forms of exploitation" (Halberstam). Even with good intentions of fighting social inequality, some students look too hastily to nearby targets by leveling harsh criticism of courses and professors rather than using their energies to fight greater threats to political and social justice. While the epidemic of campus sexual assault demonstrates a major threat for which both students and faculty should mobilize, it can be frustrating to see a disproportionate response to smaller campus controversies when much larger dangers and injustices loom, both on campus and beyond. At the same time, many students during the past few years of the trigger warning debates (2014–2017) were in fact actively and courageously involved in larger political struggles, from the Occupy and Me Too movements to Black Lives Matter and the U.S. presidential elections (2011–2017).

As we look to new macroaggressions in 2017–2020—amid presidential threats to women and transgender people, immigrants and refugees, Muslims and Mexicans, and both domestic and global stability—these students may be increasingly called on (like their professors before them) to take up larger battles against misogyny, racism, and xenophobia. We can only hope that the texts and ideas they read and discuss in our courses might help them better confront such challenges, with the same passion and sensitivity that we model for them, in both our own sympathy for and our challenges to their demands for trigger warnings and pedagogical consent.

II. TEACHING WAR AND SEXUALITY (2010–2017)

Amid this complex debate on the uses and abuses of trigger warnings, how then might one walk the pedagogical line between safety and censorship? How can instructors negotiate the teaching of textual violence so that their students will consent to read? In several undergraduate courses, I teach texts that include domestic violence, sexual assault, warfare, genocide, suicide, and various forms of misogyny, homophobia, and racism. I've chosen such challenging texts because of the way they reflect the social injustices of their time and to educate students about this history so that we can—as Suk Gersen and Halberstam have argued—better understand and combat these forms of human exploitation, discrimination, and violence in the present. These are not easy conversations, but they are important and necessary ones.

Among the more controversial texts I teach in courses on the French nineteenth- and twentieth-century novel and in advanced seminars titled Sexuality and Seduction, Danger and Desire, and Paris on Fire are several titles that include domestic violence and sexual assault. In Honoré de Balzac's *The Girl with the Golden Eyes* (1835), Paquita Valdes is brutally murdered by her jealous lover in Paris, and in Balzac's *Sarrasine* (1830), the young sculptor Ernest-Jean Sarrasine falls into a wild rage and attempts to kill the operatic diva La Zambinella, with whom he is infatuated. In Émile Zola's *La Curée* (1872), a young woman named Renée Béraud du Châtel is raped by an older man and then forced to marry a man of her family's choosing in order to quell the scandal of her unwed pregnancy. In Zola's *Thérèse Raquin* (1867), Thérèse and her lover, Laurent, murder her husband, Camille. Wracked with guilt, Laurent beats Thérèse, who accepts such brutality as punishment for her crime. And in Zola's *L'Assommoir* (1877), a violent alcoholic named Bijart mercilessly beats his wife and eight-year-old daughter Eulalie until he eventually kills them both. Guy de Maupassant's *Boule de suif* (1880) centers on a prostitute named Elisabeth Rousset, who is coerced into sex with an enemy officer during the War of 1870, while Maupassant's *Story of a Farm Girl* (1881) recounts the suffering of Rose, whose husband, Vallin, beats her for not conceiving a child. And in Maupassant's *Yvette* (1884), the title character is assaulted by Jean de Servigny when she refuses to kiss him during an evening walk.[10]

Other texts that I teach examine both self-inflicted and state-sanctioned violence. Like Maupassant's *Yvette*, Gustave Flaubert's *Madame Bovary* (1857) ends with a woman who poisons herself when suicide seems the only option amid the suffocating misogyny of nineteenth-century France. Victor Hugo's *Claude Gueux* (1834) and *The Last Day of a Condemned Man* (1829) both examine the effects of murder and the death penalty. Hugo's *Les Misérables* (1862) compares the miseries of crippling poverty, police harassment, and excessive incarceration (for Jean

Valjean) as well as the sexual exploitation and misogyny of nineteenth-century prostitution (for Fantine). In addition to Hugo's *Les Misérables* and Maupassant's *Yvette* and *Boule de suif*, prostitution is also at the center of Balzac's *Cousine Bette* (1846), Jules Barbey d'Aurevilly's *A Woman's Revenge* (1874), Maupassant's *Bed 29* (1880), and Zola's *Nana* (1880). And like these last three texts, in which prostitutes suffer both public humiliation and painful deaths to syphilis, Hervé Guibert's *To the Friend Who Did Not Save My Life* (1990) recounts the analogous humiliations and miseries of those living with and dying of AIDS.

All of these texts are potentially triggering for students who are survivors of sexual assault, violence, disease, racism, homophobia, misogyny, exploitation, and discrimination. But as Suk Gersen has argued, it is vital for us to read texts that denounce human suffering so that we might be better equipped to both understand the struggles of the past and to combat social injustice in the future. How then do we get students, who have been raised in a generation that often expects trigger warnings and who may be reluctant to confront such issues in the classroom, to take our courses, engage with such texts, and consent to read?

In September 2014, following the request of two students that I consider using trigger warnings, I decided to make an addition to my syllabus for a course titled Paris on Fire: Incendiary Voices from the City of Light (1830–2005). Under absolutely no pressure from my campus administration, department, or colleagues and despite my initial skepticism and concerns, I added the following text to my syllabus: "The texts and films for this course examine two centuries of conflict, revolution, and social change. You should be aware that several of these works demonstrate different forms of violence, including the death penalty (Hugo), domestic violence (Balzac), war, genocide, and torture (Truffaut, Sartre, Duras, Clément), as well as racism and urban violence (Charef). If you have any concerns, my door is always open to discuss them with you in private, and to let you know about resources on campus (including the Rape and Sexual Assault Network, Dean's Office, Health Center, and Chaplains' Office) that can offer extra support." Having admired those two students for their own social engagement against sexual assault on campus, I was willing to give this a try. That semester, there was no noticeable decline in enrollments for this course because of this warning or the material it describes. To my knowledge, no students avoided or dropped the course for its challenging material. Despite my reluctance, this experiment succeeded in respecting student concerns and reassuring them that these difficult topics would be treated with sensitivity and that there were other resources on campus to provide support if they should need it.

In subsequent semesters, I made similar additions to my other syllabi, including the following for my course on Adversity and Modernity in the Twentieth-Century Novel:

The texts for this course examine a century of adversity, conflict, and social change. You should be aware that several of these texts demonstrate different forms of emotional and physical suffering, including social rejection (Colette, Begag), illness and death (Camus, Guibert), racism and colonialism (Duras, Begag), and urban violence (Ernaux, Begag), as well as misogyny (Colette, Ernaux, Duras), homophobia (Guibert), and sexual vulnerability (Colette, Duras, Guibert, Ernaux). We will pay particular attention to the ways these texts empathize with human suffering and denounce injustice and discrimination. If you have any concerns, my door is always open to discuss them with you in private, and to let you know about resources on campus (including RASAN, the Dean's Office, Health Center, and Chaplains' Office) that can offer extra support.

Yet again, my students appreciated this addition to the syllabus. If my institution or department had forced me to provide such a warning or to alter my course material, I would have felt much differently. Rather than capitulating to censorship, however, I merely tried to respond to what is—unfortunately, frustratingly, but palpably—a serious concern for safety from this generation of students. I've learned in a personal way that, as with every new generation, teachers sometimes need to engage with students where they are, in their own time, and within their own historical, cultural, and generational context.

My most valuable lesson, however, came from my course on war literature, titled War and Resistance: Two Centuries of War Literature in France (1804–2004). Amid the many discussions of sexual violence in these recent debates on trigger warnings, far less attention has been paid to the effects of military violence and warfare. Ironically, war narratives have been largely ignored by the trigger wars, even by those who are concerned with triggering flashbacks to past trauma.[11] In addition to survivors of rape and sexual assault, war veterans, refugees, and school shooting survivors also suffer from post-traumatic stress disorder (PTSD), whose very name was coined during the Vietnam War to describe soldiers suffering from the effects of what had previously been called "shell shock" and "combat fatigue" during the First and Second World Wars.[12]

Since the more recent wars in Iraq and Afghanistan (starting in 2001), many American universities have had—as they did during the Vietnam War and the Gulf War before them—increasing numbers of veterans and refugees on campus. As Syrian, Afghan, Iraqi, and other refugees reach both European and North American shores (especially amid the ongoing refugee crisis that exploded in 2015), we need to be aware of new students in our classrooms who may be living with PTSD. This became clear to me when I was teaching my war seminar several years ago.

During the fall of 2010, one of the students in my course on War and Resistance was a survivor of the genocide in Rwanda and Burundi from 1993 to 1994 and the ensuing civil war in Burundi from 1993 to 2006, when ethnic cleansing among Hutus and Tutsis in both countries led to more than one million deaths.[13] This student, whom I'll call Joseph, first told me about his war trauma in an essay for the course.[14] Moved by our reading of Elie Wiesel's *Night* (1958) and its account of the Nazi death camps, Joseph wrote in his essay about his own experiences as a survivor of genocide, when he fled the butchery in his native town, hid in the forest, and eventually made his way to the United States in search of safety and a new life. For Joseph, Wiesel's Holocaust memoir offered a model and context for articulating his own experiences of war. I was moved by Joseph's essay and worried that I had not known of his war trauma earlier, so that I could have reached out to offer extra support. When we met to discuss this later that week, Joseph reassured me that my detailed course description in the catalog had explicitly described and appropriately warned him about the seminar's focus on warfare and its content on genocide.

> In 1883, Maupassant called on his fellow war veterans and writers to join him in speaking out against warfare and violence, crying "Let us dishonor war!" From the Gallic Wars against Caesar (during the first century) to France's controversial role in the "War on Terror" (during the twenty-first century), the French literary tradition is rich in texts that bear witness to war and speak out against its monstrous inhumanity. While war literature in France can be traced back to ancient and medieval texts on Vercingétorix, Charlemagne, William the Conqueror, and Joan of Arc, this course will focus specifically on literary representations of war during the nineteenth and twentieth centuries, from the Napoleonic Wars, to the First and Second World Wars, to the Algerian and Cold Wars, and the "War on Terror." Discussions will examine the impact of war on soldiers and civilians, patriotism and pacifism, history and memory; the implications of war as invasion and conquest, occupation and resistance, victory and defeat; the relationship of war to gender, sexuality, and ethnicity; and the role of war in colonialism and genocide. Texts and films to include works by Balzac, Stendhal, Hugo, Rimbaud, Daudet, Maupassant, Zola, Cocteau, Wiesel, Duras, Resnais, Pontecorvo, Alleg, Camus, and Fanon.

Joseph further explained that this course description had inspired him to take the class in order to consider the effects of genocide and survival, from the French context to his own. This conversation also gave me the opportunity to offer Joseph additional support and help him connect to other resources on campus, including mental health services, the dean's office, and the college chaplains.

Since then, I have added the following text to my syllabus for this course, in the hopes that it will serve as both a warning and an invitation for other war survivors, refugees, and veterans in my courses to come and speak with me and to reach out to services on campus that can offer expert help and support: "The texts and films for this course examine two centuries of human warfare, violence, and genocide. You should be aware that all of these works demonstrate some form of violence, including combat and bombings, executions and torture, ethnic cleansing and genocide, racist and colonial brutality, sexual coercion and assault, biological and nuclear warfare. If you have any concerns, my door is always open to discuss them with you in private, and to let you know about resources on campus (including RASAN, the Dean's Office, Health Center, and Chaplains' Office) that can offer extra support." As we see more combat veterans, war refugees, and school shooting survivors on our campuses and in our classrooms, texts such as these may offer a way to better inform, understand, and support our students.[15]

CONCLUSION

As I learned from this student in my war seminar several years before the trigger warning debates, explanatory texts in both course catalogs and syllabi can be helpful pedagogical tools and serve as invitations to deeper engagement between students and faculty. Rather than a gateway to censorship, such texts might help us offer better information, context, and support for students who—because of their need for a greater sense of safety and their desire to discuss and transform a chaotic and frightening world—may flock to rather than flee from our courses. By offering such texts and using such tools, we can provide a more effective context for gaining the confidence and pedagogical consent of our students. But this can only happen if both students and teachers can focus more on solidarity and trust, a respect for generational differences and individual vulnerabilities, and a renewed commitment to open dialogue in the classroom.

NOTES

1. The White House Task Force confirmed the findings of other studies on campus rape and sexual assault, including a report for the U.S. Department of Justice in 2007 and a poll by the *Washington Post* and Kaiser Family Foundation in 2015 that both found that one in five women is sexually assaulted in college (White House Task Force; Kessler; Namako). In September 2015, the Association of American Universities (AAU) issued yet another report on this alarming rate of campus sexual assault (Anderson and Clement; Cantor et al.).
2. At McGill University, students Sajdeep Soomal and Samuel Kessler organized a Trigger Warning Reading Group at the Institute for the Public Life of Arts and Ideas in 2015–2016. I am grateful to them for their bibliographical suggestions. As this group at McGill makes clear, the trigger warning debates have not been limited to American colleges and universities. In an April 2017 cover story in Montréal's *Le Devoir*, Jean-François Nadeau documents recent events at McGill, the Université de Montréal, and the Université du Québec à Montréal in which students and faculty clashed over free speech and censorship, including issues

on trigger warnings. This debate thus extends beyond the United States to Québec and from Anglophones to Francophones.

3. Among many others, Medina provides a good summary of this call for literary warnings and exclusions.

4. Haidt and Lukianoff further argue that this "perpetual state of outrage" demonstrates the need for behavioral therapy to correct several "common cognitive distortions" among students, such as, "catastrophizing," "labeling," "overgeneralizing," and "blaming."

5. Lythcott-Haims explains that "millennials have been called the 'Everyone Gets a Trophy' generation" (22). Having seen an "increasing numbers of our students lacked the wherewithal to cope with adversity," she warns that a "lack of ability to cope with struggle isn't only a problem among young adults at Stanford or Harvard. It's a growing facet of life in middle- and upper-class America today" (228–229).

6. This generational difference was in some ways paralleled by clashes between younger supporters of Senator Bernie Sanders and older supports of Secretary Hillary Clinton during the 2016 Democratic Primary for president, who shared common progressive principles but often clashed over how to achieve them.

7. For more on this ongoing "crisis in the Humanities," see Belkin and Levitz, Bérubé, Brooks, Flaherty ("Major Exodus"), Jaschik, Klinkenborg, Lewin, and Silver.

8. See "SUNY Albany to Cut Language, Classics, and Theater Departments" (2010).

9. For more on these cuts at SUNY, see Courtine, Foderaro, Lawrence, and Québec Ministry of International Relations.

10. For further research on sexual violence in literature, see Barnett, Catty, Greenstadt, Gunne and Thompson, Robertson and Rose, Sielke, Stockton, and Tanner.

11. Consent is also at the center of debates on both the First and Second World Wars. Echoing Goldhagen's *Hitler's Willing Executioners: Ordinary Germans and the Holocaust* (1997), Becker and Audoin-Rouzeau argue in *14–18: Understanding the Great War* (2002) that ordinary citizens and soldiers bear part of the responsibility for consenting to violence. While this argument on "patriotic consent" relies on what political philosophy calls "the consent of the governed," others (notably the French historian Frédéric Rousseau) believe that this unjustly blames soldiers and citizens who were forcibly conscripted under penalty of imprisonment and execution and were exploited by nationalist discourses from 1914 to 1918.

12. Shephard writes in *A War on Nerves: Soldiers and Psychiatrists in the Twentieth Century* (2001) that the "the diagnostic eras of shell shock, battle fatigue, and post-traumatic stress disorder" (xix) are associated with the First World War, the Second World War, and the Vietnam War.

13. For more on the genocide in Rwanda and Burundi, see Dallaire, Kidder, and Tuhabonye and Brozek.

14. I'm using this pseudonym to protect the safety of my student, amid renewed violence and instability in Burundi, from 2015 to 2017.

15. For more on trigger warnings, see Ahmed, Duggan, Filipovic, Freeman et al., Hanlon, Jarvie, Johnson, Kang, Marcotte, Noonan, Schlosser, and Stoeffel.

WORKS CITED

Ahmed, Sara. "Against Students." *The New Inquiry*, 29 June 2015. www.thenewinquiry.com/against-students/.

American Association of University Professors (AAUP). "On Trigger Warnings." Aug. 2014, www.aaup.org/report/trigger-warnings.

American Library Association (ALA). "Labeling and Rating Systems." 1 July 2014, www.ala
.org/advocacy/intfreedom/librarybill/interpretations/labelingrating.

Anderson, Nick, and Scott Clement. "College Sexual Assault: 1 in 5 College Women Say They
Were Violated." *Washington Post*, 12 July 2015, www.washingtonpost.com/sf/local/2015/
06/12/1-in-5-women-say-they-were-violated/?utm_term=.afd2f50d1035.

Audoin-Rouzeau, Stéphane, and Annette Becker. *14–18: Understanding the Great War*. Translated by Catherine Temerson, Farrar, Straus, and Giroux, 2002.

Barnett, Pamela. *Dangerous Desire: Sexual Freedom and Sexual Violence since the Sixties*. Routledge, 2004.

Belkin, Douglas, and Jennifer Levitz. "Humanities Fall from Favor: Far Fewer Harvard Students Express Interest in Field with Weak Job Prospects." *Wall Street Journal*, 6 June 2013,
www.wsj.com/articles/SB10001424127887324069104578527642373232184.

Bérubé, Michael. "The Humanities Declining? Not According to the Numbers." *Chronicle of
Higher Education*, 1 July 2013, www.chronicle.com/article/The-Humanities-Declining
-Not/140093.

Brooks, David. "The Humanist Vocation." *New York Times*, 20 June 2013, www.nytimes.com/
2013/06/21/opinion/brooks-the-humanist-vocation.html.

Butler, Judith. "Report from the MLA Committee on Academic Freedom and Professional
Rights and Responsibilities (CAFPRR)." Modern Language Association, 26 Sept. 2015,
www.mla.org/content/download/39397/1741167/rpt-CAFPRR-J16.pdf.

Cantor, David, et al. "Report on the AAU Campus Climate Survey on Sexual Assault and
Sexual Misconduct." Association of American Universities, 21 Sept. 2015, www.aau.edu/
sites/default/files/%40%20Files/Climate%20Survey/AAU_Campus_Climate_Survey
_12_14_15.pdf.

Catty, Jocelyn. *Writing Rape, Writing Women in Early Modern England*. Palgrave Macmillan,
1999.

College Art Association. "About CAA." 11 Nov. 2004, www.collegeart.org/about/.

Courtine, Jean-Jacques. "Campus américain: Le français en déclin." *Le Monde*, 11 Jan. 2010,
www.lemonde.fr/idees/article/2010/11/01/campus-americains-le-francais-en-declin
_1433858_3232.html.

Dallaire, Romeo. *Shake Hands with the Devil: The Failure of Humanity in Rwanda*. Random
House, 2003.

Downs, Linda. "Trigger Warnings." College Art Association News, 22 June 2015, www
.collegeart.org/news/2015/06/22/trigger-warnings/.

Duggan, Lisa. "On Trauma and Trigger Warnings, in Three Parts." *Bully Bloggers*, 23 Nov.
2014, bullybloggers.wordpress.com/2014/11/23/on-trauma-and-trigger-warnings-in
-three-parts/.

Filipovic, Jill. "We've Gone Too Far with Trigger Warnings." *Guardian*, 5 Mar. 2014, www.theguardian
.com/commentisfree/2014/mar/05/trigger-warnings-can-be-counterproductive.

Flaherty, Colleen. "Major Exodus." *Inside Higher Ed*, 26 Jan. 2015, www.insidehighered
.com/news/2015/01/26/where-have-all-english-majors-gone.

———. "Not So Fun Home." *Inside Higher Ed*, 25 Aug. 2015, www.insidehighered.com/
news/2015/08/25/duke-u-freshmen-object-graphic-novel-depicting-lesbian-relationships.

———. "Trigger Unhappy." *Inside Higher Ed*, 14 Apr. 2014, www.insidehighered.com/news/
2014/04/14/oberlin-backs-down-trigger-warnings-professors-who-teach-sensitive
-material.

Foderaro, Lisa. "Budget-Cutting Colleges Bid Some Languages Adieu." *New York Times*, 3
Dec. 2010, www.nytimes.com/2010/12/05/education/05languages.html.

Freeman, Elizabeth, et al. "Trigger Warnings Are Flawed." *Inside Higher Ed*, 29 May 2014, www .insidehighered.com/views/2014/05/29/essay-faculty-members-about-why-they-will -not-use-trigger-warnings.

Greenstadt, Amy. *Rape and the Rise of the Author: Gendering Intention in Early Modern England.* Ashgate, 2009.

Goldhagen, Daniel Jonah. *Hitler's Willing Executioners: Ordinary Germans and the Holocaust.* Vintage, 1997.

Gunne, Sorcha, and Zoë Brigley Thompson, editors. *Feminism, Literature, and Rape Narratives: Violence and Violation.* Routledge, 2004.

Haidt, Jonathan, and Greg Lukianoff. "The Coddling of the American Mind." *The Atlantic,* Sept. 2015, www.theatlantic.com/magazine/archive/2015/09/the-coddling-of-the -american-mind/399356/.

Halberstam, Jack. "You Are Triggering Me! The Neo-liberal Rhetoric of Harm, Danger, and Trauma." *Bully Bloggers,* 5 July 2014, www.bullybloggers.wordpress.com/2014/07/05/ you-are-triggering-me-the-neo-liberal-rhetoric-of-harm-danger-and-trauma/.

Hanlon, Aaron. "My Students Need Trigger Warnings and Professors Do Too." *New Republic,* 17 May 2015, www.newrepublic.com/article/121820/my-students-need-trigger -warnings-and-professors-do-too.

———. "The Trigger Warning Myth." *New Republic,* 14 Aug. 2015, www.newrepublic.com/ article/122543/trigger-warning-myth.

Jarvie, Jenny. "Trigger Happy." *New Republic,* 3 Mar. 2014, www.newrepublic.com/article/ 116842/trigger-warnings-have-spread-blogs-college-classes-thats-bad.

Jaschik, Scott. "The Shrinking Humanities Major." *Inside Higher Ed,* 14 Mar. 2016, www .insidehighered.com/news/2016/03/14/study-shows-87-decline-humanities-bachelors -degrees-2-years.

Johnson, Angus. "Why I'll Add a Trigger Warning." *Inside Higher Ed,* 29 May 2014, www .insidehighered.com/views/2014/05/29/essay-why-professor-adding-trigger-warning -his-syllabus.

Kang, Jay Caspian. "Trigger Warnings and the Novelist's Mind." *New Yorker,* 21 May 2014, www.newyorker.com/books/page-turner/trigger-warnings-and-the-novelists-mind.

Kessler, Glenn. "One in Five Women in College Sexually Assaulted: An Update on This Statistic." *Washington Post,* 17 Dec. 2014, www.washingtonpost.com/news/fact-checker/wp/2014/12/ 17/one-in-five-women-in-college-sexually-assaulted-an-update/?utm_term=.59ed2e9e8a2a.

Kidder, Tracy. *Strength in What Remains.* Random House, 2009.

Klinkenborg, Verlyn. "The Decline and Fall of the English Major." *New York Times,* 22 June 2013, www.nytimes.com/2013/06/23/opinion/sunday/the-decline-and-fall-of-the -english-major.html.

Lawrence, Jesse. "Broadway Just Had Its Highest-Grossing Year Ever." *Forbes,* 10 July 2015, www.forbes.com/sites/jesselawrence/2015/07/10/broadway-just-had-its-highest -grossing-year-ever/#2f7fd78875b6.

Lewin, Tamar. "As Interest Fades in the Humanities, Colleges Worry." *New York Times,* 30 Oct. 2013, www.nytimes.com/2013/10/31/education/as-interest-fades-in-the-humanities -colleges-worry.html.

Lythcott-Haims, Julie. *How to Raise an Adult: Break Free of the Overparenting Trap and Prepare Your Kid for Success.* Henry Holt, 2015, pp. 1–28.

Marcotte, Amanda. "The Year of the Trigger Warning." *Slate,* 30 Dec. 2013, www.slate.com/ blogs/xx_factor/2013/12/30/trigger_warnings_from_the_feminist_blogosphere_to _shonda_rhimes_in_2013.html.

Medina, Jennifer. "Warnings: The Literary Canon Could Make Students Squirm." *New York Times*, 17 May 2014, www.nytimes.com/2014/05/18/us/warning-the-literary-canon-could-make-students-squirm.html.

Modern Language Association. "About the MLA." 9 July 2008, www.mla.org/About-Us/About-the-MLA.

Nadeau, Jean-François. "Liberté d'expression sous pression: La censure contamine les milieux universitaires," *Le Devoir*, 1 Apr. 2017, www.ledevoir.com/societe/education/495389/liberte-d-expression-sou-pression-la-liberte-d-expression-en-crise.

Namako, Tom. "Joe Biden Writes an Open Letter to Stanford Survivor." *BuzzFeed News*, 9 June 2016, www.buzzfeed.com/tomnamako/joe-biden-writes-an-open-letter-to-stanford-survivor?utm_term=.qe955p06on#.ydO002W57l.

Noonan, Peggy. "The Trigger-Happy Generation." *Wall Street Journal*, 22 May 2015, www.wsj.com/articles/the-trigger-happy-generation-1432245600.

Pérez-Peña, Richard. "1 in 4 Women Experience Sexual Assault on Campus." *New York Times*, 21 Sept. 2015, www.nytimes.com/2015/09/22/us/a-third-of-college-women-experience-unwanted-sexual-contact-study-finds.html.

Price, Erika. "Hey, University of Chicago: I Am an Academic. I Am a Survivor. I Use Trigger Warnings in My Classes. Here's Why." 25 Aug. 2016, www.medium.com/@erikadprice/hey-university-of-chicago-i-am-an-academic-1beda06d692e.

Québec Ministry of International Relations. "New York State: Québec's Main American Partner." 6 Sept. 2013, www.mrif.gouv.qc.ca/en/salle-de-presse/actualites/12926.

Robertson, Elizabeth, and Christine Rose, editors. *Representing Rape in Medieval and Early Modern Literature*. Palgrave Macmillan, 1999.

Schlosser, Edward. "I Am a Liberal Professor and My Liberal Students Terrify Me." *Vox*, 3 June 2015, www.vox.com/2015/6/3/8706323/college-professor-afraid.

Shephard, Ben. *A War on Nerves: Soldiers and Psychiatrists in the Twentieth Century*. Harvard UP, 2001.

Sielke, Sabine. *Reading Rape: The Rhetoric of Sexual Violence in American Literature and Culture, 1790–1990*. Princeton UP, 2002.

Silver, Nate. "As More Attend College, Majors Become More Career-Focused." *New York Times (538 Blog)*, 25 June 2013, www.fivethirtyeight.com/features/as-more-attend-college-majors-become-more-career-focused/.

Stockton, Sharon. *The Economics of Fantasy: Rape in Twentieth-Century Literature*. Ohio State UP, 2006.

Stoeffel, Kat. "Why I Stopped Rolling My Eyes at Trigger Warnings." *New York Magazine*, 21 May 2014, www.thecut.com/2014/05/stop-rolling-your-eyes-at-trigger-warnings.html.

Suk Gersen, Jeannie. "The Trouble with Teaching Rape Law." *New Yorker*, 15 Dec. 2014, www.newyorker.com/news/news-desk/trouble-teaching-rape-law.

"SUNY Albany to Cut Language, Classics, and Theater Departments." *Huffington Post*, 4 Oct. 2010, www.huffingtonpost.com/2010/10/04/suny-albany-to-cut-langua_n_749437.html.

Tanner, Laura. *Intimate Violence: Reading Rape and Torture in Twentieth-Century Fiction*. Indiana UP, 1994.

Tuhabonye, Gilbert, and Gary Brozek. *This Voice in My Heart: A Runner's Memoir of Genocide, Faith, and Forgiveness*. HarperCollins, 2006.

Turkle, Sherry. *Alone Together: Why We Expect More from Technology and Less from Each Other*. Basic Books, 2015.

Verne, Jules. *Paris in the Twentieth Century.* Translated by Richard Howard, Random House, 1996, pp. 6–8.

White House Task Force to Protect Students from Sexual Assault. "Not Alone: The First Report of the White House Task Force to Protect Students from Sexual Assault." Apr. 2014, www.title9.us/wp-content/uploads/2014/04/Not-Alone-White-House-Task-Force -on-Sexual-Assault.pdf.

8 · AMBIVALENT DESIRES

Blue Is the Warmest Color, Luce Irigaray, and the Question of Consent

CAROLINE GODART

Yes and no typically frame the issue of consent: violation, as it is understood legally, involves overcoming somebody's objection or resistance. And yet perhaps even more than power, consent brings up the question of difference: to spurn a no is to show disregard for the other's singularity, for their own approach to the world, for the integrity of their needs, affections, and desires. The purpose of this chapter is to raise the issue of consent through that of difference on the basis of Abdellatif Kechiche's *Blue Is the Warmest Color* (France, 2013), looking at the way the film addresses these two interrelated questions. Consent and its absence hover over *Blue*, even though the film, which received the Palme d'Or at the 2013 Cannes Film Festival, does not depict any kind of violation.[1] Rather, its focus is on a fully consensual love story between two young lesbians. Yet the explicit sex sequences that made it famous cannot be detached from its main actresses' complaints that they were mistreated on the shoot. More generally, the film brings up the questions of alterity and consent in a particularly complex way that underscores the essential connection between these terms—and it is precisely this relation that I want to study in these pages. With this purpose in mind, I will begin my argument with an analysis of Kechiche's approach to difference in the film and then use it as a basis to examine the concept of consent.

Based on Julie Maroh's graphic novel *Le Bleu est une couleur chaude*, the film tells the story of Adèle (Adèle Exarchopoulos), a teenage girl, and Emma (Léa Seydoux), a young woman a few years her senior, who fall in love and embark on a passionate story. A couple of years pass, and Adèle begins feeling unable to compete with her girlfriend's ambitions and her interest in another woman.

Neglected and upset, she has sex with one of her male colleagues. Emma finds out and puts a sudden, brutal end to their relationship. Adèle, desperately brokenhearted, is thrown into deep, long-lasting sorrow.

A large number of moviegoers were shocked by *Blue's* explicit depiction of lesbian sex, which earned the film a rating of NC-17.[2] Although these scenes only make up nine minutes, their crudeness, as well as Kechiche's editing choices (the first one lasts for a full six minutes, quite long for a scene in which not a single word is uttered), have made them central to critical discussions of the film. Furthermore, the young actresses reported in an interview with the *Daily Beast* ("Stars") that Kechiche had abused them verbally and emotionally during the shoot, imposing unreasonable demands on them,[3] and their most stringent critiques concerned the sex scenes themselves.

This type of behavior inscribes Kechiche within a distasteful tradition of sexist emotional and sexual abuse in art films.[4] This brutality is often a feature of the script, as sexual violence is a habitual trope in art cinema (Russell 3). Many male art filmmakers (including Roman Polanski, Stanley Kubrick, and Claude Chabrol) have depicted the sexually aggressive man as a rebellious figure who subverts bourgeois norms and conventional values by engaging in supposedly transgressive desire and sexual practices[5] (although it can be argued that nothing is more conventional than the oppression of women). Kechiche depicts neither such a figure nor any violation, but all the ingredients of the genre are still present; the length of the sex scenes, the characters' youth and homosexuality, and, most importantly, Kechiche's own violence during the shoot all betray his incarnation as a rebel male figure who uses his ascendancy over women to *choquer le bourgeois* (i.e., to confront his spectators with the inanity of their own repression) through sexuality.

Thus it comes as no surprise that the film has been accused of voyeurism, most prominently by Maroh, Manohla Dargis (*New York Times*), and Amy Taubin (*Film Comment*).[6] Voyeurism is by definition a gaze that does not honor difference; the voyeur acts like a thief, surreptitiously taking hold of that which does not belong to him rather than offering a space in which the other's subjectivity can unfold. Kechiche frequently objectifies his actresses, offering them up to the spectator's (and presumably his) desire. This is evident, as both Dargis and Taubin have noted, in his taste for showing Exarchopoulos's behind, including in the film's very first scene, which depicts Adèle walking to the bus stop in the morning, her bottom framed squarely in the middle of the screen.

This fixation peaks during the sex scenes, whose explicitness has made the headlines and fueled intense debates. Some spectators, like Jonathan Romney, consider them true to life. Others, such as Dargis and Taubin, find the sex sequences to be forced, artificial, and needlessly aestheticized. In particular, many lesbians (myself included) have taken issue with the representation of lesbian sex in the film,[7] and several critics, such as Marcie Bianco and Maroh herself, have established parallels with pornographic representations of lesbian sex, thereby underscoring their artificiality.[8]

However, Linda Williams remarks that the sex scenes in *Blue* do not in fact follow the cinematic conventions of pornography, as they suggest sexual acts more than they clearly show them. For example, the sex scenes depict no full frontal nudity, and the film departs from today's hardcore porn by never picturing fingers or mouths on or in genitals (14). Further, she comments that most of the sex scenes "are shot to reveal vast expanses of intertwined flesh and not particular parts" (14), thereby countering the fetishization of women as body parts rather than whole beings. She maintains that the scenes' explicitness is only "relative" (9) and therefore the film cannot be cited as an example of pornographic material.

I agree and would add that another key generic element is missing: contrary to pornographic conventions, neither Adèle nor Emma seem to be enjoying themselves very much during sex, and with few exceptions, pleasure appears to be largely absent. I could not help but feel, like Maroh, that the two actresses were lost and unconvincing in their attempts to perform unfamiliar sexual routines. Adèle and Emma's blank stares, evidently meant to suggest that their sexual passion has brought them into another realm altogether, rather evoked boredom to me. In other words, the problem with the sex scenes is not that they are too much like pornography but that they resemble it too little, failing in their representation of sexual ecstasy. Also curiously absent are any signs of love during sex, a singular omission in the depiction of an *amour fou*, perhaps especially between two women. The lesbian poet Eileen Myles, in a series of tweets that circulated virally on social media, summed up the scenes' issues incisively when she noted that *Blue* was "a no lesbian sex movie renowned and lauded for its bold lesbian sex."

Exposing issues of verisimilitude, which is needed to understand Kechiche's approach to alterity, is of course inherently problematic: as Williams points out, "The ink spilled over whether the film's depiction of sex is 'authentically' lesbian seems misplaced since authenticity in sex acts only exists relative to previous stylizations. In other words, there is no such thing as authentic sex whether in art films, R-rated films, or pornography" (15). Indeed, a film can do no more than give its viewers an impression that what they are seeing on the screen reproduces a hypothetical reality—and far from being absolute, our impressions of what constitutes a faithful depiction of the world have evolved historically. Movies are shaped by and in constant dialogue with the films that came before them. But these arguments do not invalidate the fact that *Blue* offers a problematic portrayal of lesbian sex. Rather, they make it clear that what needs to be underscored is not that the sex scenes are inauthentic but that they form a failed *attempt* at verisimilitude.

This is quite perplexing coming from a director who is obsessed with realism and very apt at conveying an impression of the real. Kechiche said in an interview, "I don't want [cinema] to look like life, I want it to actually *be* life. Real moments of life, that's what I'm after" (Romney, "Abdellatif Kechiche Interview"). And, indeed, he often renders minute details that make the screen appear truer than life itself—for instance, through location shoots and the absence of extradiegetic music. His sense of rhythm is outstanding, and he is able to draw out exceptionally fine performances from his actors. How then can we explain the sex scenes' artificiality? This does not appear to be a deliberate choice by Kechiche, as nothing suggests that he wanted to take a break from the overall realism of the film. For instance, he does not introduce new aesthetic elements (lighting, music, editing, etc.) in these scenes that would make it clear that he situates them in an alternate dimension, away from the real and the self-imposed necessities of verisimilitude. Rather, it seems that he was a victim of his own lack of interest in the particular experiences of lesbians.

Maroh writes of the unconvincing sequences, "It seems clear to me that that is what was missing on the set: lesbians" (Maroh). Whether or not gay women were present (and consulted) during the shoot remains unclear, but Kechiche himself confirms his ignorance of LGBTQI experiences and cultures. When asked at the 2013 New York Film Festival which queer and especially which lesbian films had influenced *Blue*, he hesitated a little and then replied, without a trace of irony, William Wyler's 1959 *Ben-Hur* (Film Society of Lincoln Center). Perhaps this explains the forced atmosphere that reigns in *Blue*'s lovemaking sequences.

It is difficult not to conjecture that the strained looks on Exarchopoulos's and Seydoux's faces are also tied to the rough treatment to which Kechiche subjected them. The two young women made revelations to the press about his directing methods, saying, for instance, that they hardly knew each other before shooting the first sex scene and that they could not rely on clear directions or even reassurances that they were doing well.[9] Kechiche did nothing (except for having them wear fake vaginas) to desexualize the acts, denying his actresses a professional, theatrical distance that would have made their work less brutally intimate. Exarchopoulos pointed out that not receiving directions while hardly knowing anything about lesbian sex made acting especially hard for her. To the question "Did [you] ever worry [you] were merely playing out a male fantasy?" Seydoux replied, "Yes. Of course it was kind of humiliating sometimes, I was feeling like a prostitute. Of course, he uses that sometimes" (Aftab). To make things worse, the shoot was endless. It took ten days to make the longest sex scene because

Kechiche follows what Exarchopoulos has called a "strategy of exhaustion," by which the director brings his actors to their very limits in search of what he decides is a moment of a grace (Exarchopoulos, "Je voulais que le nu soit un déguisement"). The scene where Adèle and Emma see each other on the street the first time was shot more than one hundred times in the course of a single day (and Kechiche exploded in anger when the two women once burst into nervous laughter after repeating the same instant for more than ten hours).

His method is effective in the sense that Exarchopoulos and Seydoux offer extraordinary performances in *Blue*. Their work was recognized by the Cannes jury, which awarded the Palme d'Or not only to the director but also to the two actresses. And if the implausible sex scenes are disregarded, Kechiche may be said to be exceptionally gifted at drawing out the ineffable from actors. But it comes at a great cost, and this is especially sensitive in the case of *Blue*, as he chose to work with two young women, one of whom was barely of age (Exarchopoulos was eighteen when she began working on the film, Seydoux twenty-five). In this context, his "strategy of exhaustion" is no longer simply wearing out actors but becomes endowed with sinister undertones of sexism, sexual exploitation, and abuse of power.

The two actresses' own sexual volition is so thoroughly ignored in this shooting method, so irrelevant to Kechiche's vision that the question of whether they did or did not agree to his demands was not raised in interviews. That Kechiche cared so little for Seydoux's and Exarchopoulos's needs, that he used his power as a director, as an older man, and as an established artist to impose specific sexual demands on them shows that he felt entitled to circumvent the issue of consent altogether. Yet the lack of an explicit no is by no means a yes.

Maroh, and in her wake Dargis and Taubin, point out that Kechiche's problematic engagement with women (his abuse of power and his self-positioning as a figure of ultimate authority and knowledge, both of which fuel the erasure of difference and consent) is enunciated explicitly within the film: at a party thrown by Emma and Adèle, a male gallery owner in his forties talks about female pleasure and its representation in art to an almost silent audience of women. He insists that the female orgasm is "mystical" and argues that women retreat into a "beyond" when they come, thereby endowing their experience with a disturbing aura of esoteric essentialism. He backs his claim with incontrovertible evidence by citing the mythological figure of Tiresias, who, having experienced both male and female orgasms, declares the latter to be ten times superior. The man registers as both suave and pedantic. Yet he is also knowledgeable and sophisticated, and the film does not invite us to brush aside his opinion, as the women around him listen carefully and do little to contradict him. He goes on to add that while male artists have been obsessed with representing women's ecstasy, female artists have hardly depicted their own orgasms (as Dargis points out, none of the women in the assembly retort that their predecessors were usually not allowed to work with nude models). The gallerist is not unlike Kechiche himself: the male artist/intellectual pontificating about female pleasure through phallic clichés while lacking interest in the actual experiences of the women around him—the latter only serve to reinforce his authority as an astute cultural and social critic.

Yet the film did not come across as sexist to many spectators, perhaps because of *Blue*'s ostensible focus on class disparities. The movie offers a careful study of the imbalances between Emma, who comes from a wealthy and cultured family, and Adèle, whose background is working class and pragmatic. Both women's prospects are shaped by their respective milieus: whereas Emma has the luxury of pursuing an artistic career that may never be lucrative, Adèle, even though she is still a teenager, prioritizes financial security in her choice to become a nursery school teacher. Class inequality also manifests in their relationship, as Emma's condescension for her girlfriend's cultural habitus and worldview is often perceptible. Because of the film's focus on class discrimination, criticisms of its sexual politics are often brushed away with the argument that *Blue* is "actually" about class. Kechiche himself used this very reasoning to dismiss the actresses' accusations that his behavior during the shoot had been abusive: he tweeted, "Workers suffer, not celebrated actresses who walk down the red carpet." Hence sexism and homophobia in *Blue* happen three times: first on the set, then on the screen, and lastly in their very dissimulation within the film itself.

Kechiche conveys a fundamentally masculine and heterosexual point of view (let us recall his appreciation for *Ben Hur* as a lesbian classic) cloaked in a reflection on class. Therefore, the most problematic aspect of *Blue* is not so much phallic domination as the director's reluctance to engage with difference itself; he fails at representing lesbians because he is, at a very deep level, uninterested in them. Luce Irigaray proposes an astute theoretical model to account for this disregard for difference and its operation in discourse, sex, politics, relationships, and so on. Her analysis, I contend, is relevant to make sense of sexual politics in *Blue* and beyond; it can be used to think about gender and power dynamics in cinema and the issue of consent at large.

Irigaray defines phallocentrism as that discourse that denies women the opportunity to define themselves. She raises a fundamental question: What would the world look like if women were able to exist in accordance to their own needs?[10] What new modes of being, what new knowledges would arise if they were no longer interpreted and written by male artists and intellectuals a la Kechiche and his filmic avatar? Instead of thinking women on the basis of their own bodies, phallocentric discourse has only envisaged them as complementary, inferior, or contrary to their male counterparts (Grosz 112). But female bodies are not simply not-male: they have a specific ontological position, and their collective relation to the reproduction of life can by no means be reduced to that of men.[11]

Irigaray argues that we do not know who women are and only have access to them, as we do in *Blue*, through their definition by masculine parameters. This does not mean, however, that the feminine does not exist. It is real, leading a virtual existence in women's bodies, waiting for a chance to become actualized. Therefore, Irigaray presses her readers to experience the ontological uniqueness of their bodies and to create a new organization of life that affirms their distinct modes of being to the world. She demands more from feminism than a critique of patriarchy: what she calls for is the production of something entirely different from life as we know it. A dive into the unknown and the creation of the new.

The operation of phallocentrism is to render woman imperceptible by making her function as a space from which man can develop his subjectivity.[12] The negation of woman's singularity is not only a pervasive, abstract phenomenon but one that finds a very precise incarnation in what is perhaps the most foundational act of phallocentrism: heterosexual intercourse. At the core of straight phallic understandings of sex lies the assumption that the vagina is a dormant repository meant to receive an active penis.[13] In this (ubiquitous) scenario, woman serves as a passive expanse upon which man can demonstrate or, in the worst cases, enforce his activity. Woman disappears and man is caught in a dead end, fed by, on the one hand, the destructive compulsion to own her sex and, on the other, a regressive and necessarily fruitless wish to be in the womb again. Therefore, even for men, true satisfaction cannot be reached. Desire becomes driven by lack and yields both frustration and anxiety, as well as to varying degrees fear, spite, or violence. Hence phallocentric heterosexual intercourse is a hierarchical, necessarily violent act that stems from a simplistic, essentialist understanding of male (and to a lesser degree, female) desire.

This logic of occupation, effacement, and generalized discontent spills over to all aspects of phallocentric societal organization. Film, one of the most popular art forms by which modern societies represent themselves, brings these tensions into focus and often exacerbates them. Actresses find themselves in a doubly feminized position: their profession demands that they disappear as subjects so another person's vision can develop, and the roles that are offered to them too frequently serve to reinforce gender hierarchies. This phenomenon occurs in various degrees: some directors are tyrannical and controlling, others privilege collaborations.[14]

It appears that Kechiche's actresses served as expanses upon which his creative endeavor could unfold. This is especially noticeable in the prominent featuring of Exarchopoulos's and Seydoux's bodies. Phallocentric logic also occurs at the narrative level, and *Blue* has made many lesbians uneasy, not only because of its representation of sex, but also because of its account of a relationship between two women. What is at stake is not that Kechiche portrays an unbalanced couple, in which Adèle suffers from Emma's seemingly innocuous but unmistakably patronizing comments. Rather, many gay women have objected to the highly gendered nature of this relationship, as Adèle comes to embody a perfect Eisenhower-era wife, fulfilling all traditionally female functions (cooking, hosting, etc.), while Emma thrives in her career. Moreover, as the latter's "muse," Adèle becomes a passive expanse for her girlfriend to utilize; indeed, she poses naked for Emma in the film's only example of full frontal nudity. Adèle has literally become an object for the gaze, not only on the screen, but also within the film. In turn, Emma has morphed into a stand-in for Kechiche himself, performing the artist's phallic aloofness and self-centeredness as well as his infamous demands that others abide by his every whim.

Irigaray shows that the most fundamental operation of phallocentrism is to erase difference. Kechiche's own interest in alterity is limited, and it does not include lesbianism, which is of course problematic in a film that addresses precisely that topic: much more than the dykey Emma, the director appears intrigued by Adèle, a young woman who is in the closet about her same-sex relationship and never explicitly identifies as a lesbian or a queer woman. The sex scenes bring the filmmaker's ignorance of queer lives to the fore, and other sequences confirm this unfamiliarity. For example, Adèle, during her visit to a lesbian bar as a teenager, is approached by no fewer than three older, lustful, predatory women. While this would not be an extraordinary event if it involved men at a straight bar, it is highly improbable that an underage, straight-presenting young woman who is obviously out of her element would be courted in such a way and so systematically in a lesbian environment, especially by older women. Kechiche's unawareness of lesbian mores erases the very experiences that he claims to depict. This rejection of the other's singularity is echoed in his phallocentrism; the objectification of female characters that pervades the film forms a way of denying them subjecthood. The same can be said of his mystification, by proxy, of female orgasms.

The ghost of the two actresses' accusations against Kechiche hovers over *Blue*, and especially its sex scenes, making of consent a central yet simultaneously eluded issue in the film: no violation is shown on the screen, but the abuse on the shoot has become an integral part of the movie itself, as it is virtually impossible to watch it without thinking of the actresses' accusations. What is at stake in the question of consent is not simply whether a person can accept or refuse a sexual encounter and sexualized gaze. Instead, there is a deep collusion between the rejection of difference and the disregard for the other's volition: for Irigaray, the possibility of affirming one's desire is endangered, even nonsensical, in a world that denies difference. What does it mean for a woman to claim singularity and personhood if the feminine cannot be actualized? To put the question differently: In a phallocentric context of male domination and female alienation, how can a woman consent if she does not know what she wants? Can we still speak of consent in the absence of fundamental self-knowledge? Hence the question of difference is crucial—yet rarely evoked—in order to understand that of consent.

It should be noted that Irigaray's approach at once differs from and resembles other theorizations of consent. Like Catharine MacKinnon, she notes a connection between phallocentrism and heterosexuality on the one hand and consensuality on the other. MacKinnon's subject in her work on consent is a woman who knows what she wants but either is unable to express it (because she is drunk or asleep or dead) or remains unheard (because she is married, dressed in a certain way, or a prostitute). This woman is the victim of laws made by men in the interests of phallocentric male bodies, and the concept of "consent" that sustains them endows a fundamentally unequal relationship between a woman and one or several men with a veneer of equality. Through this false equality, the legal notion of consent often serves to dissimulate rape (it is, let us recall, the prosecution that has to prove nonconsent, which is often impossible). The present reading of Irigaray goes further than MacKinnon, as I claim that since many women are thoroughly ignorant of their own desires, the issue of consent is even more complicated: To what does a woman really assent when she says yes? What is then revealed is the artificial and manipulative nature of a legal ploy that serves to cover over the actual obliteration of womanhood in phallocentrism by pretending that women and men enter a sexual relationship on equal footing. Irigaray does not, like Elaine Scarry, question the categories of the active and the passive in relation to consent or establish the existence of consent in the body so much as she implicitly raises a more radical and fundamental question, that of the actual possibility of assenting to anything in a world that deprives women of an access to their own needs and desires.

Kechiche offers a telling illustration of this problem, as no authentic—or at least verisimilar—form of female desire can be expressed in *Blue*: the two actresses cannot possibly "know what they want" since they are entirely ignorant of the lesbian sex acts that they are supposed to perform. This lack of knowledge is part of a deliberate strategy on Kechiche's part to overpower his actresses: his "strategy of exhaustion" demands that actors be unaware of their own needs and desires.

But the film cannot be reduced to its sexism, nor can Kechiche simply be categorized as a filmmaker who is blind to imperatives of difference. Surprisingly, he also engages in a true and profound approach to alterity, and the question of consent both within and outside the film cannot really be grasped without understanding *Blue*'s relation to difference.

A negative assessment of the film alone does not do it justice. *Blue* is so successful—and disturbing—because it manages to engage with two very different modes of looking, which remain in constant tension throughout the film: one objectifying and alienating and the other one rich and subtle. Whereas the sex scenes rest on a lack of interest in difference and in the brutal treatment of the two actresses, other sequences demonstrate a deep investment in a nuanced and respectful approach to alterity. In these other scenes, the film creates a specular world in which consent can come into being and raises the following questions: How must we train our eyes to look if we want to foster a world in which the other's volition—which means, in the first instance, the other's difference—can safely appear? How can we look to let Adèle know what she wants, and beyond her all women and all those whose deepest longings are not heard? The answers *Blue* proposes are not without ambivalence. In what follows, I will focus on two of the film's main aesthetic features (Adèle's mouth, which is recurrently featured, and Kechiche's use of the close-up) and a short scene to study the ambiguities at the heart of *Blue* as well as their relation to difference and consent.

Adèle's mouth is almost always half-open; whether she is listening to professors or friends or lying on her bed, Adèle's lips are slightly split in a seemingly permanent state of lust and surprise. On the one hand, the mouth evokes the desire that she experiences and that she triggers, and it can be read as another vector of objectification: she typifies the hungry young woman whose lascivious body is offered up to the spectator's gaze. However, on the other hand, her gaping mouth is also a literal manifestation of her openness to the world, as Adèle appears to live with a sense of constant questioning. She is a deep, intense teenager with an ardent appetite for food and sex and an unquenchable curiosity for literature. But the type of knowledge that interests her is not, like Emma's interests, primarily intellectual. Rather, and this is clearly a mode of being that the film privileges, Adèle has a rich, intuitive, and sincere relation to the world that focuses on emotions.

Alongside Adèle's half-open mouth, one of the most noticeable aesthetic traits in *Blue* is the film's consistent use of the close-up. Close-ups are typically used to convey a character's subjective experience: by coming nearer, the camera can register more of an actor's facial expressions, which can in turn create a deeper connection than a long shot. Close-ups form *Blue*'s main mode of relating to its characters, and especially to Adèle. A. O. Scott (*New York Times*) notes that the camera and its close-ups never depart from her for very long, and he praises the film for its "ardent and sincere commitment to capturing the fullness of Adèle's experience—sensory, cerebral and emotional." In contrast, for Dargis and Taubin, the close-ups do nothing more than gesture at Adèle's interiority, only to ultimately reduce it to her lust and sex appeal. I see no reason to choose, as these critics invite us to do, between a reading of the film that praises its fine-tuned, sympathetic gaze and one that condemns its sexism. Rather, I want to foreground both.

Exarchopoulos herself has commented on this ambivalent approach, noting about the extended casting process (Kechiche interviewed her many times in the course of several months), "Abdel observes you a lot, with a certain reserve but also with intrusion" (Exarchopoulos, "La vie d'Adèle"). This combination of reserve and invasion captures the two opposite movements that define not only Kechiche's relational mode but also his approach to his characters, especially Adèle. This combination makes the film both dismaying and disarming: we feel for Adèle, are curious about her, and, at the same time, are invited to objectify her.

Kechiche's dual approach makes it complicated to resort to psychoanalysis to understand the film, even though psychoanalytical feminist film criticism, which dominated film studies between the 1970s and 1990s, still continues to inflect reflections on film and gender today. To a large extent, *Blue* lends itself to such a critique: the film's pervasive objectification of female bodies, its voyeurism, and Kechiche's preference for a forceful directing style can all be explicated successfully within a psychoanalytical framework (as the first part of the present argument, though not couched in psychoanalytical terms, performs). But this paradigm also has its limitations. Foremost among them is the fact that psychoanalysis is very apt at analyzing power relations but is not as relevant in accounting for difference: at psychoanalysis's heart lies the postulate that women are castrated, or as Lacan put it, "not-all"—that is to say, defined on the basis of male parameters (for Freud, the little girl is a little boy). Further, psychoanalysis mostly enables a negative approach: it excels at debunking symptoms but usually fails at producing positive, life-affirming readings, since it rests on the assumption that desire functions as a lack (of the phallus, of the mother's breast, or of any other figuration of what Lacan called *objet petit a*).[15]

In other words, psychoanalysis can only shed light on the first of Kechiche's modes of looking. But we need a model that can account for both or we risk needlessly impoverishing the film and our understanding of consent. Irigaray's account of spatiality in phallocentrism, which I evoke earlier, is useful for this purpose: not only does she offer a sophisticated account of power imbalances between women and men, but she goes beyond a simple critique to propose a positive description of what life could be like if we moved past phallocentrism.

As stated previously, Irigaray argues that desire in phallocentrism functions as a lack, as desire is inherently incapable of reaching absolute satisfaction. However, she also claims that this does not need to lead to frustration. Whereas phallocentrism, by leading lovers to believe that consummation is attainable, leaves them with a bitter sense of disappointment, an alternative is possible in which the unquenchable nature of lust becomes a source of wonder and plea-sure: Irigaray suggests that through mutual admiration and the affirmation of each other's difference, lovers can produce a truly amorous encounter, one that is both a leap of faith and a visceral experience of the transcendence of flesh and of life.

Whereas in phallocentrism, woman functions as space for man and consent is a complicated category, as woman has no access to her own desire, in this alternative (the mode of difference), which is grounded in mutual consent and the development of self-knowledge, both woman and man are forging a place for themselves from which they can elaborate their own subjectivity based on their specific needs. However, while having one's own place is necessary for a true encounter to happen between two subjects, it is also insufficient, as two impermeable beings would not be able to meet. A dual movement is necessary, whereby one is both nourished by one's place and moves toward the place of the other. Irigaray calls this threshold the interval. The interval is the mobile, constantly moving opening (Hill, "Interval, Sexual Difference" 129) that gath-ers lovers while guaranteeing their singularity; it is the force of desire and dif-ference that constitutes two subjects as such (as opposed to a subject and an object) through the distance that separates and brings them together. In other words, this distance is also a closeness, and it is the condition of both intimacy and independence within loving relationships.

In the mode of difference, the insatiability of desire is a source of change: it comes to form an interval from which an authentic form of sexual differentiation could emerge and where the feminine would elaborate itself not as a response to masculinity but on its own terms. Desire becomes a political force, the most efficient and crucial of political forces, for it is only through desire that new rela-tions between human beings can emerge, relations that affirm the other in her/his singularity rather than seeking to impose a preconceived grid on her or him.[16]

As noted earlier, Kechiche's gaze toward Adèle frequently goes well beyond objectification to perform a delicate, inquisitive approach. This look is in effect a form of interval: the director moves toward Adèle rather than reducing her to an attractive body. What interests him then is her interiority, not so he can break her down to a set of characteristics, but rather in a contemplation of her elusive complexity. Desire, congruent with Irigaray's interval, remains at the heart of this approach. But it is no longer alienating and objectifying. Rather, it affirms the young woman's singularity and her irreducible difference.

Let us examine one particular example. Upon her eighteenth birthday, Adèle's friends and family treat her to a surprise house party. It is the end of the school year, the warm nights of early summer, and we see her dancing with her friends in the family garden to Lykke Li's song "I Follow Rivers." The camera follows her gestures very closely, intimately capturing her adolescent glee and openness to life. These close-ups of Adèle are interspersed with others of her friends. Exar-chopoulos herself has commented on the camera's precision in interviews; she has praised Sofian El Fani, the film's director of photography, for knowing intui-tively how to move seamlessly along with her and Seydoux's movements ("La vie d'Adèle"). Adèle's joyful, sensual dancing with her schoolmates, which lasts for fifty-six seconds, is followed by a long shot, taken from across the back of the garden, about thirty yards away.

This very short scene is one of the best in the film. It conveys with a striking economy of means (a pop song, a few close-ups) the richness of this adolescent universe—its all-important friendships, its grace and sensuality. But even more interesting is the long shot that follows and provides a retrospective commen-tary on the dancing itself. While the dancing scene conveys the teenagers' wide expanse of energy, hope, and desire and the youthful impression that the uni-verse itself is becoming larger following one's own growth, the long shot shows the opposite—a suburban garden and the actual smallness of these young lives, enclosed in a neighborhood, a school, and one or two sets of friends. This ten-sion draws on a familiar method in documentary filmmaking, which features a close-up immediately followed by a long shot and which is normally used to indict or even to mock, drawing on the contrast between intimacy and distance to evince a person's foolish behavior or their misguided trust in a set of values. But here, the remote gaze is not superior. Instead, the long shot reveals that a paradise got lost in our lucid, adult realization that these worlds are minuscule in spite of adolescents' faith in their boundlessness. In other words, it is the adult gaze that is feeble, having lost touch with the preciousness of life, and while still able to notice transcendence on the screen, effectively incapable of finding it in the quotidian.

This alternation between closeness and distance calls to mind Irigaray's inter-val of sexual difference: the look of the male director at his female character is mobile and tender, close enough to enable intimacy but also remote enough to allow her to exist in her singularity. Rather than seeking to consume Adèle, it thrives on the open-endedness of its own movement and the impossibility of capturing her. Whereas, in the sex scenes, the closeness between the actresses appears to be emptied out of meaning and to function as a form of distance, the dance scene draws us to Adèle's mystery, not in the sense of a mystification of her experience, but of a real admiration for her and the force of her youth, of that which is not us.

The question of consent emerges exactly at this point. Adèle may not agree to being observed by the camera, and indeed, feminist film critics have shown that the inherent voyeurism of cinema colludes with its connotation of women as to-be-looked-at-ness. But if we agree that cinema holds a necessary element of voyeurism that cannot be removed (the camera looks at actors who are seemingly unaware of its presence) and if we move past psychoanalytical system-aticity and suspicion (which holds that the gaze is necessarily phallic), it appears that Kechiche's approach in these scenes opens up the door to new horizons. By watching her dance in this way, he allows Adèle to find out who she may be, as dancing is precisely that intuitive, embodied becoming that allows for self-exploration. The director portrays it with great finesse and respect, suggesting to the viewer that this form of coming-into-one's-own is superior to our adult haughtiness. In this process, he also gives time and space to Adèle to probe the truth of her desire—and the latter may be sexual, but not exclusively, as eroti-cism, through dance, becomes the urge for life itself. Here, consent is no longer limited to the yes or no of sex but comes to form both the condition and the con-sequence of a true embrace of the other's difference: for Adèle to be in a position to say yes, she must know who she is and what she wants, and for her to know this, she must be allowed to unfold in her singularity. Hence the interval, incar-nated in the filmmaker's gaze in this scene, offers a new way of understanding consent, in which the latter is no longer confined to the mere absence of a no but amplified as an affirmation of difference.

The film rests on the tension between two irreconcilable tendencies: on the one hand, objectification, voyeurism, sexism, and on the other, an exceptional example of a nuanced and gracious character study. Kechiche offers a particu-larly interesting instance of these features, for his virtues are as remarkable as his faults are infuriating. Not only does he engage in objectification, but he hides behind class violence to cover over gender and sexual discrimination. At the same time, many scenes, such as the birthday dance party, convey a sincere curiosity for otherness. This dual investment is typical of art cinema, a genre that is at once appallingly alienating (disavowed sexual violence forms one of its con-ventions) and simultaneously, through the affirmation of alterity and innovative aesthetics, a source of artistic renewal and potential societal transformation.

Disavowing the other's will implies a fundamental denial of her individuality. Therefore, the issue of consent and its disregard will not be resolved until we have taken the measure of our inability to affirm alterity: Irigaray suggests that foster-ing a world that can sustain as many singularities as there are individuals without seeking to reduce them to the demands of a male (and, one could add, straight, white, cis, able-bodied) standard is the necessary condition for the creation of a viable environment in which consensual relations can become the norm. The interval is precisely that mobile, paradoxical close distance that can guarantee at once the preservation of one's space and the safe openness to others.

NOTES

1. The Palme d'Or (Golden Palm) is the highest prize awarded at the Cannes Film Festival, Europe's most prestigious film competition.
2. Not all movie theaters chose to honor this decision. For instance, New York's IFC Center opened its doors to high school students (and since the movie had been banned in Idaho, they also offered a free ticket to anyone who had traveled from Idaho to see the film).
3. The film technicians had already made similar claims about their own working conditions (Fabre).
4. Tippy Hedren's, Maria Schneider's, and Björk's accusations against, respectively, Alfred Hitchcock, Bernardo Bertolucci, and Lars von Trier immediately spring to mind.
5. Although the figure of the abusive film director is prevalent, perhaps especially in art film, it is by no means universal. In her book on Irigarayan film studies, *Feminine Cinematics*, Caroline Bainbridge offers examples of female art directors who deliberately cultivate a highly collaborative mode of working; she cites, among others, Sally Potter, Jane Campion, Marleen Gorris, and Moufida Tlalti (61–76).
6. I use "voyeurism" in its general sense, as the sexual pleasure gained from watching others naked or having sex, as I do not wish to inscribe this argument in the very specific framework of psychoanalytical feminist film theory.
7. This is by no means true of all female gay viewers; Linda Williams and B. Ruby Rich are two well-known exceptions.
8. One could also add that Kechiche's abusive behavior on set is reminiscent of the many accusations that actresses have leveled at porn directors (as in *Deep Throat* star Linda Lovelace's autobiography, *Ordeal*). It should be noted that "porn" here denotes movies and videos made with a straight male audience in mind. But of course, the genre is much wider than its primary market. In particular, queer women directors and performers have developed a fascinating alternative subgenre (see, for instance, Shine Louise Houston, Émilie Jouvet, Courtney Trouble, and Madison Young).
9. In contrast, one of the norms of queer and feminist porn is to create a healthy, nonabusive environment on the set—for instance, by establishing a connection between actors (see Tristan Taormino's *Chemistry* series, in which professional actors are grouped together in a house and decide when, how, and with whom to have sex).
10. Although Irigaray (very frustratingly) limits herself to a discussion of cissexual subjects, her insights into the untapped potentialities of bodies could lend themselves to a conceptualization of all ontologies, including trans, intersex, and gender nonconforming (TIGNC). For a pointed critique of Irigaray's approach to TIGNC subjectivities, see Tim Johnson's "Questioning the Threshold of Sexual Difference."
11. This does not mean that Irigaray believes that all women "should" have children. Her point is rather that women come from bodies that look like theirs and belong to the group that gives life (whereas the opposite is true of men) and that this specificity puts them with a particular position with regard to existence.
12. Irigaray develops this analysis in "Le lieu, l'intervalle," a chapter from *Éthique de la différence sexuelle*.
13. The fear of castration at the teeth of the *vagina dentata* is only the other face of the same coin: the aggressive vagina must be tamed so it can function "normally"—that is to say, passively.
14. For example, Claire Denis, another French art filmmaker, prefers a shooting technique that relies on trust and close-knit relations with her actors.

15. The question of love and violence could have been examined through Freud's work on masochism and sadism, as well as through the long and rich array of interventions in feminist film theory (I am thinking in particular of Laura Mulvey's "Visual Pleasure and Narrative Cinema" and Gaylyn Studlar's *In the Realm of Pleasure*). In this chapter, I deliberately choose to avoid this approach, as part of my aim here is to open up new avenues of reflection for feminist film criticism, moving away from psychoanalysis and the theory of the male gaze.

16. Irigaray focuses on straight sex, but as Hill suggests (*Interval* 73–81), her work can be used to think about all forms of queer sex as well; what we need is to tap into the productive force of desire and to use it to affirm and intensify difference, between women and men, but also between women and between men and other forms of gender identification.

WORKS CITED

Aftab, Kaleem. "Blue Is the Warmest Colour Actresses on Their Lesbian Sex Scenes: 'We Felt like Prostitutes.'" *Independent*, 4 Oct. 2013, www.independent.co.uk/arts-entertainment/films/features/blue-is-the-warmest-colour-actresses-on-their-lesbian-sex-scenes-we-felt-like-prostitutes-8856909.html.

Bainbridge, Caroline. *Feminine Cinematics: Luce Irigaray, Women and Film*. Palgrave Macmillan, 2008.

Bianco, Marcie. "Is 'Blue Is the Warmest Color' a 'Lesbian Film'?" *AfterEllen*, 25 Oct. 2013, www.afterellen.com/movies/199835-blue-is-the-warmest-color-comes-stateside.

Dargis, Manohla. "The Trouble with 'Blue Is the Warmest Color.'" *New York Times*, 25 Oct. 2013, www.nytimes.com/2013/10/27/.../the-trouble-with-blue-is-the-warmest-color.html.

Exarchopoulos, Adèle. "Je voulais que le nu soit un déguisement." Interview for *Telerama Officiel*, 9 Oct. 2013, www.youtube.com/watch?v=obAzZb4pafg.

———. "La Vie d'Adèle a bouleversé la mienne." Interview by Patrick Simonin for *TV5 Monde*, 8 Oct. 2013, www.youtube.com/watch?v=22jXWJp-UeA.

Fabre, Clarisse. "Des techniciens racontent le tournage difficile de *La vie d'Adèle*." *Le Monde*, 24 May 2013, www.lemonde.fr/festival-de-cannes/article/2013/05/24/des-techniciens-racontent-le-tournage-de-la-vie-d-adele_3417150_766360.html.

Film Society of Lincoln Center. "NYFF51: 'Blue Is the Warmest Color' Press Conference with Abdellatif Kechiche, Adèle Exarchopoulos." *YouTube*, 12 Oct. 2013, www.youtube.com/watch?v=2WOLjfxuPeo.

Grosz, Elizabeth. *Sexual Subversions: Three French Feminists*. Allen & Unwin Academic, 1989.

Hill, Rebecca. *The Interval: Relation and Becoming in Irigaray, Aristotle, and Bergson*. Fordham UP, 2012.

———. "Interval, Sexual Difference: Luce Irigaray and Henri Bergson." *Hypatia*, vol. 23, no. 1, 2008, pp. 119–131.

Irigaray, Luce. *Ethique de La Différence Sexuelle*. Éditions de Minuit, 1984.

Johnson, Tim. "Questioning the Threshold of Sexual Difference." *GLQ*, vol. 21, no. 4, pp. 617–633.

Lane, Anthony. "New Love." *New Yorker*, 28 Oct. 2013, www.newyorker.com/magazine/2013/10/28/new-love.

Mac Kinnon, Catharine A. "Rape Redefined." *Harvard Law and Policy Review*, vol. 10, 2016, pp. 431–477, www.harvardlpr.com/wp-content/uploads/2016/06/10.2_6_MacKinnon.pdf.

Maroh, Julie. "Le Bleu d'Adèle." *Les Coeurs Exacerbés*, 27 May 2013, www.juliemaroh.com/2013/05/27/le-bleu-dadele/.

Rich, B. Ruby. "Blue Is the Warmest Color: Feeling Blue." *The Criterion Collection*, 24 Feb. 2014, www.criterion.com/current/posts/3072-blue-is-the-warmest-color-feeling-blue.

Romney, Jonathan. "Abdellatif Kechiche Interview: 'Do I Need to Be a Woman to Talk about Love between Women?'" *Guardian*, 27 Oct. 2013, www.theguardian.com/film/2013/oct/27/abdellatif-kechiche-interview-blue-warmest.

———. "Cannes 2013: Up Close and Physical." *British Film Institute*, 20 Feb. 2015, www.bfi.org.uk/news-opinion/sight-sound-magazine/comment/festivals/cannes-2013-close-physical.

Russell, Dominique, editor. *Rape in Art Cinema*. Continuum, 2010.

Scarry, Elaine. "Consent and the Body: Injury, Departure, and Desire." *New Literary History*, vol. 21, no 4, 1990, pp. 867–896.

Stern, Marlow. "The Stars of 'Blue Is the Warmest Color' on the Riveting Lesbian Love Story." *Daily Beast*, 1 Sept. 2013, www.thedailybeast.com/articles/2013/09/01/the-stars-of-blue-is-the-warmest-color-on-the-riveting-lesbian-love-sory-and-graphic-sex-scenes.html.

Taubin, Amy. "Masculin Féminin." *Film Comment*, July/Aug. 2013, www.filmcomment.com/article/cannes-2013-amy-taubin/.

Williams, Linda. "Cinema's Sex Acts." *Film Quarterly*, vol. 67, no. 4, 2014, pp. 9–25.

PART 3 CONSENT, PERSONHOOD, AND PROPERTY

9 · THE ART OF CONSENT

DREW DANIELLE BELSKY

> We attempted to recreate the conditions of Zimbardo, to confirm whether evil is inherent in human nature and always manifests itself whenever we consent.
>
> —Artur Żmijewski, *Repetition*, qtd. in Murray 82

In 2005, Polish video artist Artur Żmijewski set out to reenact the infamous Stanford prison experiment, conducted by social psychologist Philip Zimbardo in 1973. Zimbardo recruited college students to take on randomly assigned roles of prisoners or guards in a makeshift "prison" in the basement of a Stanford University building. Though it had been planned to last two weeks, the research team ended the experiment after six days due to the increasingly unstable and inhumane behaviour of participants. Żmijewski's reenactment, titled *Repetition*, took place on a set constructed in Warsaw, and he recruited unemployed Polish men to play the roles of guards and prisoners. Much of the original version was copied, including psychological tests and interviews and the offer of money in exchange for participants' time. *Repetition* lasted one day longer than Zimbardo's experiment before the participants themselves voted to end it. With the help of five cameramen and infrared surveillance cameras, Żmijewski video-recorded the week's events and has presented the edited results as a looped video installation, varying in length from thirty-nine to seventy-five minutes.

Like most of his work, the footage is presented in a no-frills documentary style that reads as objective. Żmijewski's interventions in the experiment (such as by encouraging escalation on the part of guards or prisoners) are largely effaced, and even his presence as the orchestrator of the events in *Repetition* is acknowledged only briefly in the video. Speaking to a camera, presumably wielded by Żmijewski, one guard reflects at the end of the video, "We brought it off together. You devised, I did" (qtd. in Downey 77). Although the inclusion of such an accusation implicates the artist in the events that have unfolded, it is easily missed in the context of a looped video installation, and because *Repetition* is a reperformance of a well-known experiment, responsibility for the situation is ultimately displaced onto the experiment's originator, Zimbardo.[1]

Like Zimbardo's, Żmijewski's role in the pseudoexperiment can be likened to that of the white-coated "scientists" in Stanley Milgram's 1961–1962 electroshock experiments, who, with the weight of cultural capital behind them, encouraged participants to behave with more ruthlessness than they might have otherwise.[2] Zimbardo's and Milgram's experiments have become canonical references in discussions of human brutality, power dynamics, and suggestibility. As Stephen Bottoms points out, they were also the impetus for tightening and restructuring standards of ethics and informed consent in research settings and are thus unrepeatable from within that framework. Hence Żmijewski uses the aesthetic conventions of objectivity to adopt the legitimating role of the social scientist while using his position as an artist to reject the ethical responsibilities that role entails.

Many of Żmijewski's artworks follow patterns similar to *Repetition*: a group of strangers, often members of marginalized and/or vulnerable groups such as unemployed or disabled people, is recruited to participate in a scenario of the artist's devising, such as playing tag in the nude in various places including a defunct Nazi gas chamber (*Game of Tag*, 1999), learning and performing a choral work (*The Singing Lesson I* and *II*, 2001 and 2003), acting as limbs for people with missing limbs in daily chores (*Eye for an Eye*, 1998), or carrying paralyzed people (*Out for a Walk*, 2001). These scenarios, filmed and edited by the artist and shown as videos, are usually described by reviewers as documentary, realist, or objective accounts. Unlike much of his work, *Repetition* does show, at least to a degree, the apparatus of consent and its withdrawal through documentation of the screening process, scenes of the participants' withdrawal, and exit interviews.

Questions of ethics and the role of the artist that arise from *Repetition* are emblematic of the questions arising from Żmijewski's practice more broadly: What is the artist's responsibility to participants? What does consent mean in the context of social art? Who can give it, and can it be withdrawn? For whose benefit does the work exist? That these questions are raised in the reenactment of a canonical social scientific experiment is not incidental. Rather, in this work and others, the performance of scientific objectivity is a key modality by which Żmijewski simultaneously justifies his interventions and obscures his responsibilities.

I focus here on the ways in which these works take on the guise of social science while eschewing its ethical apparatus. I argue that refusal to engage with questions of consent, reflexivity, and accountability in art are counterproductive to artistic claims to disrupt or intervene in the social and political milieu precisely because they assert an artificial separation between aesthetic and ethical concerns. Ethical questions of consent and agency make evident the social relations between participants, artists, and audiences, the very structures into which social artists ostensibly wish to intervene aesthetically. While Żmijewski professes to engage with the interrelatedness of embodiment and political and social agency, his work does so in ways that not only foreclose the possibility of broader interpretive frameworks of embodiment but also reinscribe the removal of political and social agency from those bodies. Like science, art is inseparable from the political and social milieu in which it is practiced; to treat either as distinct from the contexts in which it is produced risks fixing representations as natural facts and undermines any potential for intervening constructively in those milieux.

I begin by examining the apparatus of consent in 1960s and 1970s performance art. I explore the ways in which art critics have attempted to account for the shifts that have occurred as nonartists become integral to artwork. Despite the incorporation of social science practices and methods into artwork, critics have tended to treat ethical and aesthetic considerations as separate, if not opposing, concerns while ignoring questions of consent altogether. I discuss the work of Artur Żmijewski and French artist Sophie Calle with disabled participants. I argue that the critical evaluation of the aesthetic power of these works is predicated upon excluding participants from the putative audience and positioning artists as passive observers. Through the performance of scientific objectivity, social artists obscure the complex social, political, and historical contexts in which scientific representations are produced. Finally, by examining the ways in which social scientists and anthropologists have grappled with questions of consent and representation, I challenge artists and their critics to incorporate this reflexivity into their artistic practices. I consider consent as part of a broader ethical framework of ongoing responsibility toward social others, with aesthetic consequences. Following Donna Haraway, I argue that a situated approach that acknowledges the partiality of perspectives offered by both art and science, including radical attention to questions of consent and to the agency of both artists and participants in social art projects, offers new aesthetic possibilities.

CONSENT AND SOCIAL ART

Since the last decades of the twentieth century, contemporary artists have adopted strategies characterized by some social element, which I refer to in this chapter as "social art."[3] These practices have also engendered new forms of art criticism that aim to make sense of a shift away from the singular artist who works apart from society toward artists who engage directly with communities and/or audiences. Such critique has tended to separate ethical and aesthetic concerns, implying that the status of art and the cultural position of the artist provide a privileged perspective outside of society and ethical norms.

In the 1960s and 1970s, performance art began to trouble boundaries between seeing, witnessing, watching, and participating. Despite this fundamental move away from viewers as passive consumers to more active participants, critical attention to the role of consent in such situations has been sparse. Kathy O'Dell's *Contract with the Skin* explores the performance of uncomfortable and disturbing acts in canonical performance and body artworks of the 1970s, positing an implicit contractual arrangement between the artist-performer and the audience.[4] Drawing on Deleuze's notion of the "masochistic contract," O'Dell explores the mechanisms by which artists, in subjecting their own bodies to various tasks before an audience, signal the contract between parties through the understanding that both "the artists and their audience members had the freedom to stop or walk out of their temporarily incarcerating circumstances" at any time (6).

For O'Dell, the contract as a theoretical unit of analysis vacillates between highly codified legal terms and "everyday agreements—or contracts—that we all make with others but that may not be in our own best interests" (2). However, despite her formulation of a contractual logic in masochistic performances, O'Dell rarely addresses consent—the act symbolized by the contract—explicitly. Consent on the part of the performing body is implied by the fact that it is the artist's body, over which the artist is understood to exercise agency. Consent on the part of viewers is inferred from the assumption that they have the capacity to revoke it by leaving or intervening.

Since the 1970s, a growing number of artistic performances include volunteer or hired participants. These participants may be interviewed, contracted to perform various tasks or scenarios, or observed and documented by the artist. These practices were first loosely grouped under the category "relational aesthetics," a term coined by Nicolas Bourriaud in his 2002 essay of the same title. The term describes both an observed trend in art and his own critical approach to it. For Bourriaud, relational art is potentially transformative because it engages social interaction and therefore engenders new and different subjectivities (although it is unclear what is different or how this difference will result in substantive political change).

Clare Bishop raises concerns about Bourriaud's implication that social interaction is inherently positive and transformative as well as the replacement of "aesthetic judgment with an ethicopolitical judgment of the relationships produced by a work of art" ("Antagonism and Relational Aesthetics" 65). In "The Social Turn," she critiques a tendency among art critics to evaluate social artworks according to the social interactions involved (such as the mechanics of consent, collaboration, and participant autonomy) and not their aesthetic outputs. She argues that aesthetics, not ethical conduct, should form the basis of critical analysis.[5] For Bishop, the dynamics of consent at play between artists and their participants are irrelevant, if not antithetical, to the production of what she considers to be good art.

Predating both Bourriaud's and Bishop's formulations of social art, Hal Foster's 1995 essay "The Artist as Ethnographer" also examines the adoption of methods reminiscent of social research, such as involving marginalized non-artists as part of the process of research in art production. For Foster, the projection of artistic values and intentions onto communities and sites often results in a perfunctory harvesting of material and content without substantive input or direction from those communities. Such projects, Foster argues, romanticize ethnography and treat marginalized communities as "readymade for representation" (306), fields of authenticity onto which the artist's practice is projected. In Foster's reading, simply obtaining consent to do an art project cannot be the end point of an artists' responsibility to participants.

While I am sympathetic to Bishop's critique of Bourriaud's utopian fantasies, like Foster, I am equally suspicious of a critical stance that absolves artists of any responsibility toward the individuals that they recruit as human material for their work. Both Bishop's argument and those she critiques are based on the premise that ethics and aesthetics can (and should) be addressed separately. On the contrary, I propose that the mechanics of consent and agency embedded in social art make it impossible to address its aesthetic outputs as independent of the means of production, both of which are embodied in the participants themselves. I focus on Artur Żmijewski's use of disabled participants as emblematic of the impossibility of separating ethical questions from aesthetic ones. Żmijewski's work makes clear the complex articulations of consent and agency at play in social artwork, particularly that which adopts methods of social research in its process of production.

SOCIAL ART AND SOCIAL OTHERS

Żmijewski's subjects are often asked to respond to potentially painful or traumatic requests and situations, such as cajoling a former Holocaust victim into freshening up the tattooed number on his arm (*80064*, 2004), bringing ideologically opposed groups together to create (and then destroy each other's) artwork (*Them*, 2007), or interviewing a young woman with advanced osteoporosis about her experience of pain (*Karolina*, 2002). The extreme vulnerability enacted in these performances has much in common with the masochistic performances of the 1970s, yet the contours of consent are far less clear. The inclusion of nonartists demands an evaluation that accounts for the participants as subjects with agency who are nevertheless enmeshed in unequal power relations; these dynamics are inseparable from the aesthetic qualities of the work.

Performance art of the 1960s and 1970s entails an explicit acknowledgement of the artist's body as both author and performer. Consent in a situation where the performer's body is subjected to tasks of her own devising and the audience members are presumed competent to make decisions about their own participation as fully enfranchised subjects is palpably different from consent in Zmijewski's practice. First, the inclusion of participants who are neither artists nor spectators introduces a third party to the performative contract. However, as I will explore, the staging of participants' marginalized status reduces them to objects whose consent is no longer relevant. Second, the presentation of the work as video documentation collapses the perspectives of artist and spectator, reducing the audience's consent to the capacity to look or to turn away from a fait accompli. Intervention is impossible.

Unlike performances of the 1960s and 1970s in which the artist puts his or her own body on display, contemporary social art like Żmijewski's often seeks the participation of marginalized Others such as racialized immigrants, disabled people, and poor and/or unemployed people.[6] Historically, marginalized Others have been rendered as objects of representation and scientific study without agency, from traveling displays of indigenous and colonized bodies to eugenic arguments for racial and gender superiority. Growing acknowledgment of racist, sexist, and eugenicist practices perpetuated by the sciences has led to increasing efforts to articulate and regulate the ethical frameworks within which such research takes place, particularly the apparatus of consent and accountability on the part of researchers. However, a tendency to cling to an ideal of art as an autonomous and distinct domain, exempt from social and political norms, short-circuits a similar reckoning for social art. (Ironically, similar claims of social and political autonomy have been made for science, a point I will return to later.)

Critical analysis that separates ethics from aesthetics continues the tradition of making the Other into a metaphorical or symbolic object. This critical perspective is made clear in Bishop's discussion of Żmijewski's videos *The Singing Lesson I* and *II*, in which the artist portrays a group of Deaf students learning and performing classical music:

> The opening shot is staggeringly hard: An image of the church interior, all elegant Neoclassical symmetry, is offset by the cacophonous, distorted voice of a young girl. She is surrounded by fellow students who, unable to hear her efforts, chat with one another in sign language. . . . The artist's editing, compounded by my inability to understand sign language, seems integral to the film's point: We can

only ever have limited access to others' emotional and social experiences, and the opacity of this knowledge obstructs any analysis founded on such assumptions. Instead we are invited to read what is presented to us—a perverse assemblage of conductor, musicians, and deaf choir that produces something more complex, troubling, and multilayered than the release of individual creativity. ("The Social Turn" 182)

Bishop is not alone in her reactions. Like Bishop, other critics base aesthetic evaluations on their experience of the disjuncture between the Deaf students and themselves. Parveen Adams offers an even more visceral reading of the films, which I quote here at length:[7]

> The sound is unearthly. Which doesn't make it like the sound of angels, but these are not animal sounds either. It is unutterably awful; we are full of awe. We cannot locate this sound within any known parameters. Occasionally we glimpse the effort at music, when a group of children translate high and low (in response to a conductor) through some dark and distant analogy with something in their world, unknown to us. The tall girl with blond hair, perhaps the "soprano", lets out a sound which is a cross between a wail, a scream, a shout but whatever it is, it is in fact devoid of human expression. . . . It is a completely different world from ours, a point Żmijewski emphasizes. If there is such a thing as a singing body we do not find it here. Here are the bodies of deaf children trying to play a game whose rules they do not know. We dimly perceive that they are enjoying their bodies which become strange to us. This is an effect that Żmijewski wants. He aims to underline the difference between the deaf and the hearing and he does so in an almost brutal way. . . . The difference of normal and disabled bodies captures us in the wordless space in-between and makes us think. The unrepresentable event, that which is heterogenous to language, surfaces to allow different thoughts and different series at the level of the symbolic. (Adams 90–91)

Both readings locate the aesthetic power of the work in the disjuncture it creates between the critics viewing the work and the Deaf children depicted in it. Adams's reading makes clear that, like Bishop, the author's response to viewing these performances is one of profound disidentification. The bodies engaged by Żmijewski are not only the bodies of others but that of the Other: forms of life assumed to be utterly different from those of the artist or putative audience, potentially not even human. The sight of Deaf youth singing is "unearthly," "devoid of human expression," and "completely different." Adams only dimly appreciates the possibility that the children might feel something like enjoyment (an arguably human expression), concluding feebly that the brutal depiction of disabled bodies as utterly foreign and possibly inhuman "makes us think." Further, she links this "unrepresentable event" (conveyed in the conventionally representational medium of video) to "the level of the symbolic."

Bishop seems more inclined to grant the students their humanity, remarking upon their laughter and discussions in sign language while describing their performance as "staggeringly hard" and "strained wailing." However, Bishop's later descriptions of the piece emphasize the fact that the video form "allows Żmijewski to direct the viewer's attention away from the individuals in order to draw out larger points about religion, harmony, community, and communication" ("Outsourcing Authenticity?" 121). Although their performance is the very matter of the work, the singers themselves are understood as symbolic or metaphorical objects. For Bishop, the aesthetic (and therefore political) value of contrived, delegated performances like *The Singing Lesson* is their ability to provoke an affective response. She concludes elsewhere that although not a "privileged political medium," participatory art's potential for political transformation lies in its capacity "to elicit perverse, disturbing, and pleasurable experiences that enlarge our capacity to imagine the world and our relations anew" (Bishop, *Artificial Hells* 284). Despite this lofty ambition, what possibility for new worlds is opened up by the discovery that "we can only have limited access to others' emotional and social experiences" is unclear.

I am struck in these accounts by two things: First, the assumption that "we" the audience can hear and will judge the sounds as aesthetically "cacophonous, distorted," "unearthly," and "devoid of human expression" based on a familiar baroque standard. This assumption is clear in Adams's evocation of a "wordless space" and her assertion that the event is "heterogeneous to language," omitting the presence of a fulsome sign language that, as Bishop acknowledges, is not available to her. Both base their readings on the assumption that the audience will experience sound, language, and difference as they do, not as the singers do. Second, while the artist is understood to be the author of this scenario, he is absent from the work. Although the readings rely on assumptions about the artist's intentions, the bodies on display are not his. Thus unlike performance art, which melds material and agency by using the artist's own body as a medium, participants are engaged as materials for artistic expression but cannot be the authors of it. Indeed, for Bishop, the fact that the artist maintains ultimate control over the situation (even while appearing not to) is the very aspect that makes such work *aesthetically* superior to more collaborative work.

In his commentary on the work of French artist Sophie Calle, hearing-impaired artist Joseph Grigley addresses the relationship of process to product in terms of the availability of the final work to those who helped create it. In 1986, Sophie Calle asked a number of people who have been blind since birth to describe "what their image of beauty was" (Grigley 31). From these descriptions, she produced a series of tripartite renderings: a photograph of the speaker, a transcription of the speaker's answer (or a short portion thereof), and a photograph representing Calle's interpretation of the text (*The Blind*, 1986). The conceit of the work is in the play between what is seen and unseen, who sees and who is seen. Grigley engages with Calle's work at length through a series of thirty-two "postcards" (Grigley 57). In short vignettes, Grigley's letters trace a range of reactions to the work—visual, affective, and intellectual. Grigley is both "entranced" and "uncomfortable" with these words and images that "do not, because of their visual modality, return themselves" to their subjects (Grigley 33–34).

Far from being an irrelevant detail of the production process, this tension is an integral part of the aesthetic. Consent to take part in such a project entails consent to be the medium of work for which one can never be the audience. While participants may well draw benefits from their participation, the mining of their experiences as material for these works is explicitly designed to highlight the lack of reciprocity and the reduction of the process of consent to a blanket permission to be used as the artist sees fit—in other words, to be made into an object.

The ease with which social Others can be made into metaphors rests on their status as objects or materials; they are neither the author nor the intended audience of representation. To what degree can participants meaningfully consent to be "use[d] as a medium" (Bishop, "Delegated Performance" 112) or as a metaphorical object? For Bishop, whether the participants can meaningfully consent to the process is hardly the issue because the aesthetic reception of the final work is what matters: the ends justify the means. However, this only works by denying participants the personhood required to meaningfully consent, a perverse logic for social art. The result is an aestheticized recapitulation of the existing social order. If the work is indeed social, involving people not objects, then the dynamics of consent (or lack thereof) enacted in the process of production are inseparable from their aesthetic products.

The aesthetic and affective power of these performances is tied to their ability to incite dis-ease—what Julia Gruson-Wood has termed a "sublime mis-identification"—in the viewer, who is presumed to be "normal" (3). Calle's and Žmijewski's works are explicitly designed to stage the differences that separate the artist (and his or her imagined audience) from the participants. While ostensibly allowing for the participants' autonomous actions, the results are overdetermined from the outset and disseminated in a mode to which participants themselves explicitly do not have access. The reactions of a viewer like Grigley are complicated precisely by the fact that his identification with the subjects of the work is changed by their shared social status as "disabled" and his choice to remain with them as Other rather than to disavow that status.

Far from "enlarging our capacity to imagine the world and our relations anew," the performance of difference orchestrated by Żmijewski encourages normatively embodied audiences to reify their existing assumptions about Deafness and sensory difference. The confrontation of traditional Western icons of beauty with bodies that were always already excluded from them evokes an affective reaction that ends in cathartic release from the experience of disability back into culturally acceptable normalcy, not unlike the freak shows, human zoos, and teratological *cabinets de curiosités* of previous eras.[8] Rather than offering a novel aesthetics of disability or social relations, the discourses of incommensurable difference and lack that are provoked by this form of social art simply reiterate normative understandings. The potential to propose the kind of aesthetic intervention with political ramifications that social art promises (even for Bishop) is short-circuited precisely because it does not engage meaningfully with the relationship between aesthetics and social structures that the involvement of the participants entails.

Unlike Calle, Żmijewski relies heavily upon resemblance to methodological norms of social science research to justify his experiments, even as he eschews the ethical norms of those methods such as explicit informed consent or anthropological reflexivity. Żmijewski is often described by critics and reviewers as a "disengaged" (Murray 80), "straightforward" (Verwoert), or "dispassionate" (Kleeblatt 159) observer, "allowing events to unfold without intervention" (Murray 80). This aesthetic of "unflinching objectivity" (Kleeblatt 159) serves to distance Żmijewski from the events that he has instigated. The artist is invisible: seeing, recording, and presenting events he does not seem to control without comment. Contrary to Bishop's assertion that delegated performances "testify to a shared reality between viewers and performers" ("Delegated Performance" 112), the audience is located on the same side of the camera as the artist; they are viewers of a performance they do not control, with the participants on the other side. By presenting the events after the fact, as though they were unmediated, Żmijewski dissolves the performative contract. Unlike in the performances that O'Dell describes, there is no simple two-way contract, easily entered into or revoked in the moment. Where body art and performances collapsed artist and performer/medium into one party, with audience as counterparty, Żmijewski's video performances collapse audience and artist into one while rendering participants as artistic materials whose consent is moot.

SOCIAL ART AND SOCIAL SCIENCE

Żmijewski often appeals to the legitimacy of science as an aspiration for art. In manifestos such as *Applied Social Art*, the artist suggests "encroach[ing]" upon the discourses of science "as a way of proving oneself" (Żmijewski). Elsewhere, in relation to *Repetition*, he asserts that the difference between art and science is precisely art's ability to act outside of the ethical frameworks imposed on science but that the price of such immunity is also the acceptance of the idea that art cannot intervene in the world (Matt and Żmijewski 22). As an artist who professes a desire to render art politically useful and deliver it from "political impotence" (Miller 4), Żmijewski's assertion seems to illustrate precisely the double bind at the core of much of the last century's art and criticism: if art is a unique and autonomous kind of practice, then it is also incapable of any real material effects in the world; on the other hand, if art is not separate from life, then it isn't uniquely exempt from the social and political milieu in which it is created. In this final section, I propose a third way: like science, art is both part of the social and political world in which it is practiced and also a unique method of intervening in that world. As such, its aesthetic outputs *include* the process of production just as the evolution of research ethics in science is inseparable from the representations it produces. This formula neither denies the power of aesthetics to intervene in the world nor sets ethics as a prerequisite for intervention; rather, it acknowledges that representations and interventions are always productive of each other, not separate.[9]

In order to unpack the relationships between social science, representation, and consent, I return to Foster. Foster critiques artistic versions of "'ethnographic self-fashioning' in which the artist is not decentered so much as the other is fashioned in an artistic guise" (306). James Clifford's essay "On Ethnographic Self-Fashioning: Conrad and Malinowski," from which Foster draws the term, offers a somewhat more subtle analysis of the play of subjectivities in the twinned practices of fieldwork and writing that came, via Malinowski, to characterize contemporary cultural anthropology. Clifford examines Malinowski's *Argonauts of the Western Pacific* (1922) in conjunction with the diaries he kept during his time in the field, which were published as *A Diary in the Strict Sense of the Term* (1967) some forty years later. *Argonauts* is a canonical text in cultural anthropology that not only presents Malinowski's anthropological arguments about the nature of Trobriand culture but also sets out his research methodology, participant observation, as the defining method of cultural anthropology. He presents his findings in a self-consciously objective and detached manner, mimicking the discursive forms of so-called hard sciences. The diaries, on the other hand, shocked many because unlike the ethnographic text, they revealed the cultural and personal subjectivities of the prototypical participant-observer and, by comparison, the constructedness of *Argonauts'* scientific account of Trobriand culture.

Through stylistic recourse to the aesthetic conventions of documentarian, pseudoscientific "objectivity," Żmijewski's interventions foreclose any examination of "the fashioned, contingent status of all cultural descriptions (and of all cultural describers)" with which ethnographers following Malinowski have grappled (Clifford 100). Żmijewski's works are presented as Malinowski's *Argonauts*: functional accounts of a scientific study of cultural others. The contingencies and contradictions of the encounter and of the artist's subjectivity, like the ambivalence, self-doubt, sexual desire, and hatred of his subjects that emerge in Malinowski's diaries, are sanitized in order to build a seemingly omniscient and scientifically objective narrative.

Critics like Bishop argue that the adoption of social art methods like delegated performance is justified precisely because artists are free from the ethical constraints of traditional social sciences. Such arguments seem to want to have it both ways: to benefit from the epistemic legitimacy of scientific practices without acknowledging the ideological parameters upon which that legitimacy is constructed. Żmijewski has repeatedly asserted that he seeks to treat art as an "equal partner with other discourses" (Kleeblatt 156) such as science or politics and has himself critiqued mythologizing approaches to art that "[protect] the artist form any real responsibility for his or her actions" (Kleeblatt 156). Yet the interventions that he proposes do not address this need for accountability but rather perform the myth of scientific objectivity upon which so much of Western ideology is based (not least the categories of normal and disabled).[10]

Bishop takes fellow art critics to task for privileging discussions of ethics and process in social art over aesthetics, concluding that "authorial intentionality (or a humble lack thereof) is privileged over a discussion of the work's conceptual significance as a social and aesthetic form" ("The Social Turn" 181). Her argument assumes an inevitable dichotomy: on the one hand, the self-effacing or self-sacrificing community artist who "renounce[s] authorial presence in favor of allowing participants to speak through him or her" and, on the other, the artist as aesthetic interventionist, "act[ing] on their desire without the incapacitating restrictions of guilt" ("The Social Turn" 183). This binary proposition presents an unintentional rehashing of the constructivist and positivist forms of knowledge production critiqued by Donna Haraway. The quasi-positivist artist, who conducts experiments with human subjects, maintains his distance, and presents his findings guilt-free, performs the "god trick" of positivism wherein researchers cast themselves as evanescent omniscient gods able to see "everything from nowhere" (Haraway 581). On the other hand, the constructivist/relativist viewpoint is embodied in the self-effacing artist and the inherent authenticity of the community. Though it aims to give voice to often-ignored perspectives, the constructivist position runs "the serious danger of romanticizing and/or appropriating the vision of the less powerful while claiming to see from their positions" (Haraway 585). Both approaches assert the artist/scientist's ability to see and know but not be changed by or implicated in what is perceived.

Haraway challenges the supposed dichotomy between this (positivist) objectivity and (constructivist) subjectivity by proposing that, while the ontological assumptions may be different, the epistemological position of the viewer (the researcher) remains the same: a vanishing point that sees but is never seen. She proposes instead a shift in perspective that would bring the researcher into view and actively acknowledge the limitations of both "objective" and "subjective" accounts. Objectivity, according to Haraway, is not a matter of omniscience but is rather situated, limited, and contextual. She emphasizes the performative aspects of knowledge production, exhorting a reflexivity that "allows us to become answerable for what we learn how to see" (Haraway 583).

THE ETHICS OF AESTHETICS

Haraway's argument for partiality is embedded in an allegory of vision, which ties it not only to the dominant epistemological practices of science but also to visual arts practice. As Grigley points out, reliance on allegories of vision runs the risk of reifying the dominance of the visual over other modes of perception; however, in discussions of visual art production, the analogy is apt. Though they work in very different ways, both science and art are knowledge practices that operate by representing and intervening in the world. Treating art or science as separable from the social and political contexts in which they are practiced risks fixing representations as natural facts. Without acknowledging the perspective that limits the range of perception, the gaps in that vision remain unacknowledged and therefore invisible and unknowable.

The idea that science is autonomous from politics or the social contexts in which it is practiced, which was taken for granted prior to the Second World War, has since been challenged repeatedly. Social and historical studies of science have shown that the methods and outputs of scientific endeavour are both produced by and productive of social and political relations.[11] Similarly, art has often been theorized as autonomous, a realm of the sensory separate from the social and political world. Social practices not only challenge distinctions between art and life, as their proponents are fond of reiterating; they also make clear the ways in which artists are bound to and act within the dominant systems they purport to challenge. Like scientific practices, such practices construct unnatural (social) circumstances with the professed goal of generating phenomena that will convey the truth of (human) nature. In both cases, underlying assumptions about the nature they seek to reveal predetermine the kinds of circumstances they construct as well as the interpretations that are drawn from them.

The efforts of the social sciences to articulate and enact complex subjectivities in their research practices and outputs are helpful in exploring possibilities for rethinking social practices in art. As Clifford points out, the field of cultural anthropology has struggled (and continues to) with questions of authorship and subjectivity as well as the process of representing the cultures and lives of others.

Pushback from those Others they study, such as poor, racialized, and indigenous research subjects, has forced the social sciences to become more reflexive and to consider new models of ethics and consent. A similar reactive force has been building on the part of disabled people, including disabled artists. Disabled artists and audiences have begun to contest the use of disabled bodies as uncanny objects in art and to reassert their agency and subjecthood. It remains to be seen whether these movements, along with the diversification of critical commentary on social and relational art practices, will result in a reframing of disability and embodied difference, but it is clear that artistic practices cannot claim political relevance in one breath while eschewing accountability in the next.

Like social science, the outputs of social art like Żmijewski's are dependent on their means of production—the embodiment of participants themselves—thus they are dependent upon either obtaining their ongoing consent or violating it. Questions of consent are only moot if participants are assumed to lack agency. Hence particularly for groups who have historically been treated as objects, consent is a productively specific place to begin reorganizing the social order in art. Questions posed explicitly in the case of social research often remain implicit in social art: What constitutes informed consent, and who can give it? To what benefits and harms does participation expose them, and how will harms be minimized or managed? Will the participants be compensated, and if so, how? What other terms have they agreed to when accepting payment? Will they have control over their information or its dissemination? Will their anonymity be maintained? How far does the consent of the participants go? Have they been given accurate and complete information about the nature of the experiment and what they will be asked to do? Can they withdraw their consent, and if so, how or when? I am not advocating bureaucratic answers to these questions; as the proliferation of ethics review boards in the social and practical sciences can attest, they are not neatly resolved. However, whether or not they are acknowledged, such questions are always embedded in any attempt to represent and intervene in the world, precisely because practices of knowing are inseparable from politics.

I believe that the social turn in contemporary art is symptomatic of a sincere desire among artists to intervene in the world's becoming and to achieve political and social change through artistic means. However, if this is so, then it is incumbent upon artists to discard the god tricks of the self-effacing social artist and the invisible documentarian. Creative production entails the potential to acknowledge the performative role of the artist, embedded within the world they seek to understand. If the social is considered not merely as material for artistic creation but as a means inextricable from its ends, then any intervention must first acknowledge participant bodies as active agents and potential viewers, not simply as objects or metaphors. The political potentials of art, if they exist at all, cannot be realized unless artists, viewers, and critics become "answerable for what we learn how to see" (Haraway 583).

NOTES

1. Bottoms provides an excellent analysis of Żmijewski's work in relation to Zimbardo's, concluding that, far from revealing any timeless truths about human nature, Zimbardo's experiment was itself a kind of performance. Downey also provides a useful analysis of the aesthetics of surveillance in *Repetition*.

2. Stanley Milgram's 1960s experiments constructed a faux learning environment wherein research subjects were assigned the role of "teacher" and encouraged by scientists to administer electroshocks to students to see if it would improve memory. The electroshocks were not real and the "students" were actors.

3. A variety of terms have been used to describe contemporary artworks that rely upon participants' contributions, audience interaction, or some combination thereof to form the basis for works of art, including "relational aesthetics" (Bourriaud), "participatory art" or "delegated performance" (Bishop), or "do-it-yourself art" (Dezeuze). I use Bishop's term "delegated performance" in order to signal ties to performance art as well as the term "social art" in reference to methodological and ideological ties to social science and Żmijewski's own characterization of his work as "applied social art" (Żmijewski).

4. O'Dell focuses primarily on artists Gina Pane, Vito Acconci, Chris Burden, and Marina Abramovic, all of whom engaged in physically and/or emotionally painful acts as part of their live performances.

5. Some of Bishop's preferred examples include Żmijewski, Santiago Sierra, and Thomas Hirschhorn.

6. I use the capitalized form "Other(s)" to refer specifically to these kinds of socially marginalized groups. I use the noncapitalized form to refer to those who are not the subject but not necessarily marginalized.

7. While Adams's reading is certainly the most hyperbolic of those I have encountered, it is not inconsistent with more tempered critical reactions.

8. See, for example, Garland-Thompson and Blanchard as well as Eli Clare and Julia Kristeva on anxiety and fascination in relation to disabled bodies.

9. For a philosophical inquiry into representing and intervening in scientific practice, see Ian Hacking.

10. Numerous scholars have documented the ways in which the social and political construction of race, gender, social class, and ability as salient axes of classification relies upon scientific representational practices while simultaneously producing such categories as objects of study. See especially Bowker and Star, Dumit, and Hacking's "Making Up People." For a canonical treatment of the scientific categories of "normal" and "pathological," see Canguilhem.

11. For example, Shapin and Shaffer argue that the rise of experimentalism as the defining method of science was a direct product of the social and political organization of seventeenth-century England. Similarly, Daston and Galison have traced the relationship between practices of seeing and representing and the evolution of the very concept of scientific objectivity.

WORKS CITED

Adams, Parveen. "The Art of Repetition-Exploitation or Ethics?" *ArtMonitor*, vol. 3, 2008, pp. 82–101.

Bishop, Claire. "Antagonism and Relational Aesthetics." *October*, 2004, pp. 51–79.

———. *Artificial Hells: Participatory Art and the Politics of Spectatorship*. Verso Books, 2012.

———. "Delegated Performance: Outsourcing Authenticity." *October*, spring 2012, pp. 91–112.

———. "Outsourcing Authenticity? Delegated Performance in Contemporary Art." *Double Agent*, edited by Claire Bishop and Mark Sladen, Institute of Contemporary Arts, 2008.

———. "The Social Turn: Collaboration and Its Discontents." *Artforum*, vol. 44, no. 6, 2005, pp. 178–183.

Blanchard, Pascal, ed. *Human Zoos: Science and Spectacle in the Age of Colonial Empires*. Liverpool UP, 2008.

Bourriaud, Nicolas. *Relational Aesthetics*. Les Presses du réel, 2002.

Bowker, Geoffrey C., and Susan Leigh Star. *Sorting Things Out: Classification and Its Consequences*. MIT, 1999.

Calle, Sophie. *The Blind*. 1986, series of photographic prints and text. Various galleries and private collections.

Clare, Eli. "Gawking, Gaping, Staring." *GLQ: A Journal of Lesbian and Gay Studies*, vol. 9, nos. 1–2, 2003, pp. 257–261.

Clifford, James. "On Ethnographic Self-Fashioning: Conrad and Malinowski." *Konteksty*, vols. 1–4, 2000, pp. 80–105.

Daston, Lorraine, and Peter Galison. *Objectivity*. Zone Books, 2007.

Dezeuze, Anna. "Blurring the Boundaries between Art and Life (in the Museum?)" *Tate Papers*, vol. 8, 2007, www.tate.org.uk/download/file/fid/7345.

Downey, Anthony. "The Lives of Others: Artur Zmijewski's Repetition, the Stanford Prison Experiment, and the Ethics of Surveillance." *Conspiracy Dwellings: Surveillance in Contemporary Art*, edited by Outi Remes and Pam Skelton, Cambridge Scholars, 2010, pp. 67–82, www.anthonydowney.com/2010/10/01/conspiracy-dwellings/.

Dumit, Joseph. *Picturing Personhood: Brain Scans and Biomedical Identity*. Princeton UP, 2004.

Foster, Hal. "The Artist as Ethnographer?" *The Traffic in Culture: Refiguring Art and Anthropology*, edited by George E. Marcus and Fred R. Myers, U of California P, 1995, pp. 302–309.

Garland-Thomson, Rosemarie. *Freakery: Cultural Spectacles of the Extraordinary Body*. New York UP, 1996.

———. *Staring: How We Look*. Oxford UP, 2009.

Grigley, Joseph. "Postcards to Sophie Calle." *Points of Contact: Disability, Art, and Culture*, edited by Susan Crutchfield and Marcy Epstein, U of Michigan P, 2000, pp. 31–58.

Gruson-Wood, Julia Frances. "Ableism Kitsch: The Aesthetics of Disability-Related Ethics." *Critical Disability Discourse/Discours Critiques dans le Champ du Handicap*, vol. 1, 2009, www.cdd.journals.yorku.ca/index.php/cdd/article/view/23387.

Hacking, Ian. "Making Up People." *The Science Studies Reader*, edited by Mario Biagioli, Routledge, 1999, pp. 161–171.

———. *Representing and Intervening: Introductory Topics in the Philosophy of Natural Science*, Cambridge UP, 1983.

Haraway, Donna J. "Situated Knowledges: The Science Question in Feminism and the Privilege of Partial Perspective." *Feminist Studies*, 1988, pp. 575–599.

Kleeblatt, Norman L. "Moral Hazard." *Artforum International*, vol. 47, no. 8, 2009, pp. 154–161.

Kristeva, J. "At the Limits of Living: To Joseph Grigely." *Journal of Visual Culture*, vol. 5, no. 2, 2006, pp. 219–225.

Matt, Gerald, and Artur Żmijewski. "Philosophie À L'acte." *Hypertexte*, vol. 1, 2008, pp. 13–24.

Miller, Jason. "Activism vs. Antagonism: Socially Engaged Art from Bourriaud to Bishop and Beyond." *FIELD*, vol., 3, winter 2016, pp. 165–183, www.field-journal.com/wp-content/uploads/2017/01/FIELD-03-Miller-ActivismVsAntagonism.pdf.

Murray, Derek Conrad. "Sujets Carceraux: Le Jeu Du Pouvoir Dans Repetition D'Artur Zmijewski." *Parachute: Contemporary Art Magazine*, 124, 2006, pp. 78–91.

O'Dell, Kathy. *Contract with the Skin: Masochism, Performance Art, and the 1970s.* U of Minnesota P, 1998.

Rosaldo, Renato. "Grief and a Headhunter's Rage." *Death, Mourning, and Burial: A Cross-Cultural Reader*, edited by Antonius C. G. M. Robben, Blackwell, 2004, pp. 167–178.

Verwoert, Jan. "Game Theory." *Frieze*, 1 Apr. 2008, www.frieze.com/article/game-theory.

Żmijewski, Artur. "Applied Social Art." *Krytyka Polityczna*, nos. 11–12, 2007, www.peterkilchmann.com/files/a207_applied_social_art_1.pdf.

———. *80064*, 2004, video. Foksal Gallery Foundation, Warsaw.

———. *Eye for an Eye.* 1998, video. Galerie Peter Kilchmann, Zurich.

———. *Game of Tag*, 1999, video. Kadist Foundation, Paris.

———. *Karolina.* 2002, video. Galerie Peter Kilchmann, Zurich.

———. *Out for a Walk.* 2001, video. Galerie Peter Kilchmann, Zurich.

———. *The Singing Lesson I.* 2001, video. Galerie Peter Kilchmann, Zurich.

———. *The Singing Lesson II.* 2003, video. Museum of Modern Art, New York.

———. *Them.* 2007, video. Foksal Gallery Foundation, Warsaw.

10 · SARDANAPALUS'S HOARD

Queer Possession in Henry James's *The Aspern Papers*

ANNIE PFEIFER

In Lord Byron's play *Sardanapalus* (1821), the eponymous character declares before succumbing to the flames, "Rather let them be borne abroad upon / The winds of heaven, and scattered into air, / Than be polluted more by human hands / Of slaves and traitors. In this blazing palace, / And its enormous walls of reeking ruin, / We leave a nobler monument than Egypt / Hath piled in her brick mountains, o'er dead kings" (166). Sardanapalus was the apocryphal Assyrian king, legendary for his decadence and depravity—a favorite figure for Romantic poets such as Lord Byron. Rather than fall into the hands of his enemies, he ordered that his eunuchs, his male and female concubines, and his entire collection of treasures be amassed on a huge funeral pyre to be burned alongside him. Sardanapalus can be seen as the most extreme version of a hoarder who identifies himself so closely with his possessions that his own death mandates the destruction of his hoard.

The violent, nonconsensual dynamics of Sardanapalus's orgiastic self-immolation is most vividly portrayed in Eugène Delacroix's *La Mort de Sardanapale* (1827), inspired by Byron's play. In the foreground of the painting, a man in Oriental garb is poised to stab his naked victim while Sardanapalus watches dispassionately from his opulent bed, littered with the corpses of his female victims. Mounting the woman from behind while forcefully grasping her arms, the man simultaneously appears as a rapist who forces himself on his victim by threatening violence. This slippage between hoarding, rape, and murder implies that a material acquisitiveness also extends to a person's social and sexual behavior. The hoarding of objects becomes an index for improper, coercive behavior toward other people. A hoarder like Sardanapalus treats individuals as extensions of his objects, raping, killing, and violating the social contract between a ruler and his people.

Sardanapalus's actions prefigure the schemes of many of Henry James's infamous hoarders, who would rather destroy their own valuable collections than see them fall into the wrong hands. From James's short story "Sir Dominick Ferrand" to *The American*, the motif of the burned hoard pervades James's fiction; it is also a feature of his own biography. In James's novella *The Aspern Papers*, Miss Bordereau, the eccentric centenarian and hoarder, is described as "an old woman who at a pinch would, even like Sardanapalus, burn her treasure" (39). Throughout the novella, she tries to keep the papers of her former lover, the late Romantic poet Jeffrey Aspern, out of the hands of the meddling, conniving, and obsessive narrator, who vows to obtain them at any cost. The narrator's unbridled rapacity sets off a struggle for possession with far-reaching ramifications, facilitating Miss Bordereau's death, her niece's unrequited love, and a climactic conflagration that ultimately consumes the entire Aspern collection.

Drawing on Scott Herring's *The Hoarders: Material Deviance in Modern American Culture* (2014), I treat hoarding in *The Aspern Papers* as a social construct rather than a psychopathological category. Establishing an alternative material genealogy outside of marriage, procreation, or inheritable property, the hoarder presents a queer threat to both the dominant heteronormative and economic order. By repeatedly characterizing Miss Bordereau as a senile hoarder and eccentric witch, the narrator seeks to justify his predatory pursuit of her papers—a tactic that seems to be condoned by his friends, fellow editors, and the broader literary community. From Miss Bordereau's hoarding tendencies to the narrator's devious plot to the niece's bonfire, there is no room for consensual or contractual possession in this novella. For both James's narrator and Sardanapalus, sex functions only as a means of possession and plunder rather than intimacy. By refusing the wedding proposition of Miss Bordereau's niece, Miss Tina, and resorting to deception and force, the narrator exemplifies the way that the struggle for possession is more about exercising power and coercion than eliciting mutuality or consent. Not coincidentally, as I will show, the narrator's nocturnal entry into Miss Bordereau's bedroom to try to steal her papers carries with it all the connotations of sexual assault. According to contemporary rape laws, the same criteria of consent is necessary to justify a person's "access" to or "use" of another person's body, property, and personal domain (Whisnant 2013). The violent underpinnings of theft reveal that plunder, like rape, is rooted in the same form of nonconsensual coercion.

I read James's thematic preoccupation with hoarding as a way of dealing with his own anxieties about clutter, specifically textual clutter. The ethical dimension of possession is at the forefront of James's critical concerns as a writer and in his writing. James is deeply troubled by the prospect of a meddling editor who might revise his work without his permission or consent and possibly disclose private or compromising information. My reading of *The Aspern Papers* explores James's fictional dramatization of theft and hoarding against the backdrop of his own methodological approach to writing—namely, his continued attempts to exert authorial and editorial control over his own work after its publication. Indeed, by obsessively editing, framing, and reworking his own texts and destroying any compromising letters, James himself could be accused of a form of textual hoarding that resembles the dubious actions of his own characters. Comparing James's actions to those of his own characters, I conclude by positing that hoarding can also function as a bulwark against the threat of plunder and rapacity. In contrast to Sardanapalus's solipsistic, orgiastic hoard, Miss Bordereau's hoarding, like James's obsessive editorial control, acts as a defensive measure against the perceived threat of the intrusive editor.

QUEER HOARDERS

The unnamed narrator of James's short story embarks on an obsessive quest to obtain the famed Aspern papers, rumored to be in the possession of Miss Bordereau, Aspern's former lover. An aspiring writer, he is willing to go to any lengths to secure his prize, claiming, "There's no baseness I wouldn't commit for Jeffrey Aspern's sake" (6). He plots to become a lodger in Miss Bordereau's dilapidated Venetian palace in hopes of gaining access to Aspern's papers. When the narrator's attempts to acquaint himself with the aging spinster fail, he begins to court Miss Tina, her naïve niece, who was also "of minor antiquity" (3). On one oppressive Venetian summer night, the narrator thinks Miss Bordereau's bedroom is empty and is seized by "an acute, though absurd sense of opportunity" and tries to open the cupboard believed to contain the papers (62). His transgression is witnessed by Miss Bordereau, who stands in the doorway, uttering her famous last words, "Ah you publishing scoundrel!" before she collapses, dying soon thereafter (66). Upon Miss Bordereau's death, Miss Tina inherits the collection, promising to "give him everything" on the condition that the narrator marry her (76). When he refuses her offer, she burns all the papers, in the vein of Sardanapalus, leaving him scarcely able to "bear his loss" (80).

An "ancient" spinster who lives with her unmarried, aging niece, Miss Bordereau epitomizes the stereotypical portrait of a hoarder as old, reclusive, unmarried (or long widowed), and possibly queer. In literature as well as society, the hoarder is often represented as a marginalized, reviled figure who threatens social, economic, and sexual norms precisely by operating outside of traditional property relations. Not only does the hoarder accumulate in a pathological way; he or she fails to discard things at the appropriate time. In James's novella, as well as our own clutterphobic culture, the asocial, unhygienic activities of the hoarder have often served as a pretext or justification for forceful interventions.[1] Beginning with the Collyer brothers in Harlem and culminating in the cluttered East Hampton mansion of "Big Edie," the first cousin of Jacqueline Kennedy Onassis, Herring's *Hoarders* traces the way unusual habits of accumulation become correlated with hygiene and social propriety in twentieth-century American culture. Yet as I will show, Miss Bordereau's status as a social misfit suggests that the negative cultural associations around hoarding began to coalesce well before the postwar preoccupation with the Collyer brothers.

Throughout the novella, Miss Bordereau is depicted as a miserly hoarder who clings to all sorts of rubbish. Her "room was a dire confusion; it looked like the room of an old actress. There were clothes hanging over chairs, odd-looking, shabby bundles here and there, and various pasteboard boxes piled together, battered, bulging and discoloured, which might have been fifty years old" (59). According to hoarding experts Randy Frost and Gail Steketee, hoarding is characterized by three features: "1) the failure to discard a large number of possessions that appear to be useless or of limited value, 2) extensive clutter in living spaces that precludes activities for which the rooms were designed, and 3) significant distress or impairment in functioning caused by hoarding" (3). From a contemporary psychopathological perspective, Miss Bordereau's room might be characterized as a manifestation of senile squalor syndrome—namely, the combination of hoarding rubbish, severe self-neglect, and social alienation that sometimes accompanies old age. Sensing the narrator's disdain, Miss Tina explains, "She likes it this way; we can't move things. There are old bandboxes she has had most of her life" (57). This sentiment prompts the narrator to suspect that she, like Sardanapalus, would "cling" to her letters until she "should feel her end at hand" (20).[2] Imbricated with senility, Miss Bordereau's hoarding tendencies become a cultural index for improper aging as well as inappropriate social and sexual relationships.[3]

Together with her niece, Miss Bordereau lives "in obscurity, on very small means, unvisited, unapproachable, in a dilapidated old palace on an out-of-the-way canal" (2). Their life of "domestic isolation" behind "closed shutters" (6) is repeatedly derided by both the narrator and his confidant, Mrs. Prest, who appear to represent the normative perspective of the rest of the community. Frustrated with his attempts to engage the two women, the narrator finally concludes, "I had never met so stiff a policy of seclusion; it was more than keeping quiet—it was like hunted creatures feigning death" (23). Not only is their behavior deemed to be asocial and reclusive, but their lifestyle appears to threaten the rest of the community.

Their characterization as uncanny specters is not coincidental; the narrator and his friends often malign the women as witches or ghosts. At one point,

Mrs. Prest declares, "Perhaps the people are afraid of the Misses Bordereau. I daresay they have the reputation of witches" (4). The narrator flippantly repeats this claim several times, stating, "She was such a subtle old witch that one could never tell where one stood with her" (35). Building on Mary Douglas's *Purity and Danger* (1966) and Stanley Cohen's *Folk Devils and Moral Panics* (1972), Herring draws a parallel between the role historically occupied by witches and the contemporary status of hoarders. Linking the "representations of hoarding as mysterious forms of deviance, disorder, and perversion," Herring analyzes the way the hoarder is typecast as a "material deviant" who threatens contemporary social and economic norms the way "folk devils" such as witches did in earlier epochs (7). Indeed, the two types share many similarities; like witches, hoarders are characterized as eccentric, old, reclusive, unmarried, and often female.[4]

The site of squalor and chaos, the hoarder's home also exists outside of the regimes of purity, cleanliness, and order enforced by bourgeois social norms. Once the narrator finally gains access to the dilapidated mansion, he finds their rooms to be "all dusty and even a little disfigured with long neglect" (13). This neglect is echoed in the personal hygiene of Miss Tina, who is "not young" and had "a great deal of hair which was not 'dressed,' and long fine hands which were—possibly—not clean" (7). Herring's application of Douglas's *Purity and Danger* to hoarding is particularly relevant here: "A messy hoarder comes to exemplify moralized forms of disorder vilified by the social body . . . little wonder that hoarders seem dangerous when their residences are thought to reek of 'unsanitary deviancy'" (8). An exotic, "orientalized" zone located on the periphery of Western Europe, Venice itself represented an unclean, disordered, and potentially infected space. With its pungent canals and narrow alleys, Venice harbors the same kind of strange "esotericism" and "wasted antiquity" that inhabit the uncanny personage of Miss Bordereau (17).

Miss Bordereau's cohabitation with her niece evokes the same specter of queerness that was associated with the Collyer brothers—two notorious American hoarders who were found dead in their Harlem brownstone in 1947, surrounded by more than 140 tons of clutter that they had amassed over several decades.[5] When normally solitary hoarders do live in pairs, they are often of the same sex, like the Collyer brothers in Harlem and Big and Little Edie in East Hampton. Both Miss Bordereau and her niece are repeatedly referred to as "aging spinsters" who prefer the company of each other to any kind of romantic relationship. Like the Collyer brothers, their lack of concern with any kind of procreative sexual reproduction or offspring also makes them threatening to the existing social order of private property transmitted through inheritance. Similarly, the widowed Mrs. Gereth in James's *Spoils of Poynton* (1897) is portrayed as a brilliant but narcissistic hoarder who is willing to disinherit her own son in order to preserve her invaluable collections. In keeping with the same-sex affinities of the other hoarders, Mrs. Gereth forms a close bond with Fleda Vetch, who shares her aesthetic taste. Circumventing primogeniture and accepted familial patterns of inheritance, Mrs. Gereth undermines the social order by destroying her own hoard upon her son's marriage to an "unworthy" woman.

Even in our contemporary psychological understanding, reflected in A&E's hit television series *Hoarders*, hoarding is portrayed as a threat to heterosexual marriage and family life and thus worthy of intervention. The show's team of psychologists and personal organizers typically step in to help hoarders save their marriages or regain custody of their children. Herring asks, "Why are hoarders presumed to be a threat to reproductive heterosexuals who have created offspring? Could it be that hoarding rattles our ideas of the normal family or the material cultures thought to inform this fantasy of domestic life?" (11). The home as an orderly, bourgeois domestic space is predicated on the appropriate and timely disposal of objects once they have achieved their purpose. Holding onto objects beyond their expiration date not only is unsanitary and potentially dangerous but quite literally imposes on the space occupied by other family members. Episodes of *Hoarders* feature countless scenes where spouses and children are shut out of portions of the house to make room for growing clutter.

The thematics of consent provide us with another perspective on Herring's questions. Namely, one could argue that by evading procreative, heterosexual reproduction, hoarders operate at the margins of the legal-economic framework of contracts and consent that governs private property and inheritance in a capitalistic society. Returning to Byron's play, we can see Sardanapalus's coupling of material acquisitiveness and deviant sexuality as a reflection of the way inappropriate accumulation becomes an index for the practice of aberrant sexual behavior. Unrestrained sexual impulses are as inimical to domestic family life as unfettered accumulation. Already by the 1880s, Herring notes, the word "curiosa" had become a euphemistic term for "erotic or pornographic books" (42). The semantic ambiguity between "curiosa" as both a collectible rarity and a deviant object attests precisely to the slippage between aberrant material practices and sexual deviance. Even for James, who is notoriously squeamish about the representation of sex, the hoarding practices of these women seem to imply other unseemly behavior. As the narrator recounts, "In these windows no sign of life ever appeared; it was as if, for fear of my catching a glimpse of them, the two ladies passed their days in the dark. But this only proved to me that they had something to conceal; which was what I had wished to demonstrate. Their motionless shutters became as expressive as eyes consciously closed" (24). One can easily apply Eve Sedgwick's observation about the "highly equivocal, lexical pointers to a homosexual meaning" in James's *Beast in the Jungle* to *The Aspern Papers* (103). In light of James's sexual reticence, hoarding could be seen as a coded way to describe atypical same-sex relationships outside of the discourse of sex.

Hoarding, I am arguing, has historically been treated as a feminized perversion of "normal" patterns of material acquisition as practiced by men. Already according to the Greek historian Diodorus Siculus, Sardanapalus "lived the life of a woman . . . assumed the feminine garb and so covered his face and indeed his entire body with whitening cosmetics and the other unguents used by courtesans, that he rendered it more delicate than that of any luxury-loving woman" (427). In Byron's play, he is similarly described as "femininely garbed, and scarce less female / The grandson of Semiramis, the Man-Queen" (42–43) who was "nursed in effeminate arts from youth to manhood" (222). In most versions of the myth, Sardanapalus is depicted as an effeminate king whose sexual depravity threatens the entire kingdom as much as his material greed. Sardanapalus's aberrant relationship with objects becomes part of his femininity and monstrous sexuality, which is not only queer but coercive. Accused of a range of ignoble deeds from perverting youths to burning his entire household, Sardanapalus represents the extreme case of the effeminized hoarder whose despotic actions toward others are a manifestation of his inappropriate relations with objects. Effectively, I am arguing, the hoarder becomes the feminized, potentially queer perversion of the orderly masculine collector. In *The Aspern Papers*, the narrator continually demonizes Miss Bordereau as a hoarder in order to justify his rapacious attempts to seize her papers, which he legitimates under the auspices of collecting. The portrayal of hoarding as a female perversion is noticeably absent from Herring's account, which represents hoarding as a phenomenon that "cuts across gender" even as it draws attention to the interplay between material accumulation and queer sexuality (128).

TRIANGULATED DESIRE

In light of James's queer hermeneutics, the hypermasculine collector isn't as straightforwardly heteronormative as he may initially appear. Matching the intensity of Miss Bordereau's obsession with her hoard is the narrator's insatiable desire to obtain it at any cost. In fact, the narrator's single motivating force seems to be his passion for the dead poet. Jeffrey Aspern was most certainly "not a woman's poet," the narrator repeats several times, as if to reclaim him for himself and the homosocial community (3). According to the narrator, Mrs. Prest, instantly seizes on this obsession, finding "my interest in my possible spoil a fine case of monomania (2). 'One would think you expected from it the answer to the riddle of the universe,' she said, and I denied the impeachment only by replying that if I had to choose between that precious solution and a bundle of Jeffrey Aspern's letters I knew indeed which would appear to me the greater boon. She pretended to make light of his genius and I took no pains to defend him. One doesn't defend one's god: one's god is in himself a defence" (2). When he finally comes face-to-face with Miss Bordereau, he is compelled by "an irresistible desire to hold in my own for a moment the hand Jeffrey Aspern had pressed" (17). After learning that Miss Bordereau is in possession of the papers, "these words caused all my pulses to throb" (44), and he "flushes" when he sees Aspern's portrait (53). As Miss Tina muses, "'How much you must want them!' 'Oh I do, passionately!' I grinned, I fear, to admit" (62).[6] Later, when he learns that Miss Tina has burnt them, "real darkness descended on my eyes" (80). It is as if his thirst for these objects stands for the unspeakable—the narrator's romantic passion for Aspern. Negotiated through Aspern's material traces, the narrator's latent desire for Aspern is couched in a more socially acceptable manner as a lust for things.[7] Indeed, it is the narrator with his unfettered desire, more than Miss Bordereau, who begins to resemble Sardanapalus.

The narrator couches his quest for material objects in the language of sexual desire. Initially, he attempts to woo the women with "floral tributes," as if sexual conquest provided a socially acceptable pretext for his more sinister motive (37). Whereas material objects often act as a means of attaining sex, here sex functions as a vehicle through which to acquire objects. This dynamic is heightened by Miss Tina's proposal, which promises to "give him everything" on the condition that he marry her (76). Sex, for the narrator, like for Sardanapalus, is linked to possession, theft, and plunder and disassociated from any romantic attachment. As the narrator furtively sneaks into Miss Bordereau's bedroom one night, he can "feel himself close to the objects I coveted" (56). Stealing into the female chambers would normally smack of sexual conquest, but here even the slightest sexual undertone is channeled into his lust to be close to his beloved "objects." Ultimately, by refusing the contractual means of securing his treasure, the narrator foregrounds the extent to which possession in James's novella is framed in coercive, nonconsensual terms.

Contemporary rape laws provide another lens for us to examine consent as it relates to James's novella. The legal scholar Rebecca Whisnant argues, "In most contexts, there is a standing presumption that one does not have access to and may not make use of another body, property, personal information, or other elements of his or her personal domain. This presumption is reversed, however, when (and for as long as) the other consents to such access." Effectively, the same criteria of consent is required to justify a person's "access" to and "use" of another person's property as to their "access" to or "use" of another person's body. When the narrator steals into Miss Bordereau's bedroom to try to seize Aspern's papers, he is violating consent, both on the material level of personal property and on the physical level of the body. The fact that his unscrupulous action is couched in his idealized, homoerotic love for Jeffrey Aspern does little to mitigate its coercive underpinnings.

Even the narrator's rationalization is framed in dubious rhetorical terms that smack of the self-serving justifications of rape. He is so single-minded in his quest that when he tries to break into the cabinet that he believes contains the papers, he reads the most trivial circumstances as a secret sign left by Miss Tina: "If she wished to keep me away, why hadn't she locked the door of communication. . . . That would have been a definite sign that I was to leave them alone. If I didn't leave them alone she meant to come for a purpose—a purpose now represented by the super-subtle inference that to oblige me she had unlocked the secretary. She hadn't left the key, but the lid would probably move if I touched the button" (65). In his twisted logic, he reads the placement of objects as stand-ins for consent, just as rape victims are often alleged to be inviting violation by dressing provocatively or going somewhere alone with an attacker.[8] Only the monomaniacal narrator can be so solipsistic to believe that Miss Tina would have thought to make such arrangements while tending to her dying aunt. In his deluded conviction, the narrator even believes the poet himself consecrates his efforts: "I had invoked him and he had come; he hovered before me half the time; it was as if his bright ghost had returned to earth to assure me he regarded the affair as his own no less than as mine and that we should see it fraternally and fondly to a conclusion" (24). Overriding any consensual framework, the poet's posthumous blessing seems to further validate the narrator's violent tactics.

PLUNDER AND CONSENT

By repeatedly labeling Miss Bordereau as a crazy old hoarder, social deviant, and witch, the narrator seeks to rationalize his plunder. On a basic legal level, theft, or the unlawful taking of another person's property without his or her permission, is a type of forced possession that circumvents the standard contractual relationship between individuals and private property. Thus theft, by its very definition, is nonconsensual, as it strips the aggrieved party of his or her possessions without consent. William James, the famed philosopher and brother of Henry, notes in *Principles of Psychology* (1890), "In civilized life the impulse to own is usually checked by a variety of considerations, and only passes over into action under circumstances legitimated by habit and common consent" (286). In other words, it is only through consent that the instinctual human desire to possess is tempered and channeled into a governable social framework. Consent also plays an important role in the distinction between theft, where consent is nonexistent, and fraud, where consent is obtained through deception.

In keeping with the gendered cultural norms of property ownership, the narrator's illegitimate seizure of property seems to be socially vindicated, while the spinster's legitimate claim to secure her own property is labeled devious and aberrant. Indeed, his unscrupulous actions are condoned, even sanctioned by Mrs. Prest, John Cumnor, his coeditor, and the literary community more broadly. Characterizing Miss Bordereau as a volatile eccentric who might destroy her own papers, the narrator highlights her incompetency as a cultural steward in order to justify his own aggression. In other words, the young male editor can justifiably strip valuable treasures from the clutches of the aging female hoarder who would probably misuse or damage them. Once again phrased in gendered terms, hoarding is a queer, female subversion of the masculine imperative to dominate through ownership and control. While in reality, the narrator is far greedier than Miss Bordereau, his actions are sanctioned in the name of the public good, while hers are deemed a violation of hygiene and decency. She is denigrated as a hoarder, while he is publicly celebrated as a collector and editor.

As if to underscore the social legitimacy of his quest, the narrator is unabashedly forthright in his desire to possess the papers by any means. Early in the story, Mrs. Prest suggests approaching Miss Bordereau with money; the narrator protests indignantly:

The old woman won't have her relics and tokens so much as spoken of; they're personal, delicate, intimate, and she hasn't the feelings of the day, God bless her! If I should sound that note first I should certainly *spoil* the game. I can arrive at my *spoils* only by putting her off her guard, and I can put her off her guard only by ingratiating diplomatic arts. Hypocrisy, duplicity are my only chance. I'm sorry for it, but there's no baseness I wouldn't commit for Jeffrey Aspern's sake. First I must take tea with her—then tackle the main job. (6)

That main job quickly becomes executed as the most appropriative, rapacious means of acquisition—theft: "She would die next week, she would die tomorrow—then I could pounce on her possessions and ransack her drawers" (13). The overtly polysemous valence of the notion of "ransacking her drawers" again attests to the imbrication of material and sexual rapacity throughout *The Aspern Papers*.

Like in James's *Spoils of Poynton*, the operative word "spoils" appears several times in the aforementioned quotation as well as in the novella overall. One of the major differences between the 1896 original and James's 1908 revision is the addition of more "connotatively loaded" words such as "spoils," "tokens," "relics," and "mementoes" in place of the more neutral "documents" and "papers" (Brown 266) as if to accentuate the dynamics of spoilage.[9] In fact, it is only in the

1908 revision that James makes the reference to Sardanapalus. One of the most instructive instances of the rhetoric of spoilage is when the narrator declares, "I would pay her with a smiling face what she asked [for rent], but in that case I would make it up by getting hold of my 'spoils' for nothing" (16). His boastful phraseology of "getting hold" of his "spoils for nothing" highlights the way the narrator's predatory quest is elevated—rather than debased—through the lack of reciprocity or consent.[10]

By foregrounding the violence that inheres in possession, James exposes the nonconsensual origins of ownership as spoilage, plunder, and rape. James shows himself especially conscious of the ethical dynamics of appropriation in his Italian travel sketch "Two Old Houses and Three Young Women" (1899), where he dramatizes the detrimental effects of the Austrian possession of Venice, which officially ended in 1866. Recasting the occupation in gendered terms, James writes, "Dear old Venice has lost her complexion, her figure, her reputation, her self-respect" (347). James encounters a young Venetian girl who had recently travelled to the British Museum in London to see "a room exclusively filled with books and documents devoted to the commemoration of her family. She must have encountered at the National Gallery the exquisite specimen of an early Venetian master in which one of her ancestors, then head of the State, kneels with so sweet a dignity before the Virgin and Child. She was perhaps old enough to have seen this precious work taken down from the wall of the room in which we sat and—on terms far too easy—carried away forever" (355). Not coincidentally, James frames the annexation of Venice as a rape, whereby an innocent girl is forcefully deprived of her own cultural heritage. By reinforcing the link between rape and spoilage, James also builds on the historical understanding of women as property, where virginity was understood to be a woman's—or her father's—most important property.[11] Although in *The Aspern Papers*, it is the Americans rather than the Austrians or British who carry off the Venetian valuables, James is keenly attuned to the imperial appropriation of foreign national treasures.[12] Setting his sight on his own Venetian spoils, the narrator follows a long line of conquerors, spoilers, and collectors who appropriated the cultural heritage of a subjugated people.

Yet unlike the naïve Venetians who belatedly realize the value of their "sacrifice," Miss Bordereau is all too aware of the narrator's schemes, goading him, "Do you dream that you can get off with less than six months? Do you dream that even by the end of that time you'll be appreciably nearer your victory?" (52). While Miss Bordereau is acutely aware of the possibility of being swindled, poor Miss Tina is described as a "perfectly artless and considerably witless woman" (35) who is "capable of doing almost anything to please a person markedly kind to her" (46). Her first words to the narrator are, "Nothing here is mine," as if to dispel any illusion of power and thus shirk all responsibility (9).[13]

Sensing Miss Tina's inherent submissiveness, the narrator tries to "bribe" her with attention and "charming influences," hoping to "make her turn in some way against her aunt" (46). Yet she helplessly confesses to the narrator, "Why I have no control of her. It's she who controls me. . . . I've always done everything she has asked for" (47). Like many of James's novels, *The Aspern Papers* has no space for a functional, consensual relationship predicated on mutuality or reciprocity. Tina resembles Fleda Vetch in *Spoils of Poynton*, who is depicted as a submissive, naïve young woman under the control of a stronger, older hoarder. Like in *Spoils of Poynton*, ownership is equated with control; those who possess things are those who can manipulate other people. Yet while male collectors appear to be vindicated within the novella's social framework, their female counterparts like Mrs. Gereth or Miss Bordereau are vilified as hoarders or witches.

Either because he realizes his true passion lies with Jeffrey Aspern or because he wants to possess these papers without any of the give and take that is inherent in contractual exchanges, the narrator rejects the possibility of the most consensual, heteronormative avenue of inheritance—marriage, albeit to a woman well beyond her childbearing years. He initially justifies his behavior through the same patriarchal norms that led him to rationalize his behavior toward Miss Bordereau: "I could not accept. I could not, for a bundle of tattered papers, marry a ridiculous, pathetic, provincial old woman" (52). Yet with the passage of time, "a kind of ferocity had come into my desire to possess them," and he tries to approach Miss Tina once more (53). Again, the narrator tries to operate outside of the bounds of consent, boasting, "I would not unite myself and yet I would have them" (53). Like the Venetian masterpieces and countless cultural treasures that were gained from vanquished people through duplicitous schemes and coercive treaties, the narrator seeks to evade consensual measures in order to secure his spoils without conditions.

Miss Tina's brazen decision to burn the Aspern letters at the end of the novella frees her from these fetters of possession. Like Fleda, who ultimately refuses Owen and thus abdicates ownership of Poynton, Miss Tina comes into her own through her act of dispossession. Even for the monomaniacal narrator, Miss Tina is momentarily transfigured into an attractive, self-possessed figure: "She stood in the middle of the room with a face of mildness bent upon me, and her look of forgiveness, of absolution, made her angelic. It beautified her; she was younger; she was not a ridiculous old woman" (79). Momentarily beguiled, the ever-opportunistic narrator "heard a whisper somewhere in the depths of my conscience: 'Why not, after all—why not?' It seemed to me I was ready to pay the price" (80). Perpetually driven by "stratagems and spoils," he greedily eyes his prize until the last possible moment, when he realizes the papers have been destroyed (79). Yet for Miss Tina and Fleda, the price of self-emancipation comes at the cost of dispossession, both in emotional and material matters; they must sacrifice their love interest and their claims to a valuable collection. Pervaded by the interrelated themes of possession and renunciation, *The Aspern Papers* follows the pattern of most of James's novels, which begin with a desire to possess and end in the renunciation or loss of erotic or material satisfaction. Far from the controlling hoarder her aunt was, the meek Miss Tina effectively becomes the novella's Sardanapalus in her own surprising act of renunciation. But rather than burning the papers in order to save them from misuse, she burns them to save herself.

PUBLISHING SCOUNDREL

Ultimately, the male editor's public imperative trumps the personal memories of a voiceless old woman. As epitomized in her famous last lines to the narrator—"Ah you publishing scoundrel!"—Miss Bordereau is worried more about the possibility of publication than theft. Indeed, "it rankled for me that I had been called a publishing scoundrel, since certainly I did publish and no less certainly hadn't been very delicate" (67). The narrator acknowledges his transgressions in a curious formulation that precedes Miss Bordereau's climactic accusation: "I felt almost as base as the reporter of a newspaper who forces his way into a house of mourning" (46). Even his similes indicate the extent to which his attempt to possess the Aspern papers is predicated on his expectation of publicity. Attempting to justify his actions, the narrator tells Miss Tina it is a matter of public interest: "It isn't for myself; there is no personal avidity in my desire. It is simply that they would be of such immense interest to the public, such immeasurable importance as a contribution to Jeffrey Aspern's history" (31). In disputes over the fate of cultural treasures, the rationale of public interest combined with the alleged incompetency of the local culture is often invoked to justify why, for example, the British Museum rather than the Egyptian Museum should exhibit ancient Egyptian treasures.

The novella's plot reveals James's personal preoccupation with the meddling figure of the editor, who would possibly disclose "compromising" information (31). During a discussion with Miss Tina about her aunt's papers, the narrator inquires,

> "Does she have them out often?"
>   "Not now, but she used to. She is very fond of them."
>   "In spite of their being compromising?"
>   "Compromising?" Miss Tina repeated as if she was ignorant of the meaning of the word. I felt almost as one who corrupts the innocence of youth.
>   "I mean their containing painful memories."
>   "Oh, I don't think they are painful."
>   "You mean you don't think they affect her reputation?" (31)

Thinly veiled in the narrator's probing questions, James seems to express his own anxieties about authorial legacy and privacy, particularly in an age where "the public's interest in authors' private lives seemed to be outgrowing the interest in their literary works" (Stougaard-Nielsen 1). Notoriously guarded about his private life, James was especially concerned with preventing the publication of any details around his erotic relationships and ambivalent sexuality. As Jakob Stougaard-Nielsen concludes, "The tale reveals that questions of the public's right to knowledge and the protection of privacy are entangled and unstable positions. *The Aspern Papers* suggests that James's conception of authorial 'privacy' is of a more complicated nature than his attempt to frustrate his own executors will let us believe" (6). James's preoccupation with privacy and legacy once again constellates around the issue of consent or what may be done with an author's work and biography after death, when he or she is no longer able to grant consent.

A Sardanapalus in his own right, James "built one of the biggest bonfires in Anglo-American literary history" in 1909, when he destroyed the private papers, letters, manuscripts, typescripts, proofs, and photographs he accumulated over forty years (James *Selected Letters* 664). In early 1909, James wrote to an editor that he had "sacrificed" many items in "a great garden-fire of old rubbish and papers."[14] Here, James imitates the most defiant gestures of his own characters. In addition to Miss Tina's momentous act in *The Aspern Papers*, in *Turn of the Screw*, Miles burns his governess's letter to his guardian, perhaps in a futile attempt to save his reputation. In *The American*, Newman thrusts "a paper containing a secret of the Bellegardes—something which would damn them if it were known"—into the fire rather than using it as valuable blackmail (308). Had Mrs. Gereth burned Poynton as a final act of revenge or spoliation, she would have been in good company. Epitomized by Sardanapalus, the immolator is the ultimate hoarder who would rather destroy his collection than share it with others. Sardanapalus, Tina, and James preemptively destroy their hoards to prevent anyone from gaining possession of them after their deaths. It is the most radical gesture of evading consent.

James seeks to preempt precisely the acts of editorial appropriation that his fictional narrator-editor attempts to execute with respect to Aspern's papers. The narrator of *The Aspern Papers* claims that he acts as a mouthpiece for "the great philosophers and poets of the past; those who are dead and gone and can't, poor darlings, speak for themselves" (50). Like Miss Bordereau, James's anxieties coalesce around what others may do with his work without his knowledge or consent, particularly after his death. His act of destruction is part and parcel of his larger obsession with curating and revising his work in order to shape his own literary legacy, perhaps most evident in the New York edition of *The Novels and Tales of Henry James*, published between 1907 and 1909.[15] By arranging, editing, and providing the prefaces for his own work, James effectively usurps the role of the editor. Similarly, by burning his papers and manuscripts, writes Ellen Brown, he "reenacted a narrative of revision" that offered an alternative, noninvasive approach to dealing with the work of the dead writer (278).

Theft, fraud, and spoilage are related in their lack of any semblance of mutuality. The absence of consent pervades the often exploitative, controlling relationships that dominate James's novels, a dynamic that is mapped onto his construction of the relationship between the author and editor. Reexamining Miss Bordereau's fate through James's authorial anxieties, one could suggest that hoarding and burning are legitimate reactions to the threat of editorial appropriation. James's obsessive revisions and climactic act of destruction reveal the way authors perceive editing and revising as appropriative processes that occur outside of their consent. Fundamentally uneasy with his exposure to public scrutiny, he sought to regain control of his work at the end of his long career. Within the novella's nonconsensual patterns of ownership and possession, preemptive self-destruction seems to be the only surefire way to safeguard oneself and one's valuables.

NOTES

1. This is best exemplified by A&E's TV show *Hoarders*, where individuals labeled as hoarders are counseled by a team of psychiatrists, professional organizers, and cleanup crews.
2. Charging the narrator an exorbitant monthly rent for his shabby quarters, Miss Bordereau's miserliness and price gouging is another dimension of her tendency to hoard.
3. Perhaps not coincidentally, William James, Henry's brother, was an earlier theorizer of hoarding as a pathological, socially deviant tendency. In *Principles of Psychology*, he notes, "Now 'the Miser' par excellence of the popular imagination and of melodrama, the monster of squalor and misanthropy is simply one of these mentally deranged persons. . . . As a matter of fact his hoarding is usually directed to money; but it also includes almost anything besides" (287).
4. This link is continually reinforced by psychological studies. According to one study of sixty-two elderly hoarders conducted by Frost and his colleagues, the majority were female, unmarried, and lived alone: "Never-married status was associated with more severe hoarding and greater impairment and possibly with worse outcomes of intervention efforts" (Steketee et al.).
5. The brothers were also labeled as incestuous deviants: "Two bachelor brothers . . . dependent on each other in a way more incestuous than fraternal" (Herring 43).
6. Even his physiological responses to objects are sexualized. Although "secretary" refers to a piece of furniture, the slippage reveals the way the narrator's libidinal energy is transferred to material objects: "I stopped in front of the secretary, gaping at it vainly and no doubt grotesquely" (65). Again, Sedgwick's reading of the *Beast in the Jungle* is relevant here, as she describes the homosexual possibility that interrupts or paralyses the possibility of the narrator's heterosexual relationship with Miss Tina.
7. Or as Richard Salmon puts it, "If, on an immediate level, the narrator couches his siege of the Bordereaus in terms of a sexual conquest, structurally both Juliana and Miss Tina serve as

conduits, or instrumentalized objects, within a process of hermeneutic desire which is ultimately fixated upon the figure of Aspern himself" (92).

8. "It has too often been assumed that a woman's appearance, attire, status, location, prior sexual history, or relationship to the man in question either function as stand-ins for consent (that is, as 'asking for it') or render her consent irrelevant or unnecessary" (Whisnant 4).

9. As Ellen Brown has noted, this episode is expanded in the 1908 edition from the earlier version, perhaps to dramatize the narrator's transgression and Juliana's "virtue violated" (267).

10. Curiously, it is only once he is apprehended by Miss Bordereau that the narrator momentarily feels like a common thief: "[Her] extraordinary eyes . . . glared at me, they were like the sudden drench, for a caught burglar, a flood of gaslight; they made me feel horribly ashamed" (66). Such scenes lend credence to Maurice Rheims's claim that "many collectors have been victims of [kleptomania], for reasons of venality, or to prove their taste, or for simple love of some particular object" (37). Precisely by eschewing legitimate consent to obtain their prizes, obsessive collectors can become criminals.

11. In *Rape: A Philosophical Investigation*, Keith Burgess-Jackson notes that women were the property of men, with their value as property measured largely by their sexual "purity." Rape was thus regarded as a property crime against a woman's husband or father (44). Because a raped woman was less valuable as property, penalties for rape often involved fines or other compensation paid to her husband or father (68). I am indebted to Rebecca Whisnant's entry, "Feminist Perspectives on Rape," for this citation.

12. Scott Byrd writes, "James had long been aware of the English pillaging of Italian art collections which had occurred during the Austrian possession and which had continued, though somewhat checked by the fierce American competition in the latter part of the century" (378).

13. Yet instinctively, Miss Tina too senses the threat of nonconsensual appropriation, crying, "Oh don't take [the garden] from us; we like it ourselves" after the narrator poses as a renter seeking a house with a garden. Tellingly, even as he tries to disguise himself as an innocuous renter, he sounds abrasive, declaring, "You know I must have a garden—upon my honour I must" (9), as if to lay bare the coercion beneath his seemingly humble quest.

14. James's letter is omitted from Horne's *Henry James: A Life in Letters*. I found it in the Beinecke Library at Yale University.

15. Stougaard-Nielsen suggests, "James's practice of thoroughly revising his own author-image and not least his novels and tales for the New York Edition may, however, also be considered a complement to 'letter burning'"(4).

WORKS CITED

Blackmore, Josiah, and Gregory S. Hutcheson. *Queer Iberia: Sexualities, Cultures, and Crossings from the Middle Ages to the Renaissance*. Duke UP, 1999.

Brown, Ellen. "Revising Henry James: Reading the Spaces of *The Aspern Papers*." *American Literature*, vol. 63, no. 2, June 1991, pp. 263–278.

Burgess-Jackson, Keith. *Rape: A Philosophical Investigation*. Dartmouth, 1996.

Byrd, Scott. "The Spoils of Venice: Henry James's 'Two Old Houses and Three Young Women' and *The Golden Bowl*." *American Literature*, vol. 43, no. 3, 1971, pp. 371–384.

Byron, George Gordon. "Sardanapalus: A Tragedy." *The Works of Lord Byron Poetry*, edited by Ernest Hartley Coleridge, vol. 5, John Murray, 1901. *Project Gutenberg*, 14 Nov. 2007, www.gutenberg.org/files/23475/23475-h/23475-h.htm.

Frost, Randy, and Gail Steketee. *Compulsive Hoarding and Acquiring: Therapist Guide*. Oxford UP, 2007.

Herring, Scott. *The Hoarders: Material Deviance in Modern American Culture*. U of Chicago P, 2014.

James, Henry. *The American*. Edited by James Tuttleton, W. W. Norton, 1978.

———. *The Aspern Papers*. Dover, 2001.

———. *Henry James, Selected Letters*. Edited by Leon Edel, Belknap, 1987.

———. *The Letters of Henry James*. Edited by Percy Lubbock, vol. 2, Project Gutenberg, 2011, www.gutenberg.org/files/38035/38035-h/38035-h.htm#page_008.

———. *The Spoils of Poynton*. Edited by David Lodge, Penguin Classics, 1987.

———. *Transatlantic Sketches*. Houghton Mifflin, 1888.

———. *The Turn of the Screw*. Edited by Robert Kimbrough, W. W. Norton, 1966.

James, William. *Principles of Psychology*. Vols. 1–2, Harvard UP, 1981.

Rheims, Maurice. *Strange Life of Objects: 35 Centuries of Art Collecting & Collectors*. Translated by David Pryce-Jones, Atheneum, 1961.

Salmon, Richard. *Henry James and the Culture of Publicity*. Cambridge UP, 1997.

Sedgwick, Eve Kosofsky. "The Beast in the Closet: James and the Writing of Homosexual Panic." *Epistemology of the Closet*, by Eve Kosofsky Sedgwick, Harvester Wheatsheaf, 1991.

Siculus, Diodorus. *The Library of History*. Loeb Classical Library edition, vol. 1, Harvard UP, 1933. www.penelope.uchicago.edu/Thayer/E/Roman/Texts/Diodorus_Siculus/2A* .html.

Steketee, Gail, et al. "Hoarding by Elderly People." *Health and Social Work*, vol. 4, Nov. 2001, p. 234.

Stougaard-Nielsen, Jakob. "'No Absolute Privacy': Henry James and the Ethics of Reading Authors' Letters." *Authorship*, vol. 1, no. 2, 2012.

Whisnant, Rebecca. "Feminist Perspectives on Rape." *Stanford Encyclopedia of Philosophy*, 14 Aug. 2013, www.plato.stanford.edu/entries/feminism-rape/#Con.

11 · QUEERING AND QUARTERING INFORMED CONSENT

Genomic Medicine and Hyperreal Subjectivity

GRAHAM POTTS

Informed consent in digitally enabled direct-to-consumer personalized and preventative genomic medicine (DEDCPPGM), and e-health generally, challenges the ways that subjectivity has been constructed and deconstructed in the social sciences and humanities. Digitality impacts our understanding of subjectivity, what it means to be a subject today, and how we understand ourselves as subjects of and through digital devices and technologies.

I argue that it is productive to turn to the discourse on how we become interpellated as subjects ("hailed" by a power that is other) flowing from Louis Althusser through to contemporary queer theory in order to understand the contemporary subject as it relates to DEDCPPGM and e-health.[1] Both natural rights–based liberalism and queer theory understand the individual-as-that-particular-individual or the subject-as-that-particular-subject as bodies that matter.[2] This is a key strength of both, as I see it, and the reason to continue to use and interrogate the term "subject" from both, though I do not mean to argue with or against those who move us into a posthumanist subject framework,[3] as I find these lines of flight to be also productive. But what I would like to interject is a Deleuzian conceptualization of what has been happening to subjectivity generally as a result of digitalization and in e-health and genomic medicine in specific. I conclude with six points, an "always-already" return to

Althusser in some respects, that serve as both an outline for what is included within this piece and an indication of where future research is required.

LINE OF FLIGHT 1: A NOTE ON MEDICAL SOCIETIES THAT DISCIPLINE THE SUBJECT

I have no overarching quarrel with DEDCPPGM, including when it veers into presymptomatic diagnosis (which is common) or the potentially changed concept or experience of "living"—diagnosed, perhaps, into a feeling of foreclosure of futurity—after the use of products of this type. I find it both fascinating and something in which "I" (or what remains of it) can, and might want to, participate (although perhaps not with subjectivity or consent or as a subject that can make consenting claims).

At the same time, I am uneasy at having the orthodoxical or heterodoxical fields of genomic medicine relegated to self-regulating private market forces by virtue of being classed as services ordered on the internet, as opposed to health care, which is a field more stringently regulated. This is the same type of unease that I experience when other power nodes, such as what we generally call formal government, have the unchecked or uncountered ability to constitute the field of and over discourse, materiality, and practice (which explains part of the appeal to radical natural rights liberalism, even if it fails or has the counter-effect in being purely ideological). My specific uneasiness in the case of DED-CPPGM is informed by how private market actors have come to constitute the orthodoxical and heterodoxical for DEDCPPGM: as something that is both part of "health care" and not, as part of the regulation of digitality first and as subject to health regulation second (as is the case with 23andMe). I am especially uneasy about the legal precedents in the United States and Canada that mandate extracting things like "maximal value" and the "maintenance of competitive advantage" for shareholders from genomic data bodies, or the (human) subject. In this case, the maximal value comes from (post)human life (data), and the maintenance of competitive advantage includes the purchase of competitors to delay the entrance into the market (and into human lives) of more advantageous treatments.

This is to say a few and perhaps conflicting things. First, it is to sound a note of caution, specifically about the (neo)liberal concepts of consent and subjectivity that private market-based genomic medicine relies on to argue that subjects participate of their own free will. Second, it is to note that this analysis neither excludes "the market" (at the outset; as a dictate coming from an argued state of nature, for instance) nor denigrates research produced by market-based actors just because it comes from within a market form. Third, this is to note the possibility for perceived or real misuses and abuses of the material, for which terms like "democratic control" and "moral authority" are neither foolproof balms nor the automatically enlightened counterpoints to "self-regulation" or "market forces." Finally, it is also to note that the effects of (medical) information security (and its leaks) are not relegated to just the public or private domain or to the provision of (medical) data (assemblages).

LINE OF FLIGHT 2: A NOTE ON MEDICAL SOCIETIES THAT CONTROL THE SUBJECT

The second line of flight moves us to the contribution of (radical) constructivist language associated with Gilles Deleuze. Even in this transition, I have no over-arching quarrel with digital devices generally and the hyperreal mapping technologies that enable personalized and preventative genomic medicine today (I do retain as a "standing reserve"[4] some qualms, to which we will come). Digital devices and hyperreal mapping technologies have uses both quotidian and in cutting-edge research, and I do not advance a form of Luddism in response. To, in a "willful" way,[5] engage with digital practices and what they mean for how we understand subject(s) and subjectivization(s), including how contemporary *techné(s)*[6] might erase subjectivity, is not the same thing as saying that we should throw out or smash the *techné(s)* in question.

This is similar, then, to how I view the *techné* in my eye/glass relationship and the (en)framing(s),[7] that may also be *poiēsis*, that they provide of the world. On one hand, this eye/glass relationship is a relationship in need of constant adjustment and tuning; a relationship that I would see remade into something better, if possible; a relationship that I view, and that I view differently, each time I am approached by the event of the relationship. On the other hand, this is also a relationship that enframes, where the enframing (concept) may be sent to the standing reserve. Not because of the willful assertion of myself over the frames in question given a new (conceptual) availability of an (en)framing that secures a better grip on the image(ination) of the (hyper)real(ization) that is there, around me, in DEDCPPGM, and in the axiomatic that sits behind it, the possibility of *poiēsis* within *techné* that Martin Heidegger notes in relation to technology in general and Arthur Kroker notes in relation to digital technology in specific.[8] But because of the potential for *techné* without *poiēsis* in DEDCPPGM, we have frames and an enframing that engender a glaucoma of the (hyper)real[9] or the images of the genetic code created and then supplanted over and above the "real." Put differently, this is the possibility of fundamental foreclosure of possibility that Heidegger likewise notes and Kroker warns of.[10] This is to read into the subject of Deleuze, or into the space in which the flows of this subject operate, a fundamental "striation"[11] that is present in the early and more utopian work but more explicit in the later and foreclosing works such as the *Postscript on the Societies of Control*. Here, Deleuze notes that "we are at the beginning of something . . . for the *hospital system*: the new medicine 'without doctor or patient' that singles out potential sick people and subjects at risk, which in no way attests to individuation—as they say—but substitutes for the individual or numerical body the code of a 'dividual' material to be controlled" (7).

LINE OF FLIGHT 3: A NOTE ON MEDICAL SOCIETIES THAT DESUBJECTIVIZE THE SUBJECT

As the third line of flight, I would like to begin to address the evidence from the structures and structuration of consent and cognition that are deployed on (medical) subjects within the sociolegal, sociopolitical, and sociotechnical apparatuses of DEDCPPGM in the private sector by companies like 23andMe. This evidence shows a move from foreclosed "control" (Deleuze) to a desubjectivization (beyond the later Deleuze). 23andMe in particular offers a good example of general trends because of the explicitness of its economic, personal, and political linkages to data-assemblage companies such as Google, where initial inventories of effective and affective events in relation to subjective self-understanding under the conditions of digitality have been more explored.

In DEDCPPGM and 23andMe, we see the erasure of fundamental conditions of a natural rights-based liberal subjectivity that is, counterintuitively, premised on a business model that relies on a natural rights-based liberal subjectivity—which is also, it must be added, an erasure of what we generally think of as individual subjectivity of the type that can give informed consent and what is either prior to its (queer or posthuman) formulations[12] or rests upon them, depending on whether or not one looks at it as a liberal. Problems for actual (neo)liberal arrangements structured on this theory, such as marketization or commodification of genomic research, follow from these initial claims that I am making.

The practice of DEDCPPGM makes us consider the (queer/posthumanist) responses we can have to the literal deconstruction of the liberal subject. We see that what is consented to—access and ownership of the pieces of the self—is, in practice, "consent" by something and to something that is not, or is in excess of, a "subject" as it has generally been liberally, and even queerly and posthumanistly, understood. What this means for consent with cognition is a problem that we must encounter if we are to continue to maintain that "informed consent" (or for that matter the concepts of self, subject, state, and society) is relevant and practiced in digitalized medicine and more generally in digitalized life. This is because the modern liberal project relies on a certain type of subject in both realpolitik and theoretical formulations.

Where the realpolitik and theoretical collide and what the contemporary realpolitik formulation relies on, I would argue, is a flatlined version of views put forward by Robert Nozick.[13] This reliance is against Nozick's original premise that would rule out some if not all of private market DEDCPPGM based on a liberalism constructed on radical market transactionalism. Yet a flatlined version of views put forward in *Anarchy, State, and Utopia* undergirds in—the marketization of—personal and political discourse(s) on the boundaries of personal/subject rights: what that subject can freely and informedly consent to and what falls within the acceptable parameters for Nozick of such discourse(s) based on the acts said to occur. In this the views enumerated regarding DEDCPPGM at least mirror, and arguably reinforce in new ways (moving from the molar to the molecular in focus), the political heuristic field of the (contemporary, real time) neoliberalism/neoconservatism that we live under. DEDCPPGM makes into the same much of the orthodox and the heterodox discursive field of personal and private digital medicine and its subjects: where the orthodox field's call of "It is *your* digital and/or genetic data body, or body of data" is answered by the "heterodox" field's call of "No, it is *our/my* digital and/or genetic data, or body of data." That is to say: the same thing.

23ANDME AND DIGITALLY ENABLED DIRECT-TO-CONSUMER PERSONALIZED AND PREVENTATIVE GENOMIC MEDICINE

Much has been written about the actual or potential effects (and ethics) involved in direct-to-consumer genomic testing and the delinking from the (specific and molarly regulated) disciplinary space of the doctor's office and hospital that digital technologies allow.[14] For those who have not been introduced to 23andMe or its analogues via smart viral marketing[15] or a spit party,[16] a brief primer on the subject follows.

Since the first full sequencing of the human genome in the early 2000s, which cost billions, the cost and speed of either full or partial human genome sequencing and examinations via genetic marks (i.e., a statistically understood interpretations of single nucleotide polymorphism [SNP]) has fallen astronomically. In a little more than a decade, the price attached to the ability *in the market* to sequence a full (personal) genome dropped from the billions to under ten thousand dollars, with only a negligible investment of real time required. The 23andMe test uses SNPs and is not a whole sequencing of a person but rather a statistical matching of marks that are more and less understood, statistically, to produce a list of medical and health conditions. It retails for between one and two hundred dollars and delivers the results through an aesthetically pleasing web interface after only a few weeks.

23andMe, of comparable companies, has been an industry leader in the collection of genetic data, and it has received significant financial investments. As a result, 23andMe has been able to run a loss leader pricing strategy: it is never the intent of the company that test sales and their results generate a positive revenue flow by themselves. As the company does not provide genetic counselling—a potential add-on service to tests that could be lucrative—it is clear that their aim is collecting data banks of information linked to and constitutive of genetic profiles. 23andMe does with the data bodies that constitute their market offering as Google Inc. does with the data bodies that constitute their Gmail service. Both provide free services or services for which most consumers are charged nominal or no up-front cost that are exchanged for the data that can be collected and, most often, sold for personalized advertising purposes that are tailored not to groups but to the individual—not really the individual as a whole, that is, but at the subsubject level (i.e., to a statistically understood and anticipated mood or desire or connection that the subject may not need to be consciously aware of to enable a successful transaction). This parallel is especially relevant because Google's financial investment arm, Google Ventures, was an original investor in 23andMe and also because of the personal/political linkages between the two companies. Anne Wojcicki, 23andMe's CEO and cofounder, was married to Sergey Brin from 2007 to 2013. Brin cofounded Google in 1998 and currently directs Google's Special Projects section, which is tied to 23andMe through Google Venture.[17] Much like Google Inc.'s general trajectory to move faster than attempts to regulate it, 23andMe has expanded internationally rather than slow down in the face of warning letters from the FDA, setting up a domestic foothold in Canada in 2014, where it is under a different regulatory framework and trajectory for the marketing and patenting of human-genetic information and services.

Canadian and American users of 23andMe's services are invited to participate in research in addition to the screening that they undergo using an internet-ordered, courier-delivered and retrieved saliva test. As others have noted, concerns about the original consent to the test or further consent to the research are not just about specific customers but extend to family members and others who have not consented to the resulting genetic identification enabled by what is also "their" genetic material.[18] This extension from one subject's consent to others who have not consented and to the subsubject level and all possible futures for one's own consent compresses consent's linearity. Temporal linearity is required for consent to be made with cognition, for consent to have will, and for consent to be active as in "consenting" or "to consent." Removing a linear frame of time from consent entails a collapse of what was the subject. The human body who was to consent is turned into a finite set of *actants*, which become wholly enclosed in the present tense. This involves a set of consent(s) that cannot be taken back, as the data-profiles that have been consensually collected are not erased if consenters subsequently delete a 23andMe account. This is consent to that from which consent cannot be withdrawn, which one can see in the terms and conditions for services given to use 23andMe and the 23andMe policy on consent.

What we see being consented to in 23andMe's policy regarding research is, at the least, a copying of the subject (or collection of *actants*), of the material that was the (formerly human) subject subject to subjection. The freezing of past and future into a present-tense assemblage of data that are owned and subject is a state that is legally protected, given both the terms and conditions of use of 23andMe and the sociolegal apparatus that enforces it. This frozen state retroactively includes historical subjects or individuals such as living and dead family members whose genetic data become taxonimizable and identifiable based on present-tense testing, research, and subsequent patent applications.

Without linearity and a sequence of time frames—that is, proposition offered, proposition considered, proposition consented, possibility of a proposition reconsidered, and previous consent or nonconsent reconsidered—there is no proper way that a viable test for "informed consent"[19] can be applied. This is, arguably, more of a problem for liberal subjectivity than queer articulations of subjectivity that flow from Althusser, as the latter recognizes that unconstrained freely willed acts are, to borrow Sarah Ahmed's language, already oriented one way or another. Or as Butler puts it, "When the 'I' seeks to give an account of itself, it can start with itself, but it will find that this self is already implicated in a social temporality that exceeds its own capacities for narration" (7–8). Yet the problem for queer accounts is then that the affective *and material* spheres of life are predetermined outside of sites of human disciplinary power(s) and sites of control. In this light, the queer accounts must be reconsidered as the social temporalities themselves are now (moving) behind paywalls.

For natural rights liberalism, the problem of consent is pronounced. On the one hand, the general axiomatic logic behind DEDCPPGM undercuts the liberal subject in cutting it up and parceling it out, which we can see with 23andMe's consent documents. On the other hand, because it also plays at honouring a fully rational natural rights liberal subject, DEDCPPGM is left in an internally conflicted state. But this state and its subjecting powers, as noted earlier, dominate both the orthodox and heterodox discursive domains on health services and especially e-health service provisions. So this image of a liberal subject is what is identified and given rights—discursively, juridically, politically—in the marketing and documentation from 23andMe or direct communication from 23andMe prompting current customers to participate in specific and privatized genomic research more generally. But what is being sub-jected is a rhizomatic set that is not for the (Nozickian) liberal, property or mate-rial of a type that can be taken from "the commons" for and by the individual (or incorporated individual in the case of 23andMe). This is because subject/property/material is always also a constitutive part of other human subject(s) (or *actants* or submolar assemblages that are constituted similarly)[20]—if por-tions of the genome or their identification are designated private property, are they to be removed from me?

FLATLINING THE LIBERAL SUBJECT: SOME NOTES ON SUBJECTIVIZATION AND DESUBJECTIVIZATION

In the first instance, objections can be made from a natural rights–based liberal subjective framing of the subject based on the effects of the practices outlined earlier, from within and based on orthodox (liberal) political and theoretical space. For Nozick, for example, the only type of subject that can consent to a vol-untary market scheme—say, for research or profit—is an individual; the action of liberal subjects participating in their deindividualization violates themselves as well as the equal rights of others to be individuals and so must be rejected on these grounds.[21] We see that the subject(s) of this piece and the state they are in are a flatlined version of the type of person who holds rights for Nozick, as the actions and performative speech acts undertaken in DEDCPPGM cut off "the (nonsense) on stilts" they are alleged to stand on. I say "flatlined" in the sense that an interesting work and set of thought experiments are reduced to the brute force argument "Hands off *my* stuff," which is a translation for, really, "Hands off *our* stuff," which is a translation for, in the end, "Hands off *that stuff you think is yours but is ours.*" This formulation is one where the vibrancy of the matter of the thought has been vivisected by realpolitik utilizations that seek basic or natural (rights) credentialization for (individual) "neoliberal" or "neoconservative" proj-ects. These so-called neoliberal or neoconservative projects would, if they were put together, violate each other's' rights in just such a way as to be ruled inad-missible within Nozick's full framework. So to be clear: this useful caricature, as utilized to maximal utility by "neoliberals," is not (intended) to do a disservice to Nozick's contributions to liberalism and liberal theory; it is to note the current ownership of the image and authority of this work—presumably, one hopes, based on a series of enforced voluntary contracts[22]—by the title of (a contem-porary and real-world) "neoliberalism" and to look at the role that the flatlined version does play in the general axiomatic logic behind DEDCPPGM and as this formulation is filtered, mirrored, and projected by 23andMe specifically.

    In the second instance, when viewed through a Deleuzian lens, this sub-ject, our subject (23andMe), and the subject of DEDCPPGM (you) exist as privatized (or privatizable) submolar assemblages: a state of ownership assertion over the literal (and figurative) common stock as intellectual property, copyrighted and trademarked and otherwise restricted. Engendered as it is by a dual focus on critical theory and the insertion of living bodies into it, we see from this Deleuzian (en)framing a mapping exercise, a genealogy of the corporatization and copyrighting of bodies, and language brought about by an intrusion of exclusively held signs from the capitalist economy into and as various *techné* (i.e., nonnatural languages, brands) to the skin of subjectivity *but also within the skin of subjectivity, down to and inclusive of the molecular or virtual levels*—which, rather than being a dystopian nonfiction iteration of *Gattaca* (1997), all make sense at the level of marketing. If one wants to make surplus value greater, stamp a name onto something, especially a base commodity like a food product, and build up the name of that stamp so that the name has perceived value in and of itself and then charge as much as one can for it. All of this is allowed for under a Nozickian scheme and especially for the realpolitik iterations of the flatlined version.

If we take a critical and embodied stance toward the relevance of the "sign-exchange value"[23] of the human genome, we ought to be unsettled by the ways that pieces of human genome have become the subject of sign-exchange valuation (and reevaluation in a runaway fashion) after they are sampled and collected from a tube of your spit that FedEx or DHL picks up (from your house), after the tube and the testing has been ordered from the private pathways of the internet and delivered for a seemingly reasonable cost. To examine the sign-exchange value in play is, of course, to withhold making criticisms of the value of the test based on utility, which one could reasonably do, as 23andMe and other DEDCPPGM providers and products have been dismissed as being cosmetic medicine, pseudomedicine, and sometimes wrong in diagnoses made in publications such as the *Lancet*. However, I leave it for others to make criticisms of the axiomatic logic behind and the praxis of DEDCPPGM from that direction.

Injecting a Deleuzian usage of "molar" (homogeneous whole as opposed to heterogeneous pieces) into DEDCPPGM's liberal discourse, having it replace "individual," may help us to illuminate the issue(s) at play. This language blending, I contend, helps identify that which is not utopian or promissory. We may use submolar lines of flight of a body without organs likewise to replace the utopian or promissory quality of subindividual or *actant* in contemporary posthumanist discourses. This is to advance the view that what we have is a *submolar subjectiveness* and a present-tenseness that is a foreclosure *at the submolar level* in DEDCPPGM's praxis, animating logic, and how it hails and subjects what is no longer a subject.

This *submolar subjectiveness* and present-tenseness is most problematic for liberal accounts of the subject or the use of liberal accounts by DEDCPPGM.

Why? It is because they present a model of subjectivity that gives the individual, at the *molar* level, a body with nonporous boundaries when it comes to expressive or affective actions and spheres: rational and free choice from a selection of many sets of possibilities that can be made, and thereby be said to have been made, into consensual acts. While the (re)construction of Deleuzian language into notions of the liberal subject takes us to this striated space—that is, a dystopian reflection in a two-way mirror—I would contend that we are left outside of the conceptual boundaries of the subject drawn by Deleuze, even in his later and darker articulations. Similar to Jean Baudrillard on our becoming lost in and as part of sign-exchange value from his early work, such as *Critique of the Political Economy of the Sign*, Deleuze claims that we are subject (and I would note, still a *subject*) to "a capitalism of higher-order production . . . [where] the factory has given way to the corporation" (6). With DEDCPPGM specifically and the axiomatic logic behind it that animates the society of today more generally, we have, rather than a subject that can consent, the remains, histories, and possible futures operating in the name of and for utterly striated submolar assemblages (i.e., intellectual property), not "the corporation" (with Deleuze) but the incorporation of the submolar (less but taken to be more than the—liberal—individual) in the name of the submolar.

Digital devices generally and the mapping technologies that are required to "see" and make claims on the "virtual" of genetic code enable the total foreclosure and total collapse into the present tense of our interior focused (electronic) gaze in DEDCPPGM, with the resulting total foreclosure and total collapse of our exterior relations with the material world into this virtual/digital space. This is done, practically, by making the bodies that matter and the vibrancy of human matter reducible to binary (computer code) language and a branded language and output (e.g., subject to intellectual property) and thereby encloseable. To wit, we are given the most foreclosing characteristics of a society of control coupled with the most restrictive characteristics of a disciplinary society with a revitalization of a total preoccupation with bodily death (now in the form of presymptomatic hypothesized risk) from societies of sovereignty but where Thomas Hobbes's sovereign or its Foucaultian remains are no longer an identifiable (molar) assemblage.

It means, for example, that I do not speak on a cellular phone; iPhone® speaks through Twitter® on AT&T®. I am not using my computer right now; Microsoft Word® on Apple® MacBook Air® is producing a Microsoft Word® document. I do not look something up, search it, or research it; Google® is *what* is happening and the medium in which it *is* happening. With what Marshall McLuhan calls the "electronic exteriorization of the central nervous system" through branded and otherwise restricted bodily organs, and with the electronic interiorization of this gaze, which is the 23andMe test and the formers' inverse moment, the "I" and the subject boundaries (of self ownership) of liberal individualism are all *un*subjected. (My) 23andMe test® is what sees and enables the 23andMe test® (of me): we have a closed circuit that no longer requires, through the act of participation or through a consent given (or hypothesized to have been given), the subject. This unfolding of stratiation as a final event[24] is clearly seen, and only legally and legitimately seen, through the test and is therefore a subject of and with matter through the test. The mediated matter of a subject is otherwise registered and given a body with matter in and through restricted spaces and devices, generally, specifically, and practically by the registration of the 23andMe test and the "consents" to individual/subject/subjective dissolution involved.

The role of digital technologies—especially those that map and enclose the genetic—in the effects of DEDCPPGM should not be understated. The copyrighting of digital augmentations (our data flesh), their privatization, and their ownership by something that resembles but is not another individual (for the liberal) or other (for our inverse posthuman subject images) from a vast distance that is simultaneously instantly telematically surmountable started simply enough. The initially innocuous corporatization of language and symbolization started the deeper flip in knowledge and existence. This placed the bits and parts, knowledge of the bits and parts, and the conditions for knowing or finding those bits and parts of the (post)human over the post(human) that thought that it was running things (and may still think so, presuming we are willful and act with meaning when we consent). Admittedly, the posthumans in question, myself included, did not help things much when, for instance, in an earlier iteration of the same logic of desubjectivization, we all clicked an unthinking or unconcerned yes to Facebook's® or Gmail's® "terms and conditions of use" policies that give the (in)corporated (de)subject the real ownership and final say over those data-based replacements for our body and organs (the molar and submolar) of sociality, speech, and memory: the face for Facebook, speech for Gmail, and so on. And this process of transforming the real into the virtual so that it can be so parcelled and owned is subjected to an exponential increase in coverage of its logic when we consider the so-called consents that are given in this case to 23andMe and in general to DEDCPPGM testing companies.

This transformation takes from bodies and subjects and their states in the liberal project the ability to fully consent, and consent with cognition, as singular, liberal, or subject (natural rights liberalism); as potential multitude, multiplicity, and embodied embodiment (critical queer theory); or even as every "becoming-[s]" that is not already subject to a/the striated mapped (finite) organism at the submolar level (Deleuze or post-Deleuzian posthumanist accounts).

What has been "created" in general, which we can see through our examination of DEDCPPGM in relation to the subject that is said to and must consent for this market scheme to function (and as argued here is thereby simultaneously an undoing of its own conditions of being), is a (singular) space for posthuman subjectivity, a postenlightenment nonliberal subjectivity. The new subjectivity is not in fact about inherent finite boundaries at *any* level. It is a radical unsubjectification, but not one that is of a freeing and wilful type. We see this simultaneously occur, for instance, in the continued extensions and rollout of the enfranchisement of corporate personhood and the resulting legal arguments and precedents that make it the type of body that matters and the type whose rights can be violated (and an event that is post one that can be categorized as part of a society of control). Drawing a picture of this (bodily) state, of the intrusion through language of privatized branding into our being, and the ensuing policing of intelligible and iterative body boundaries and extensions thus becomes a praxis-oriented inquiry into this new ontological ordering of body boundaries at the microscopic level. It is an episteme that makes compost of humanism's remains, or whatever remains of humanism. The ability to consent becomes ephemeral when pieces of you, or the means to find them, become proprietarily held, privatized over you through abstraction but also within "you," or what formerly was viewed as "your parts," as with the case of 23andMe.

But in some important sense, and in opposition to the possibility of praxis, we must remember the state of things is a present-tense (biopolitical) historicism into and over the past and past the past tense. And with it, a subjection to present management of future(s), thereby foreclosing the future that was, that could have been. This is not just to find no future(s) if we push the animating logic of today's liberal subject to its extreme form but also to find no past(s) that are subjective and individually subject. We lose, furthermore, any subjectivity that might be wilfully and productively resisted, any resistive will that can be read forward into the present state of things.

Utter present remains, fundamentally, a desubjectification of subjectivity. Within a revaluation that implies that there can and will be ownership over all entities that are not an organism, of their submolar bits and bites, we see therefore a more radical dissolution. What we have is thereby a vacating into a new concept of the space that was argued to be or was the subject(ed) liberal individual that could engage in consent. What we have then is the desubjectification of subjectivity and its consents.

A (RE)CASTING OF (IN)FORMED CONSENT: SIX POINTS
ON QUEERING AND QUEERED SUBJECTIVIZATION
AND DESUBJECTIVIZATION IN DIGITALLY
ENABLED DIRECT-TO-CONSUMER PERSONALIZED
AND PREVENTATIVE GENOMIC MEDICINE

1. To put forward a retelling of the story or narrative or notion of informed consent as a retelling where informed consent is an instance of the (contemporary) hail of power and the interpellation of subjects/subjection, if looked at vis-à-vis Althusser's language. In the example provided, this is the 23andMe test and how we (inter)(re)act with it—this is to say, a lack or a failure to be able to have informed consent or to really comprehend it.

2. Where in this retelling of how subjects are hailed, what we may note as the object of the hail of power may not be subjects, but that is not to say that matter and bodies are not subjected vis-à-vis the parts that are now delinked from the whole. We have parts speaking before and with more authority than the whole (person). In this, we can link to the more general social movement toward the control of risk(y) parts. This is what the 23andMe test is looking for: the presymptomatic and the promise for the elimination of risk-at-all-of-any-chance. An analogous situation is found via the general surveillance of the subindividual actions in everyday life, or, specifically, it is similar to the general governmental approach to "terrorism," an attempt to move to presymptomatic control and the attempt to exercise a political will to eliminate all possible risk of action, down to the subsubject level. This is, of course, a movement very much away from notions of individual sovereignty or innocent until molar actions performed have made one arguably guilty.

3. Where in this retelling, it matters that matter and bodies may not be subjects but are still subjected (subjected but not as a subject), in no small part because of the position of the body/bodies in posthumanist articulations (and poststructural and postmodern retellings generally) of how we become subject/subjected to power and of the openings, fissures, cracks, and other possibilities that have been articulated in (i.e., the "failure" of) this address to bodies and plural (em)bodied response(s) that may not be (or not only be) a response to a hailing. Here I am pointing to the importance of affective (and effected) bodily states and subjectivities and scenes in these retellings, which is something that we are moved from in DEDCPPGM. As Ahmed, retelling Althusser/Butler in *Queer Phenomenology*, puts it, "Rather, in moving this way, rather than that [in response to the hail], and moving in this way again and again, the surfaces of bodies *in turn* acquire their shape" (16, emphasis in original).

4. Where what we may note in the specific deployment of the animating logics of DEDCPPGM as the general axiomatic of contemporary digitality is (dis)embodiment and (de)subjectification of bodies and matter that is simultaneously an effective and affective freezing of vibrancy and movement (and the potential possibility for it). To refer us back to *the turn* to bodies into data and into the data of others. And an other that is not a subject other (i.e., corporate incorporation of intellectual property and personhood).

5. Where this can be conceptualized as a retelling of the retellings of the Althusserian hail, as this notion of the hail of power has been drawn out and coloured in by queer and posthumanist articulations of interpellation (and poststructural and postmodern retellings generally), a retelling that builds on that work that (among other things) foregrounds the heterogeneousness of bodies and their acts that are enacted within and without of the fields and lines of orientation(s) directed by the hail of power(s) that seeks to make them subject(s). Where this is the praxis that these accounts move us toward.

6. But where this is also a retelling of the hail(s) of power(s)—by parts that are not subject as (humanist) subjects, and for bodies that are not interpellated as (molar and humanist) bodies—which calls for a redirection, to take account of "the inventory of effects" wrought by the (enforceable) dis-orientation away from bodies that is evident in the relations of power and control (i.e., for bodies, for the body to be the matter that matters) that DEDCPPGM enacts and is, importantly, also the animating axiomatic generally today (i.e., outside of medical discourse, as a coterminous symptom/cause of the present-tense contemporary moment of digitality as previously noted).

NOTES

1. This in addition to the largely philosophically liberal discourse that tends toward the natural rights end of the liberal spectrum in both the popular uptake of e-health and DEDCPPGM can be found in specialist medical and technology journals.

2. Sara Ahmed develops this in *Queer Phenomenology: Orientations, Objects, Others.*

3. See, for example, Jane Bennett and Arthur Kroker.

4. For the usage that I am invoking of this term, see Martin Heidegger.

5. I am drawing here from Ahmed's work in *Willful Subjects.*

6. I here invoke and use *techné* in the expansive sense, which is to say holding forth at least the *possibly* of also being *poiésis*. See Heidegger and Kroker's reading thereof.

7. A more lengthy argument would likely contain an argument pursuing the similarities and what can be read of them of this analogy to that put forward by Steven Lukes.

8. In *The Will to Technology and the Culture of Nihilism,* Kroker brings Nietzsche and Marx to *digital fruition before the light/darkness of Heidegger comes crashing in inverted less, and less filled with hope, than the earlier work by the Krokers.*

9. Paul Virilio explores the idea that hyperreal technologies are glaucoma inducing in an epistemological sense, in the least, in works such as *The Information Bomb.*

10. Kroker develops this warning in *Exits to the Posthuman Future*.

11. Gilles Deleuze and Félix Guattari develop these arguments in *Anti-Oedipus: Capitalism and Schizophrenia* and *A Thousand Plateaus: Capitalism and Schizophrenia*.

12. While I restrict my argument here to looking at the private sector and rhetorically argue and theoretically buttress "voluntary arrangements" between private actors, where there is no direct coercion, I would subject that the argument put forward also holds for similar practices that occur in the public sector. See Nikolas Rose.

13. The unflatlined version is a position that even Nozick retreated from. See Thomas Nagel.

14. See the discourse that has occurred in the *American Journal of Bioethics*, *The Lancet*, and *Nature* since the marketing of the test as a product.

15. 23andMe has utilized ads featuring Muhammad Ali for Parkinson's syndrome, for instance.

16. Some of the original viral advertisements were collective spit parties for DNA collection.

17. To be clear, I am not putting forward, in mentioning this, an argument of some sort of conspiracy theory, along the lines of "Google has a secret plan to harvest the genes of every living human," nor saying that this period of marriage between two key figures at both companies somehow is determinant. It is to note, rather, that both Wojcicki and Brin invoke personal influence and interest for familial reasons in moving to invest and market personalized genetics services in their public speaking and to also note a similar business strategy, and even the aesthetic look, to the interface of both Google and 23andMe.

18. Concerns about genetic data linkage not just to self but to others in limited data sets of genetic information, and identification of individuals through data not provided by themselves is well documented in publications such as the *American Journal of Bioethics*, *The Lancet*, and *Nature*.

19. The Oxford English Dictionary defines informed consent as "*n. Law* permission granted in the knowledge of the possible consequences; *(Med.)* consent to a medical or surgical procedure given after all relevant information (esp. regarding potential risks and benefits) has been disclosed to the patient or the patient's guardian; an instance of such consent."

20. Indeed, one might consider that in this (en)framing of how consent is said to be given by the subsubject, that *actants* that were previously unable to give consent, such as electronic copies of a genetic profile, are given consenting (like) powers. If so, this would, it could be argued, devitalize matter in a way that would argue against the praxis for the postsubject past humanist of Jane Bennett in *Vibrant Matter* or the praxis for the still-subject humanism in Diana Coole's work that Bennett positions against.

21. Weaker but still important objections from within liberal theory that is based, like Nozick, on radical market transactionalism can also be made over a right not to participate, which is undercut by participation of those who share partial or full genetic profiles with them. A similar possibly interesting objection could also be made because of the enclosure of historical individuals into a present-tense form by the living or the extractions from the dead, for which they have not consented, based on a reading back from the present participant to the services provided by 23andMe.

22. Elsewise Roland Barthes should enter here, "stage right."

23. Jean Baudrillard develops the idea of "sign-exchange value" in *The Mirror of Production* and *Symbolic Exchange and Death*.

24. Similar to the position put forward by Paul Virilio in works such as *The Information Bomb* and *Negative Horizon*.

WORKS CITED

Ahmed, Sarah. *Queer Phenomenology: Orientations, Objects, Others.* Duke UP, 2006.

———. *Willful Subjects.* Duke UP, 2014.

Baudrillard, Jean. *The Mirror of Production.* Translated by Mark Poster, Telos, 1975.

———. *Symbolic Exchange and Death.* Sage Publications, 1993.

Bennett, Jane. *Vibrant Matter: A Political Ecology of Things.* Duke UP, 2010.

Butler, Judith. *Giving an Account of Oneself.* Fordham UP, 2005.

Coole, Diana. "The Inertia of Matter and the Generativity of Flesh." *New Materialisms: Ontology, Agency, and Politics,* edited by Diana Coole and Samantha Frost, Duke UP, 2010.

———. "Negativity as Invisibility: Merleau-Ponty's Dialectical Adventures." *Negativity and Politics,* Routledge, 2000.

Deleuze, Gilles. "Postscript on the Societies of Control." *October,* vol. 59, winter 1992.

Deleuze, Gilles, and Félix Guattari, *Anti-Oedipus: Capitalism and Schizophrenia.* Translated by Robert Hurley et al., U of Minnesota P, 1983.

———. *A Thousand Plateaus: Capitalism and Schizophrenia.* Translated by Brian Massumi, U of Minnesota P, 1987.

Heidegger, Martin. "The Question Concerning Technology." *Basic Writings: Martin Heidegger,* edited by David Farrell Krell, HarperCollins, 1977, pp. 307–342.

Kroker, Arthur. *Exits to the Posthuman Future.* Polity, 2014.

———. *The Will to Technology and the Culture of Nihilism.* U of Toronto P, 2004.

Lukes, Steven. *The Curious Enlightenment of Professor Caritat.* Verso, 1995.

McLuhan, Marshall. *The Gutenberg Galaxy.* University of Toronto Press, 1962.

———. *Understanding Media: The Extensions of Man.* McGraw-Hill, 1964.

Nagel, Thomas. Foreword. *Anarchy, State, and Utopia,* by Robert Nozick, Basic Books, 2013, pp. xi–xviii.

Nozick, Robert. *Anarchy, State, and Utopia.* Basic Books, 2013.

Rose, Nikolas. *The Politics of Life Itself: Biomedicine, Power, and Subjectivity in the Twenty-First Century.* Princeton UP, 2007.

23andMe. "Consent." Accessed 27 Feb. 2015, www.23andme.com/en-ca/about/consent/.

———. "Terms of Service." Accessed 27 Feb. 2015, www.23andme.com/en-ca/legal/tos/.

Virilio, Paul. *The Information Bomb.* Translated by Chris Turner, Verso, 2000.

———. *Negative Horizon.* Translated by Michael Degener, Continuum, 2005.

12 · VULNERABILITIES

Consent with Pfizer, Marx, and Hobbes

MATTHIAS RUDOLF

Heidi Hurd counts consent among those "remarkable powers of personhood" that appear "remarkably magical"—magical because, "by sheer exercise of the will," they "bring things into existence that have never existed before," "effect the disappearance of things that served as barriers to others," and "generate things that present obstacles to others" (121). In consenting, we generate and circumscribe the social and material realities we inhabit: we create rights and obligations that compel us to act in particular ways, altering what it is that we can and cannot properly claim as our own. Consent's "magic" is "moral," which is to say normative and just, because it turns what would otherwise be a wrong—the transgression of one person's right—into the establishment of another's right. My consent to participate in a clinical trial transforms the poisoning of my body into a more or less risky medical experiment, and consent to another's sexual advances transforms sexual assault into consensual intimacy. Similarly, consent transforms exploitation into fair use. Consent's "magic," in other words, produces some form of value, some "good" that was not there before.

This account of consent as the production of value has a striking affinity with Marx's account of capital, whose emergence marks the historical shift from primitive accumulation and hoarding—in which wealth is amassed by deception, coercion, and exploitation[1]—to the actual production of (surplus) value. In Marx's telling, the enabling event of this shift is the discovery, within the sphere of commodity circulation, of labor power, a marvelous "commodity whose use-value possesses the peculiar property of being a source of value, whose actual consumption is therefore itself an objectification of labour, hence a creation of value" (270). Yet this means of value creation is accessible only through the laborer's consent. By consenting, laborers authorize their labor power as capital and promise that the capitalist's consumption of the commodity "labor power" will take place as the consummation of their promise—as the performance of the "words of the future" or terms of contract they freely and of their own accord bind themselves to (Hobbes 103). Consent transforms the products of labor into value things in advance of their becoming—which means that value is constituted by the form of its return: the fulfillment of the words of the promise. Consent is capitalism's condition of possibility, the magical "thing" that authorizes capital.

For Marx, however, consent occluded the violent contradiction at the heart of capital that separated individuals from themselves and their interests. In the market, the "Eden of the innate rights of man" (280), all persons appeared as equals, abstract bearers of rights, free to dispose over their labor power as a thing and to represent their subjective interests. Yet this semblance of equality and freedom concealed that as preexisting, embodied social beings, laborers were the objects of power relations whose material inequalities, enforced legally by the state, deprived them of the means to provide for their subsistence and so compelled them to "offer for sale as a commodity that very labor-power which exists only in [their] living body" (272). For Marx, the contradiction was insurmountable. Insofar as the worker's consent was unfree, consent masked capitalism's exploitative bent and obscured how coercion—the politically enacted perpetuation and ideological production of nonchoice as the only choice—underwrites the production of surplus value.[2]

For what follows, it is crucial that the laborer's unfreedom was not a consequence of economic coercion (the laborer was, after all, free) but of the political and historical forces that conditioned and compelled his entry into the market. Laborers came to the market from the outside and appeared in it otherwise than they were: as dramatis personae, actors appearing as equals on its stage. The trouble was that the same abstraction that made them equal, regardless of and without reference to their particularity, also separated them from their concrete existence, which their persons came to represent *and* stand in for. The market, in other words, separated laborers from their interest—the claim not only to formal but also to material equality and justice—by making each and every one of them a representer of their own persons and of a general humanity and compelling them to represent (and so efface) those interests in the market's ostensibly universal terms. The status of consent is thus ambivalent, effacing the vulnerability of human beings to the material conditions of their subjection and enlisting their bodies to the end of capital. By the same token, however, consent figures the performative site where economic interests are open to political contestation and refashioning, be it by renegotiating contractual terms or by withholding consent *tout court* (e.g., a strike).

Against Marx, neoliberalism maintained that abstraction was not a feature of capitalism but of an economic theory that focused on relations of production, exchange, and circulation and so substituted an abstraction for the essential thing: the economic activity of humans.[3] Far from being wage slaves, humans were rational choice actors who allocated scarce means, including their bodily capacities, to alternative and mutually exclusive ends (Foucault 222). Consenting, in other words, was the very hallmark of the human, the act that produced all individuals as universal subjects and that individualized that universality. Moreover, since individuals remained in possession of their bodily capacity throughout the labor process, they were not alienated from their labor but rather related to their bodies as to capital, investing it as they saw fit. Neoliberalism thus both denounced Marx's Eden as a fiction (not realizing that Marx, too, had insisted on the same point, albeit for different reasons) *and* naturalized it by including its outside—the state that ensured the freedom of the market and the legal and violent means of that security—in it. Henceforth the whole world would be a market, and the rules of Eden applied—or ought to apply—everywhere.

In early 1996, an unprecedented epidemic of bacterial meningitis swept through Northern Nigeria, killing twelve thousand children and leaving many more permanently disabled.[4] As the epidemic worsened, Nigerian state radio called on families to take their sick children to the Infectious Diseases Hospital (IDH) in Kano to receive free emergency treatment from doctors of the aid organization Médecins Sans Frontières (MSF). What the radio did not say was that a team of doctors sent by the American pharmaceutical giant Pfizer were also there, conducting a Phase III clinical trial on Trovan (trovafloxacin), a bactericidal antibiotic with a deflorinated side chain that made it more effective and potentially dangerous.

For Pfizer, its potential investors, and its prospective clients, Trovan was the name of a promise: a potentially child-friendly, powerful, broad-spectrum antibiotic that could be taken orally and hence eliminate the health risks and costs associated with intravenous antibiotics that required skilled health care workers. Pfizer had preadvertised it to investors and drug reps as a potential blockbuster with projected annual global revenues approaching $1 billion. But for the drug to become the commodity it was destined to be, Pfizer needed the FDA's regulatory approval, and that meant demonstrating the drug's efficacy and safety in a clinical random control trial (CRT), preferably on ill children. But bacterial epidemics had become rare in the United States, making it hard to find enough sick children in one place at one time to conduct a trial efficiently. For this reason, Pfizer invested in novel tracking tools, using the budding internet and other data sources to locate epidemics in clean or "treatment naïve" populations to test unlicensed, experimental drugs (Oldani 1444). The pediatric meningitis outbreak in Kano fit the bill: a large supply of ill children and desperate parents, few of whom had ever received prior medical treatment, likely willing to sign away rights they might not even be aware they had for the promise of treatment.

Pfizer moved quickly, receiving an import permit for the "investigational use" of Trovan from the National Agency for Food and Drug Administration and Control (NAFDAC); drawing up a trial protocol; setting up a field team under Dr. Scott Hopkins; presenting the Kano State Ministry of Health with a donation of medicines, equipment, and materials to combat the epidemic; and promising to dispatch a team to "render assistance and participate in the treatment of patients" all by March 20, 1996.[5] Pfizer's donation was not unusual—the MSF, the German Red Cross, and other aid organizations had made similar donations—but Pfizer was the only organization to donate to the Kano State government rather than the official Federal Task Force coordinating the relief effort, not an unimportant difference, it would turn out.

On March 31, Pfizer's medical director for Anglophone Sub-Saharan Africa, Dr. Segun Dogunro, and Hopkins recruited Dr. Isa Dutse as the principle investigator of the trial. Dutse was a Kano pediatrician who had previously worked with Pfizer and was chairman of the Medical Advisory Committee of the Aminu Kano Teaching Hospital, the body responsible for forming an ethics committee and granting ethical clearances for all CRTs. Dogunro and Hopkins presented Dutse with a brochure on Trovan, assured him that the Kano State Ministry of Health had approved the trial, charged him with putting together a medical team, and instructed the team to report at the IDH, where Hopkins and two other American doctors—Debra Williams and Mike Dunne—would join them (FMH 22). Dutse gave his oral consent—no contracts were signed, and Dutse never received a letter commissioning his appointment from Pfizer (FMH 24)—and four days later, on April 3, less than month after discovering the outbreak, Pfizer opened up shop in two run-down cinderblock buildings, adjacent to the MSF, and recruited the trial's first four patients (FMH 23).

When they arrived with their sick children expecting treatment by foreign aid workers, the parents, largely illiterate and unfamiliar with the visual codes of hospitals, had no way of telling that there were two medical teams—both staffed by foreign doctors relying on local staff for communication—who were pursuing altogether different aims. Unable to meaningfully distinguish between the doctors, some parents "agree[d] with [Pfizer doctors] because they already saw MSF people helping them, so they thought they, too, were MSF people," as a nurse later told BBS's Barnaby Philips, who further reported how a mother had "handed over her children to a white man—she did not know if that person was from Pfizer or MSF. She was distressed at the time—and she lost the piece of paper the white man gave her. Anyway, she cannot read." That the parents' foremost concern was to procure treatment for their children made them more likely to agree to whatever conditions the Pfizer team offered. In the words of the nurse, "Some of the parents, whatever you will do to them, they will agree because they want their children to be cured if you give them treatment" (Philips). Patients treated by Pfizer doctors said they were never told of the alternative, nonexperimental treatments the MSF doctors were dispensing just a few steps away.

The outward resemblance of the two teams belied their different goals. The MSF doctors had been on the compound since mid-March, acting on the humanitarian imperative to provide medical care to all persons, "irrespective of race, religion, creed or political convictions" (MSF). Pfizer's primary interest was to generate capital, but it saw no contradiction in framing that mission in humanitarian terms: it was providing its patients with access to state-of-the-art medication, superior to that dispensed by MSF; had donated medical aid to the Kano State government; and was testing a drug that would, both now and in the future, help relieve the burden of infectious diseases (Pfizer). Even so, while MSF was treating its patients as ends in themselves, Pfizer's medical staff, acting under the cover of altruism and masquerading as aid workers, were treating patients as means to the end of profit. Under the surface appearance of a pastoral relationship between doctors and patients lay concealed a market relationship in which the doctors were buyers and sellers at once, purchasing access to their patients' personal and medical data in exchange for "free" treatment.

Pfizer treated 200 children—99 with Trovan and a control group of 101 with an unusually low dose of the FDA-approved Ceftriaxone, at the time the gold-standard drug for bacterial meningitis (Abdullahi 6). Dutse and his two assistants, Drs. Hassan Haruna and Shehu Yusuf, implemented Pfizer's protocol and performed the bulk of medical procedures, with the American doctors providing occasional assistance. Mainly, though, Hopkins and his two colleagues screened and selected patients, collected tissue and blood samples, and kept meticulous written and photographic records of the patients' medical progress. All contacts to the outside world ran through Hopkins and Dogunro, who acted as liaisons to MSF and the Nigerian authorities. No one, however, was responsible for securing the written informed and voluntary consent of the patients required by law and for the forthcoming FDA application (FMH 29). Faced with a constant stream of illiterate villagers, Dr. Dutse and "some nurses" abandoned the prepared consent forms and instead obtained "oral informed consent" (FMH 25, 68). The forms were too complicated to be fully translated, Dr. Dutse later said, and the prospective test subjects were given "a general explanation": "You explain to them it's a new medicine and you have a right to say no" (qtd. in Stephens). Often, they asked Dr. Dutse what to do. He invariably suggested they join the trial (Stephens).

After two weeks, just enough time to evaluate the initial effectivity of Trovan, the Pfizer doctors broke camp and headed home with all of the data, leaving Dr. Dutse and his staff behind to take care of the last test subjects. Hopkins returned for follow-up studies with Dr. Dutse six weeks later, meeting once with roughly half the participants, a number not nearly sufficient to track their long-term recovery. Six months after the trial, Pfizer approached Dr. Dutse for an ethical committee clearance for the trial. Dutse duly provided one and backdated it to March 28, and Pfizer included it in its FDA application, submitted later that year (FM 23, 27; Philips). The FDA found no fault with it, but when it discovered inconsistencies in the Kano test data and the lack of follow-up care, Pfizer withdrew the application for pediatric use. Two years later, the FDA approved Trovan for adult use. It generated $600 million in profit the following year before increasing reports of liver toxicity and patient deaths led to its suspension; Pfizer withdrew the drug from the marketplace in 2001 (Oldani 1443).

In 2001, a group of Nigerian victims and their guardians sued Pfizer in U.S. court for human rights violations committed abroad by a U.S. private actor under the Alien Tort Statute (ATS).[6] Abdullahi and seventy other claimants—twenty-five of them deceased—alleged that Pfizer had used the 1996 outbreak to run a hastily organized field trial of Trovan "without obtaining the requisite authorization from the Nigerian authorities" and had conducted "involuntary medical experimentation on humans," "test[ing] an experimental antibiotic on children in Nigeria . . . without their consent or knowledge" (Abdullahi 4). The Trovan trial, the plaintiffs claimed, had led to the death of eleven children—five who had taken Trovan and six the FDA-approved control Ceftriaxone—and had left many more blind, deaf, paralyzed, or brain damaged. Pfizer had refused to provide the children with the best medical care, tested a drug it knew to cause liver damage in children, deliberately underdosed the children in the control group so as to skew the results in Trovan's favor, and subsequently failed to provide the test subjects with adequate follow-up care. But the damage Pfizer inflicted was not merely physical. By casting the trial as humanitarian aid and failing to adequately inform patients of the experimental nature of the treatment, Pfizer had violated the test subjects' human rights and dignity, deceived and robbed them of the opportunity to make a meaningful choice about their bodies and themselves, and treated them merely as a means to its own ends. It had used them as things.

Pfizer's response was categorical. In an interview with the BBC, its pharmaceutical director for West Africa, Lere Baale, denied all charges of wrongdoing and instead told a tale of Pfizer's beneficence that doubled down on the initial deception: "We forget about the scientific breakthrough [Pfizer was] able to make, we forget about the beauty of lives that were saved. . . . Indeed, society should be grateful to Pfizer because we came to help save lives, and we reduced the death rate by half relative to other common medications that were in use" (qtd. in Phillips). Pfizer publicly cast the trial as part of its humanitarian mission and effaced its profit-generating purpose. Despite all evidence to the contrary, Pfizer maintained that it had "always acted in the best interests of the approximately 200 children . . . using the best medical knowledge available at the time," that "the study plainly proved that Trovan helped save lives," and that "any deaths occurring during the Trovan clinical study were the direct result of the illness and not the treatment provided to patients" (Pfizer). Apropos of consent, Pfizer did not contest that it had not obtained written consent but asserted that all the patients had been informed about the test and had given sufficient verbal consent and implied that the plaintiffs were using onerous regulations and institutional requirements to extort financial remuneration for what were, in effect, imagined or fake wrongs.

Over the following decade and a half, Pfizer mounted a protracted legal battle to have the cases brought against it in the United States dismissed on the grounds that the ATS did not apply to consent violations by private actors. When in 2010 the U.S. solicitor general signaled Pfizer would lose its appeal against the Second Circuit Court, Pfizer maintained its denials of wrongdoing, changed forums, and settled out of court for an undisclosed amount. Pfizer faced no criminal charges and never made an admission of wrong.[7]

The Trovan trial has become a textbook example of how *not* to do clinical trials; hastily planned, insufficiently authorized, and sloppily executed, Pfizer's study has more in common with a mercenary raid than a research project. That Pfizer didn't bother to fill out the consent forms required by its own trial protocol and the FDA bespeaks both the FDA's cavalier attitude toward regulations and Pfizer's readiness to exploit them and take advantage of the regulatory weaknesses of a developing nation state. Unsurprisingly, the legal and ethical assessments of the trial have not been kind to Pfizer's conduct. The dissenting judge on the Second Circuit Court called Pfizer's actions "deplorable," and the court's decision all but convicted Pfizer of violating the "norm of customary international law prohibiting medical experimentation on non-consenting human subjects" (Abdullahi 4, 54). In the process, per the court, Pfizer had "foster[ed] distrust and resistance to international drug trials, cutting edge medical innovation, and critical international public health initiatives" and so jeopardized the "enormous health benefits for the world community" that CRTs promised (17, 40). In the critical literature, the trial figures as a "notable instance of poor ethical conduct"—its only redeeming quality being its exemplarily complex faultiness as "an important and multilayered example for understanding the ethical complexities and regulatory shortcomings of fast-tracking experimental compounds to the medical marketplace" (Okonta 189; Oldani 1446). In the court of public opinion, the *Washington Post's* assessment, echoing the Nigerian government inquiry's conclusions, became the consensus judgment: it was "an illegal trial of an unregistered drug" and "a clear case of exploitation of the ignorant" (FMH 16, 88).

In the aftermath of the Trovan scandal, most commentators argued that what was needed was more and better, especially more robust, consent (Okonta 189; Shah 149–150). But what kind of consent would actually do justice in the situation and to the persons involved? How does ensuring consent do away with the economic inequality that calls its validity into question? What consent guidelines would protect the population in Kano—and not just "persons" in general—from being used as things, as disposable people, and being treated merely as a means to the ends of shareholder value? Moreover, does not calling for more and better consent miss the myriad ways that the demand for consent and respect for human rights is complicit with the very exploitation it ought to prevent? To ask, as consent theorists are wont to, about who can consent to what and under what circumstances and what counts as consent is merely to refine the lines of demarcation that separate the permissible from the forbidden and prescribe *who* can consent to *what* under which circumstances. It is also to push a particular "universal" model of subjectivity and personhood—one uniquely qualified to quantify the relative value of wrongs insofar as they can be articulated in terms of the body—on communities that have good reasons, economic and otherwise, to reject the model of rational self-interest and human dignity it advocates.

It is thus twice ironic that consent—which is supposed to protect not only those who can afford *not* having to protect themselves against epidemic outbreaks but also the much larger group of those who have recourse to little more than what their living bodies proffer—would provide the means, all the more legitimate when they are properly and successfully solicited, by which the test subjects could join their voices, signatures, and, indeed, their bare humanity to the apparently humanitarian promise their bodies authorize.

In the following, I pursue two related thoughts: that the vulnerabilities consent exposes persons and bodies to are systemic, ingrained in the very concept and functioning of consent, and that contemporary (neo)liberal accounts of consent, by trying to make consent more robust, more attuned to the details of everyday life, exacerbates the fragility of the concept. Indeed, the more consent promises to be the means par excellence of overcoming the violent antagonisms that pervade human relations, the more it displaces and reproduces what Stanislas Breton terms the "violence of tautological propositions" (134) into the social and economic margins of an increasingly globalized world.

Consent's ostensible universality derives as much from its material grounding in the human body, as Elaine Scarry has argued, as from the *fictional* occlusion of its violent foundation. Hume argues that government was founded on "conquest or usurpation—that is, in plain terms, force"—and that consent was a myth that normalized people's habituation to such violence (271). Hobbes, acutely aware of the representational nature of authority, saw the state as founded on the self-renewing capacities of fiction. For both, consent retroactively normalizes founding violence by transforming it into a form of law-preserving violence that comes to shape the limits of a common world. The insight also informs Marx's objection that the laborers' consent is invalidated because they could not consent to the conditions of their consent. This foundational violence of consent reappears in the restrictions and exclusions that constrain its exercise: only persons who are considered persons can consent, and consent must be performed in recognizable ways. Consent renders persons and bodies vulnerable because the constraints that render it operational enact thinly veiled tautologies—a person is a person, yes means yes, no means no. To paraphrase Étienne Balibar, no one can tell the difference between a person and nonperson, between yes and not-yes other than by a tautological reference to what has already been identified as a "person" and "yes" in the Western tradition (96). Consent's constraints restrict access to the very universality in which it is ostensibly grounded; its universality is defective.

Neoliberalism casts consent as a communicative act between two persons, A and B, each a unitary, free, and autonomous individual or "collective" subject governed by a decision procedure that authorizes its choice(s) to pursue a course of action, φ. In Kleinig's pithy grammar, "A consents (to B) to φ" (5–6). Shaped by the dogmas of free markets, individual responsibility, and the person as the autonomous self who relates to its bodily capacities as to capital, the Trovan trial suggests that neoliberal consent serves as a means to globalized biomedical exploitation and the ends of capital. To use the Trovan trial as evidence that consent serves as a means to the ends of capital is, however, to tread on thin ice, first because, based on the available evidence, Pfizer manifestly *failed* to obtain informed consent and built its defense on misleading claims and outright falsehoods, and second because doing go risks blaming "consent" for the unethical conduct of individual and collective actors. Nonetheless, reading Pfizer's defense at face value—that is, however counterfactually, imagining that the patients *had* given informed oral consent—draws attention to conditions we would all too easily ignore given valid consent. The neoliberal account of consent reduces politics to ethics and reframes questions of power in terms of economics, human rights, and the value of life. Moreover, and as the increasing conduct of CRTs in poor and developing countries attests, the characterization of consent as a transaction of rights between individuals that is represented by a token—the words and actions signifying consent—reduces consent to a means whose costs are too often effaced and justified in the name of the value it creates.

For pharmaceutical companies conducting CRTs, consent is a commodity they must produce as a token and exchange for regulatory consideration. Insofar as the institutional (and to a lesser degree the scientific) validity and authority of the trial depends on the informed consent of the test subjects, consent is a necessary part of the product's development to be planned, implemented, and accounted for in human and capital costs. When CRTs are carried out in the global margins, obtaining informed consent requires the translation of ostensible universal ethical norms and medical knowledge across significant cultural divides and takes significant investments of time and human resources.[8] Yet faced with linguistic, cultural, and educational barriers, the limited reach of the "universal" values of human rights and ethical conduct becomes quite apparent. Most researchers and regulatory agencies, Sonia Shah writes, throw up their hands in exasperation, proclaiming that consent is "too Western a notion," incompatible with the traditional values of the test subjects, and worry that were they to disclose "all potential adverse effects" of a drug, patients would be "scared away" and their trials jeopardized (150–153). From their perspective, the standards of informed consent appear as onerous and costly regulatory barriers that impede the production of better, more efficacious drugs for "all." As a result, most researchers and regulators are satisfied with what Beauchamp has aptly titled "legally valid compliance" with the social rules of consent (57): they procure prima facie expressions of agreement with a proposed intervention—risk disclosure and the receipt of a signed consent sheet to protect the parties from liability—and blithely press on with their trials (Shah 151). The consequence is that in the absence of the test subjects' understanding of the trial, factors that would otherwise vitiate consent—duress and undue influence, not to speak of sheer deception—all too easily become the instruments with which to procure legally valid consent.

In Hobbes's account of the foundation of the state in *Leviathan*, civil society emerges and derives its legitimacy from the act of promising that establishes the social contract. In Hamacher's retelling of Hobbes's fable, man's exit from the state of nature is marked by his radical vulnerability: naked and bereft of any and all but his bodily means, man lays down his arms and promises.[9] Since the "promise to lay down one's arms" is prompted by nothing but the untenable conditions of existence in the state of nature, the promise responds to violence and the right of the stronger: it "occurs not in the laying down of arms, but in their violently forced surrender" (234). For Hamacher, the aporia Hobbes's account enacts—that man becomes a subject only by virtue of an act (i.e., promising) that requires the subject it is to produce—offers the possibility of "an agreement and of a (even if minimal) political bond" based on something other than the violence of conquest (242). This aporetic possibility lies at the core of consent, which Hobbes casts as the repetition and confirmation of the originary "promise to lay down one's arms." To end the threat of mutual destruction, man had to "lay down this right to all things," "abandon his right to everything," and transfer it to mortal God, the Leviathan. If "the promise to lay down one's arms" inaugurates (the possibility of) a social order, consent is the *performative* iteration of that promise that always and again authorizes the coherency and stability of that order.[10] Like the promise, consent achieves this not by *positing* an order but by *abandoning* itself to the "bare existence" of "bare language," devoid of the "multiplicity of natural interests connected to it" (225). In consenting, one gives oneself—one's words and actions—over to the order of language, not to language as spoken by individuals (what linguists call "parole"), but to language as a system of signification beyond the reach of any individual agency ("langue"), such that the manifestation of will represented in one's individual speech act comes to be authorized and transmitted by its entry into language in general, in which it finds its figural end. In this way, consent is more than the mere transfer of rights, the exchange of entitlements, or the transformation of moral relationships between persons; it is also the individual's promise to relinquish the right to determine the meaning of its own utterance, or, in Hobbes's vocabulary, to "divest oneself of the Liberty of hindering another of the benefit of his own right to the same" (100)—that is, the other's right to make one's words and actions meaningful. This delegation, not of speech but of meaning, institutes a political relation between actors, not just an economic relation. For far from being merely a transfer of meaning and signification from one person to another, in Hobbes, the other person speaks and acts one's words and actions in place of and as one's own person. It is, in other words, not just a question of properly representing (in the sense of *Darstellung*, aesthetic or tropological representation) the significance of one's words and actions but of one's words and actions standing in for and representing (in the sense of *Vertretung*, political or proxy representation) one's meaning.[11]

Hobbes's account of the person as a representer—an "actor" who represents an "author"—makes clear that this political relation not only obtains *between* persons but rather constitutes the core of a person's being:

A Person, is he, *whose words or actions are considered, either as his own, or as representing the words or actions of another man, or of any other thing to whom they are attributed, whether Truly or by Fiction.*

> When they are considered as his owne, then he is called a *Naturall Person*: And when they are considered as representing the words and actions of an other, then he is a *Feigned* or *Artificiall Person*. (111, emphasis in original)

That words and actions can be "owned" already implies their alienation, that they are proper to no one person, and that thus even natural persons are in reality artificial. Hobbes's brief etymology of the word "person" leaves little doubt about this: "The word Person is latine, instead whereof the Greeks have *prosopon*, which signifies the *Face*, as *Persona* in latine signifies the *disguise*, or *outward appearance* of a man, counterfeited on the Stage. . . . So that a *Person* is the same that an *Actor* is, both on the stage and in common Conversation; and to *Personate* is to *Act*, or *Represent* himself or another; and he that acteth another is said to beare his Person, or act in his name" (112, emphasis in original). To speak and act as a person is to act in the place of another, even if that other is one's own self. Moreover, since personhood is contingent on having one's words and actions "considered," one becomes a person at the moment the representation of one's words and actions coincides with their alienation by a *prosopon* whose performance represents them as one's own. This unwilled, inadvertent, and unavoidable separation instituted by the passage through the "one" language constitutes *all* subjects as divided and dislocated. The prosopopoeic character of Hobbesian personhood—that is, that persons are spoken by their words and actions, which constitute the "Mask or Vizard" that at once represents *and* stands in for the person speaking[12]—thus renders *every* person an artificial and *abstract* person, even "natural" persons. Indeed, it is the capacity to be owned by those same words and actions that in its very impropriety is "natural" to personhood.

Hobbes's account of consent as a prosopopoeic, performative act foregrounds the centrality of the body to personhood. Contrary to neoliberalism's characterization of "the paradigmatic subject of consent" as the individuated "nice body with a self at home in it" (Hyde 50) of which the "collective subject" is merely a logical extension, Hobbes sees the *artificial not the natural* person as the normative case. The body at stake in consent—the body whose future words and actions are obliged by the words and actions of the actor—is thus never the body of the actor personating the author but always the body of the author. Precisely because authors only ever come to presence through actors, the body of the author is, as it were, the natural body of the artificial person: the personated, prosopopoeic "body" of a "speaker" who is never present to its words. Its proper embodiment is the *prosopon*, the prosopopoeic "Mask or Vizard" that announces itself in the words and actions that constitute the surface of its being.

From this perspective, the link between Marx and Hobbes becomes clear. In consenting, I give over my words and actions as a means to an other's ends: they become things, use values, for another to consume. The other's determination of the meaning of my words and actions takes the place of and becomes the consequence of an utterance of which "I" was always already the author. Conversely and at the same time, the consequences of the other's use of my words and actions stand in for their ostensible meaning. In other words, the tokens and performative traces of consent are things that can be properly used as a means in excess of any will or intention represented by them. It is this excess that is the "magical" source of consent's value.

Recall in this context Pfizer's claim that the Trovan trial *had* been governmentally authorized, since the NAFDAC had granted them permission to import the drug "for investigational use." NAFDAC intended the phrase to *restrict* the use of the drug, but Pfizer on its own account took the phrase "also as an authority to conduct the trial" (FMH 58). Pfizer thus used NAFDAC's consent to its import request as a means with which to justify the commencement of the trial—as if the restriction brought the to-be-restricted thing into being so it could be restricted.

Pfizer's "beneficence" defense supposes a false equivalence of bodily harm and rights violations, as if not harming the body necessarily entailed not harming the person. Pfizer's argument for the ultimate beneficence of the trial—Baale stated that "society should be grateful to Pfizer because we came to help save lives, and we reduced the death rate by half relative to other common medications that were in use" (Philips)—performs a metalepsis, the substitution of an effect (the contingent experimental outcome that showed Trovan to have been statistically more effective than either Ceftriaxone or Chloramphenicol, the drug used by the MSF) for a cause (namely, the maxim of Pfizer's actions, to make money by saving lives) and so inverts or reverses their temporal relation. By substituting a forensic result (moreover one Pfizer authored and that is only available in retrospect) for the patients' (lacking) authorization, Baale obviates the question of the test subjects' willing participation in a medical experiment with uncertain outcome and replaces it with a utilitarian calculus where outcomes are already coded in terms of the value of human life and bodily well-being. According to the "facts" of this calculus, Pfizer had all along, even if unbeknown to the patients or contrary to their stated wishes, been working for their best interests. Baale's claim, a cornerstone of Pfizer's defense, erases difference in the service of likeness, equalizing the distinction between patients dying of their illness and of the drug's side effects in the name of establishing a single measure of value: the "survival rate," the "best" of which—per Pfizer—belonged to Trovan (Pfizer).

A similar pattern characterizes Pfizer's handling of consent. Pfizer appeals to the formal tautology that yes means yes, regardless of how it is communicated, to explain its failure to obtain written consent as a mere procedural lapse—as if the formal difference between oral and written consent mattered to bureaucrats but didn't constitute an ethical wrong. In both cases, Pfizer might continue, consent is a communicative act; saying yes is the same as scribbling one's name or making one's mark on a consent form. Dressed up as a tautology, the asserted, unverifiable indifference this difference makes reappears in Pfizer's claim that the test subjects' yes meant yes to Pfizer's intervention, which consisted of "treatment" for meningitis and was part of Pfizer's "contribution [to help fight] the 1996 meningitis epidemic in Nigeria" (Pfizer). Pfizer at best conflates the patients' implicit consent to medical treatment with *oral* consent to participation in the trial and thereby perversely enlists the "therapeutic misconception"—in which medical researchers fail to acknowledge "that the defining purpose of clinical research is to produce generalizable knowledge, regardless of whether the subjects enrolled in the trial may potentially benefit from the intervention under study or from other aspects of the clinical trial" (Henderson)—in its defense.

Pfizer's insistence that it obtained insufficiently documented but nonetheless valid oral consent presupposes that the children and their guardians are autonomous persons, capable of understanding the actions they were authorizing, and competent and free to make those decisions. Pfizer's conduct suggests that presumption is grounded merely in a shared common humanity. By a priori recognizing them as fully competent human beings, as partaking of the same stuff as the doctors and nurses, having the same basic wants and needs and lives of equal worth, Pfizer abstracts them from the material conditions of their existence, ignoring that they are overwhelmingly poor, illiterate, and desperate for any treatment at all, and then asserts that there is no reason to treat their consent as anything other than an autonomous, free, and valid expression of their will. To consider them as anything else would be to denigrate their humanity and their equal rights. On Pfizer's account, the guardians are neither ignorant nor incompetent, and Pfizer refuses to treat them as such. Here the appeal to human rights and equality figures a form of concealment of social and economic inequality deployed to efface discursive and medical violence.

The temptation to identify the abstract humanity of the test subjects with their bodily existence is prescribed by the material constraints that condition clinical trials. From a purely technical standpoint, Shah writes, "uniformed, coerced subjects don't impede medical research at all" (149). Since what counts is the to-be-gleaned data from the test subject's body and not the person or self that resides in it, "unknowing, docile subjects make trials easier and faster" (Shah 149). Pfizer's claims that Trovan didn't cause any bodily harm—it was "at least as effective as the best treatment available at Kano's IDH," and "any deaths occurring during the Trovan clinical study were the direct result of the illness and not the treatment provided to patients" (Pfizer)—rehearses a similar logic. Again, it is the living bodies of the test subjects whose abstraction provides the sole measure of value. Since their bodies had been helped, the test subjects had in actuality benefitted from Trovan and had no reason to complain. The harm done to the person—the violation of a person's right to choose (ironically committed in the name of providing patients with more treatment choices down the road)—is justified by the good done to the body.

It is this identification of the body with the person that, coupled with the presupposition that all humans are rational choice actors (who cannot but consent to choose, always and again, to the degree they are subject to the needs of their bodies), restricts the children and their parents from standing in for—representing by proxy—anything else than their immediate medical and biological needs. Their words and actions only represent—aesthetically and economically, as an image and a value—their personal interests as human animals rather than speaking subjects.

If consent's defective universality might yet be its paradoxical strength, it is because its fictionality opens it up to political contestation. Indeed, the hallmark of its defectiveness lays therein that consent's abstract universality can be claimed by anyone or anything because no *one* can possess that universality to the exclusion of the rest. The noncoincidence of political and economic modes of representation that consent's passage through language describes endlessly defers and simulates the identity of bodies and persons. Insofar as consent passes between one who authorizes words and actions (an author who gives them significance and value) and one who acts on and by means of them (an actor who uses them for persuasive ends), the implicit surrender of will and intention to the mediality of language implied and iterated in every act of consent institutes an asymmetrical relation between economics and political modes of representation that can never be dissolved into its constitutive elements and, precisely for that reason, im-mediates their relation. To think of consent in these terms is to recognize its relation to power, its latent violence and contingent underpinnings, and—since consent institutes and is instituted by the deployment and consumption of words and actions—consent's artificial and political nature.

NOTES

1. Merchant capital is a prime example: one accumulates wealth by buying commodities from another person in order to sell those same commodities "dearer" to a third (Marx 266). The price difference—the value gained—follows from the advantages the merchant gains over buyer and seller by "parasitically positioning himself between them" and "cheating" both (267) and does not represent a real surplus since the commodity does not add value to the market.

2. For the relation of coercion and consent in Marx, compare, for example, Gramsci and Buroway.

3. I follow Foucault's argument in *The Birth of Biopolitics*.

4. The account I present is compiled from Stephens, Phillips, the Nigerian Federal Ministry of Health's investigation, and the *Abdullahi v. Pfizer Inc.* decision, as well as Lee and Oldani.

5. Nigeria, Federal Ministry of Health 44, 28. Henceforth FMH.

6. There were two law suits filed in the United States, *Abdullahi v. Pfizer* and *Adamu v. Pfizer*. A third lawsuit, *Zango v. Pfizer*, was filed in Nigerian courts in 2001 but abandoned in 2003 under allegations of corruption after the presiding judge was removed from the bench and the second one declined to prosecute the case for personal reasons. The first two suits were consolidated as *Abdullahi v. Pfizer* in 2009 after the U.S. Court of Appeals overturned the lower court dismissals of the two cases. For a succinct history, compare *Abdullahi v. Pfizer*. Lee provides an excellent discussion of the important role of the Trovan trial in shaping the legal framework and response to violations of informed consent.

7. After the dismissal of *Zango v. Pfizer*, the Nigerian government brought a new suit in 2009, and Pfizer—again without admitting wrongdoing—agreed to settle for $75 million, $10 million of which were to be paid to government attorneys (Loue 7–8).

8. Shah points out that "several simple methods have been shown to bridge the gulf between Western investigators and patients from developing countries," ranging from hiring local people to explain the study to administering quizzes to ensure comprehension of consent forms and then counseling those with low test scores or dropping them from the trial (149–151).

9. My discussion traces Hamacher's reading of the sovereignty of language in Hobbes's *Leviathan*.

10. Consent is not originary but a response to a solicitation, hence secondary, situated and contingent on circumstance, and made under conditions not entirely under the consenter's control. Promising is integral to consent—all consents are promises—but not all promises are consents. One can promise without consenting, even to being called on having promised. And while promises need no motivation and may be spontaneous, consent always respond to another's words, be it a query, a demand, or an offer.

11. I draw on Spivak's elaboration (276–279).

12. The OED defines *prosopopoeia* as "a rhetorical device by which an imaginary, absent, or dead person is represented as speaking or acting."

WORKS CITED

Abdullahi v. Pfizer Inc., 562 F. 3d 163 (2d. Cir). 2009.

Balibar, Étienne. "The Borders of Europe." *Politics and the Other Scene*, translated by Christine Jones et al., Verso, 2002, pp. 87–103.

Beauchamp, Tom. "Autonomy and Consent." *The Ethics of Consent: Theory and Practice*, edited by Franklin Miller and Alan Wertheimer, Oxford UP, 2009, pp. 55–78.

Breton, Stanislas. *Philosophie Buissonnière*. Éditions Jérôme Million, 1989.

Burawoy, Michael. *Manufacturing Consent: Changes in the Labor Process under Monopoly Capitalism*. Chicago UP, 1979.

Foucault, Michel. *The Birth of Biopolitics: Lectures at the College de France, 1978–79*. Edited by Michel Snellart, translated by Graham Burchell, Palgrave Macmillan, 2008.

Gramsci, Antonio. *Selections from the Prison Notebooks*. Edited and translated by Quentin Hoare and Geoffrey Nowell Smith, International, 1971.

Hamacher, Werner. "Wild Promises: On the Language 'Leviathan,'" translated by Geoffrey Hale. *New Centennial Review*, vol. 4, no. 3, winter 2004, pp. 215–245.

Henderson, Gail E., et al. "Clinical Trials and Medical Care: Defining the Therapeutic Misconception." *PLoS Medicine*, vol. 4, no. 11, 2007, p. e324. doi:10.1371/journal.pmed.0040324.

Hobbes, Thomas. *Leviathan*. Edited by Richard Tuck, Cambridge UP, 1996.

Hume, David. "Of the Original Contract." *Essays, Literary, Moral, and Political*, London, 1870, pp. 270–283.

Hurd, Heidi M. "The Moral Magic of Consent." *Legal Theory*, vol. 2, no. 2, 1996, pp. 121–146.

Hyde, Alan. *Bodies of Law*. Princeton UP, 1997.

Kleinig, John. "The Nature of Consent." *The Ethics of Consent: Theory and Practice*, edited by Franklin Miller and Alan Wertheimer, Oxford UP, 2009, pp. 3–24.

Lee, Stacey B. "Informed Consent: Enforcing Pharmaceutical Companies' Obligations Abroad." *Health and Human Rights Journal*, vol. 12, no. 1, June 2010, pp. 15–28.

Loue, Sana. "Forensic Epidemiology in the Global Context: A Case Study of Pfizer and the Trovan Trial." *Forensic Epidemiology in the Global Context*, edited by Sara Loue, Springer, 2013, pp. 1–18.

Marx, Karl. *Capital: A Critique of Political Economy*. Introduced by Ernest Mandel, translated by Ben Fowkes, Penguin, 1976.

Médecin Sans Frontières (MSF). "MSF Charter and Principles." *Medecin Sans Frontieres*, 16 Jan. 2017, www.msf.org/en/msf-charter-and-principles.

Nigeria, Federal Ministry of Health. *Report of the Investigation Committee on the Clinical Trial of Trovafloxacin (Trovan) by Pfizer, Kano, 1996*. Federal Ministry of Health, 2001. Citizens for Responsible Care and Research, 17 Jan. 2017, www.circare.org/info/trovan_clinicaltrialreport.pdf.

Okonta, Patrik. "Ethics of Clinical Trials in Nigeria." *Nigerian Medical Journal*, vol. 55, no. 3, May–June 2014, pp. 188–194.

Oldani, Michael. "Trovafloxacin (Trovan) Controversy." *The SAGE Encyclopedia of Pharmacology and Society*, edited by Sarah E. Boslaugh, SAGE, 2016, pp. 1444–1447.

Pfizer. "Summary: Trovan, Kano State Civil Case–Statement of Defense." *Pfizer*, 3 Jan. 2017, www.pfizer.com/files/news/trovan_statement_defense_summary.pdf.

Phillips, Barnaby. "Nigeria's Drug Trial Fears," *BBC*, 14 Mar. 2001, www.news.bbc.co.uk/2/hi/africa/1220032.stm.

Scarry, Elaine. "Consent and the Body: Injury, Departure, and Desire." *New Literary History*, vol. 21, no. 4, 1990, pp. 867–896.

Shah, Sonia. *The Body Hunters: Testing New Drugs on the World's Poorest Patients*. New Press, 2006.

Spivak, Gayatri Chakravorty. "Can the Subaltern Speak?" *Marxism and the Interpretation of Culture*, edited by Cary Nelson and Lawrence Grossberg, U of Illinois P, 1988, pp. 271–314.

Stephens, J. "Where Profits and Lives Hang in Balance." *Washington Post*, 17 Dec. 2001, www.washingtonpost.com/wp-dyn/content/article/2007/0702/AR2007070201255.html.

13 · "I NEVER HEARD ANYTHING SO MONSTROUS!"

Developmental Psychology, Narrative Form, and the Age of Consent in *What Maisie Knew*

VICTORIA OLWELL

Why are children excluded from the class of consenting subjects in liberal democracy, and what does their exclusion tell us about the juridical conditions of consent? Considering Henry James's 1897 novel, *What Maisie Knew*, provides us with one way to approach such questions, not only because it was written during the historical moment when children's exclusion achieved its modern justifications in developmental psychology, but also because the novel absorbs the basis of these justifications within its experimental narrative form, rendering them available to scrutiny.

At the end of *What Maisie Knew*, the young heroine, Maisie Farange, negotiates with the three adult characters vying for custody of her and then finally chooses as her guardian her former governess, Mrs. Wix. Her choice concludes the struggles she has endured as the object of a complex series of custody battles, and it marks her ultimate emergence as a subject capable of exerting agency by forming consensual bonds. Maisie, who at this point is probably in her very early teens, assumes for the first time the authority to choose who has power over her and who may stand in a familial and intimate relation to her. To be sure, she faces immediate resistance to her new authority from her stepmother, Mrs. Beale, who, like Mrs. Wix, is also Maisie's former governess. Hearing Maisie's choice of Mrs. Wix, Mrs. Beale exclaims that she has "never heard anything so monstrous!"

and calls the girl an "abominable little horror" (263, 264). As Mrs. Beale's vocabulary of monstrosity and abomination suggests, she sees the possibility of Maisie's consent as a category violation, the polluting combination of elements that should remain separate. Maisie is a child who claims a power that is supposed to be antithetical to her nature and thus opens the door to the manifold disturbing implications of the consenting girl child, from the overthrow of patriarchal parental authority and the expansion of the electoral franchise beyond men to the assertion of childhood sexuality. But Mrs. Beale has no monopoly on the question of how to understand Maisie's power to consent. Sir Claude, who is Maisie's stepfather and also Mrs. Beale's lover, readily validates her consent in the familiar idiom of liberal democracy by describing it as her rightful exercise of liberty, asserting, "I only insist that she's free—she's free" (264). In his view, her capacity to consent expands liberal democracy's circle of freedom rather than troubling its foundations by undermining its exclusive character.

James contrived this fictional dispute over a child's capacity to consent at a pivotal moment in the history of childhood, when scientific scrutiny was directed toward the minds of children in new and systematic ways that far outstripped any previous approaches to children's cognition. Beginning in the 1890s, the emergent discipline of child study produced richly detailed and dauntingly voluminous data about the contents of children's minds. Child study's immediate and more sophisticated successor, developmental psychology, organized such data into narratives of intellectual and emotional growth, charting a path from the helplessness of infancy to the full powers of adulthood (Shuttleworth 267–289).

The narrative character of developmental psychology, along with its close attention to the emergence of capacities, made it a useful tool for reframing in modern terms a question that had long plagued liberal democracy and had been answered historically in a number of conflicting ways: What are the limits defining who is capable of consenting to the state's legitimacy or to the social, sexual, and economic relations conducted in a contractarian society? The developmental narrative took over from earlier models of consensual capacity—such as those based on property, status, or less elaborated accounts of children's intellectual capacities—the political task of explaining children's exclusion from consensual status and the rights of full citizenship, a task it still performs today. Moreover, insofar as the developmental model specified the terms for deciding the difference between competence and incompetence, it provided a rich and supple language for considering the potential civic competence not only of children but also of everyone else.

Written at the moment of this transition in conceptions of who merited inclusion in the democratic community of consent, *What Maisie Knew* exposes the implications of the new developmental model. In bringing together developmental psychology, political consent, and sexual consent, James's novel allows us to investigate the intricate dynamic between political authority and vulnerability that changing models of both childhood and consent set in motion. Seeing the novel in this way also permits us to perceive the broader cultural narratives according to which children's incompetence to consent, as it was coming to be understood, established one major historical and conceptual limit to the expansion of democratic rights and inclusion.

Yet as a narrative experiment—and a thought experiment—in imagining a child's psychological development toward the capacity to consent, the novel also prompts us to think beyond the model of adult subjectivity that usually grounds consent toward an open and shifting notion of consenting subjectivity. In unfolding the political implications of developmental psychology, my consideration here of *What Maisie Knew* will be both historical and theoretical. After first exploring the interventions that *What Maisie Knew* makes into the controversies about children's political and sexual consent that roiled its historical moment, I intend here to probe the novel for ways it can help us to reimagine the power to consent in more labile terms than the Enlightenment standards of rationality and the modern measures of cognitive maturity have so far allowed.

MAISIE'S CHOICE AND CHILDREN'S POLITICAL CONSENT

In the Anglo-American political imaginary, sexual and political consent have long been linked.[1] Particularly at moments of historical transition in their meaning, they operate as metaphors for each other; at other points, changes in how one is instituted in law or custom closely track changes in the other. In ways both subtle and pervasive, the issues of children's political and sexual consent are entwined in *What Maisie Knew*, though to a certain degree, they can be tracked separately.

Turning first to political consent, it is evident that Maisie, in choosing Mrs. Wix as her guardian, enacts something of a coup, both in the immediate context of her family situation and in the broader context of children's historical position in liberal democracy. Ideological antipatriarchalism is at the core of classical liberal theory, expressed perhaps most famously in John Locke's *First Treatise of Government*, which refutes Robert Filmer's defense of the patriarchal power of monarchs. Such antipatriarchalism was also widespread in the political ideology of the American Revolution, which was justified, as Jay Fliegelman memorably put it in the subtitle of his classic account, as "a revolution against patriarchal authority." In subverting the patriarchal authority of monarchs, the American revolutionaries, like Enlightenment thinkers more generally, did not mean to overturn the power of fathers in the family. What they rejected, rather, was an order of power based on inheritance, which they sought to replace with a political order grounded in the consent of the governed. In a way that is hard to read as coincidental, Maisie's choice of Mrs. Wix as her guardian reads like an allegory of Enlightenment revolution. As James wrote in his 1907 introduction of the novel for the New York edition of his collected works, Maisie, "instead of simply submitting to the inherited tie and the imposed complication, of suffering from them," would create "a fresh tie, from which [she] would then . . . proceed to derive great profit" (*What Maisie Knew* 25). Mrs. Beale and Sir Claude, as her stepparents, represent the "inherited tie" she rejects, while Mrs. Wix is the "fresh tie" that Maisie authorizes with her own consent.

The historical irony here, though, is that while Enlightenment political ideology assailed hereditary power that it figured as patriarchal, it augmented the authority of actual fathers over actual children. Brewer, in her extensive investigation of children's changing political status with the rise of democracy, reveals that under the predemocratic order of inherited power, "younger children could testify, offer judgment, and have a civil identity" (342). This was because "their legal authority and status depended more on their rank than on their age" (342). While the intellectual capacities of young children were never entirely irrelevant to their political status—no one thought that a two-year-old could make decisions about the course of a nation—their age was a factor often subordinate to their status. When Enlightenment theory gave political authority a new basis in reasoned consent, however, children were explicitly excluded. As Brewer writes, "Children became subjects incapable of consent, because they did not have reason" (341).[2] As a result of children's exile from political authority, parental, and particularly paternal, dominion over children grew.

What Maisie Knew makes an elaborate demonstration of the perils of parental power. Maisie's biological parents, Ida and Beale, are corrupt and debauched almost beyond belief, and her stepparents, Mrs. Beale and Sir Claude, may be less odious but are also selfish, manipulative, and ethically compromised. In choosing Mrs. Wix as her guardian, Maisie rejects her exclusion from consenting authority and overthrows the parental authority under which Enlightenment ideology consigned children. Maisie's ability to do this is an exception to the general rule. She can reject parental authority only because her natural parents wish to have no claim over her, and she can consent to Mrs. Wix's authority only because this is an informal arrangement rather than one inscribed in law. But while her capacity to rebel is exceptional, James's implied critique of children's exclusion from the community of consent on the basis of their supposed lack of reason has wide implications. The whole drift of the novel is to chart the emergence of Maisie's power to consent meaningfully—a narrative process that will concern us in more detail a bit later—and her powers of informed consent emerge much earlier than the age of majority recognized in law, as presumably other children's might as well. Her gendered status as a girl has particular importance here. Women's rights advocates, in the decades before and after *Maisie's* publication, argued for women's inclusion in the franchise, juries, and contract rights on the basis of their possession of reason. In making such arguments, they often sought to differentiate themselves from children. Maisie's claim to consensual power defies that differentiation and the new political boundary it implicitly establishes between women's and girls' political subjectivities.

MAISIE'S PERIL AND THE AGE OF SEXUAL CONSENT

The line between women's and girls' capacities for consent was hotly contested in another arena, the age of sexual consent. The issue of children's—or more particularly girls'—sexual consent was inflamed in the years leading up to the publication of *What Maisie Knew*, and the novel figures it conspicuously. James wrote the novel in the wake of a massive public scandal that motivated changes in age-of-consent laws for girls in the United States and Britain, from as low as seven in the United States and thirteen in Britain to as high as eighteen in the United States and sixteen in Britain. Although legislation raising the age of sexual consent had occasionally been proposed in both countries, it was not until the furor caused by William T. Stead's notorious 1885 exposé, "The Maiden Tribute of Modern Babylon," that a critical mass of public sentiment was thrown behind such laws. Stead, the editor of the *Pall Mall Gazette* in London, initiated a widespread Anglo-American sex panic by claiming that young, working-class English girls were regularly bought and sold as slaves in an international sex trade.[3] In order to make his point, Stead arranged to buy a thirteen-year-old girl, Eliza Armstrong, from her mother and smuggle her to a brothel in France in order to prove how easy it was to do such a thing. He debilitated her with chloroform, subjected her to an examination by a midwife to prove that she was still a virgin after her kidnapping, and then handed her over to the protection of the Salvation Army. For these actions he was prosecuted and sentenced to three months in prison (Walkowitz 115). His account of this stunt and of the trade in young girls more generally in "The Maiden Tribute of Modern Babylon," however, made him a hero, moving the public to demand legislation raising the age of consent. Reformers who had been advocating such a change seized the moment to publicize their agendas, and a massive demonstration in Hyde Park applied pressure to a Parliament previously reluctant to pass such legislation. As a result, the Criminal Amendment Act of 1885 raised the age of consent in Great Britain from thirteen to sixteen. The storm of publicity in London sparked agitation in the United States as well, where, state by state, the age of consent was also raised.

Like all sex panics, the white slave panic touched off by Stead condensed and allegorized a potent mix of social anxieties, but what is perhaps most striking in retrospect is how little it had to do with understanding girls' capacity to consent in the developmental terms that have come to dominate our modern conceptions of sexual consent. Framed as a means of protecting innocence, age of consent laws, as Judith Walkowitz holds, functioned less as a way of keeping children out of the sex trade than they did as a means of regulating sexuality. Such laws motivated widespread public and legal action against prostitution more generally, galvanizing "a massive political initiative against non-marital, nonreproductive sexuality . . . whose initial victims were working-class prostitutes" (Walkowitz 83). Our modern common sense is often that the rise in the age of sexual consent evidences the improving status of children and gives proof of an emerging social consensus that they need and deserve protection from harm and exploitation until they develop sufficiently to make decisions for themselves. Yet as Deborah Gorham argues of the legislative changes that followed the *Maiden Tribute* scandal, "many of the provisions of age of consent legislation were designed to protect a guardian's right to control a girl's sexuality, rather than to prevent harm to the girl" (363). Rises in the age of consent consolidated both state and parental control of girls' sexuality.

In orchestrating Maisie's development toward the ability to consent, *What Maisie Knew* alludes extensively to the "Maiden Tribute" scandal.[4] After her parents' divorce, Maisie's father's house is figured almost as a brothel, where her body is "handled, pulled hither and thither and kissed" (40). While Maisie's bodily integrity is at stake at her father's house, her sexual subjectivity is at play in her relationship with both her mother and Sir Claude. Jealous of the affection between Maisie and Sir Claude, Ida sexually shames her, exclaiming, "You hang about him in a way that's barely decent—he can do what he likes with you" (90). Sir Claude himself picks this up in a mode of irony, noting that "if he was to have the credit of perverting the innocent child he might also at least have the amusement" (94). He here mocks not only his wife's high dudgeon but also the language of the contemporary reform movement that railed against the corruption of girls for the recreation of upper-class men. As if to make the allusion to the "Maiden Tribute" scandal impossible to miss, James even has Sir Claude take Maisie off to France, as Stead took Eliza Armstrong.

Where Eliza's story ends with girls losing the power of consent, however, Maisie's ends with a girl claiming it. Stead "saved" Eliza Armstrong by taking control of her body and "saved" English girls more generally by advocating legislation that *took away* their power to consent legally to sex. Maisie, by contrast, ultimately saves herself by *claiming* the power to consent. After years of shuttling between her parents and then, after they drop out of her life, being struggled over by Mrs. Beale, Sir Claude, and Mrs. Wix, she consents to Mrs. Wix's authority. In doing so, she makes at once an erotic decision and a political one. In one way or another, Maisie has erotic attachments to all her potential guardians, and she openly claims to be in love with Sir Claude. She tells Sir Claude that she will choose him if he will break off his adulterous relationship with Mrs. Beale, and when he says that he cannot, she rejects him in favor of Mrs. Wix's sole guardianship. In rejecting him, she exerts a painful sort of agency in the erotic realm—the right to reject is integral to the right to consent. At the same time, she exerts her reason and ethical sensibility in choosing who shall have a right to authority over her. Her ability to do so, however, is neither sudden nor purely dependent on her will to self-assertion. It slowly evolves over the course of the novel's narrative of child development.

DEVELOPMENTAL CONSENT

In metaphorizing children's exclusion from political and sexual consent, *What Maisie Knew* translates these issues into the modern terms offered by developmental psychology, exposing the implications of these new terms for understanding consent and the ties it is supposed to ground in legitimacy.[5] Developmental psychology redefined childhood in ways that soon came to dominate the fields of education and family life as well as the legal status of children and even the legal theory of child citizenship. In looking to the earlier period of the early and mid–nineteenth century, Karen Sánchez-Eppler has noted that "for the nineteenth century, childhood is better understood as a status or idea associated with innocence and dependency than as a specific developmental or biological period" (xxi). The language of status, rather than development, had dominated the debates about raising the age of sexual consent during the "Maiden Tribute" scandal. As Gorham shows, the late-Victorian reformers who successfully advocated for the age of consent to be raised "did not possess a concept of adolescence as a distinct period of development with discernable developmental landmarks. It would not be until the nineties that psychologists would begin to popularize these concepts" (369). Before the pivotal emergence of developmental models of childhood, the age of consent was based on "an older conception of youth . . . that had to do with the status of the individual in relation to other groups in society" (Gorham 369). Reformers acted from their beliefs that they had a responsibility to guard and protect working-class girls until they achieved the age of majority rather than from the belief that they should measure intellectual, psychological, or sexual maturity along a developmental scale.

It is true that the age of majority itself, insofar as it is intended to mark the transition from being incompetent to consent to being competent to do so, relies on the idea of intellectual growth from one stage to another. But the discourse about the "age of reason," as this moment of transition was long known, was more a theory about the moment at which a child emerged into reason than it was about stages of cognitive development over time. By the 1890s, developmental psychology blossomed and began saturating the public discussion of childhood. Beginning in this decade, observing the minds of children and recording their growing abilities became an academic discipline, an educational mandate, a parental fixation, and a popular pastime in ways that were intertwined. Originating in the work of G. Stanley Hall, child study comprised, as Shuttleworth has argued, "a complex network of discursive and disciplinary activities, encompassing the various forms of science adumbrated by Stanley Hall, but also extending outwards into further literary, educational, and domestic fields" (270). In doing so, these disciplines helped expand the discourse of childhood in much the same way that, as Foucault has taught us, sexology expanded the discursive domain of sexuality (*History of Sexuality* 15–35). For Foucault, to be sure, the surveillance of children was central to the growth of sexuality as a discourse (*History of Sexuality*, 27–30, 38, 41–42, 153). In the late nineteenth and early twentieth centuries, however, not only did sexuality expand via the attention to childhood, but childhood itself discursively expanded. Child study and later developmental psychology elaborated childhood as what we might call a condition of mind, constituted by a vast array of ever shifting and growing abilities, affects, and attitudes. As with the sciences of sexuality in Foucault's account, the sciences of child development, predictably, extended the operations of surveillance and power, as not only psychologists and doctors but also educators and parents observed, analyzed, and categorized the capabilities and attributes of children's minds.

In its first bloom, child study was concerned with amassing data about children's abilities, but the movement soon organized its data into narratives of child development. Stanley Hall, a former student of Henry James's brother William, employed questionnaires administered by a small army of interviewers to gather information about a dizzying number of categories of children's physical and mental growth and development. Studies that focused on the mind compiled data about what thousands of children knew or could do at various times of their lives, seeing children as a population but also breaking them down by age, sex, race, region, and whether they lived in the country or the city. In his widely cited study, *The Contents of Children's Minds on Entering School*, Hall records, for instance, the percentage of children in his survey groups who fail to recognize the meaning of such words as "beehive" (81 percent of girls ignorant, 70 percent of boys), "cow" (18 percent of girls ignorant, 12 percent of boys) and "knee" (4 percent of girls ignorant, 5 percent of boys; p. 21). He further breaks down his analysis of children's ignorance of terms by race, region, nationality, and ethnicity. In summing up the significance of his findings for education, Hall concluded, "There is next to nothing of pedagogic value of which it is safe to assume at the outset of school life" (26). With this conclusion, he nearly reproduces Locke's notion of the child's mind as a tabula rasa.

Beyond Hall's observation that the relative emptiness of the child's mind should condition teachers' expectations, the possible applications for this sort of data were limited until developmental psychology and physiology soon organized it into narratives of maturation that divided childhood into progressive stages, each of which led to the next, none of which could be skipped on the way to maturity, and all of which were biologically conditioned (Turmel 250–277). Child development was measured in incremental stages, from birth (or earlier) to the late teens or early twenties. The master trope organizing the study of child development was the teleological one of human evolution. The development of each child recapitulated human evolution, from primitive origins to full modern humanity (Shuttleworth 269). This research found a by and large welcoming public reception. Middle-class parenting itself took on the features of a research project, as guidebooks and other sources of advice encouraged parents to document their children's development in lavish and minute detail. Evolutionary teleology brought grandeur to such parental surveillance. As Shuttleworth notes, "The mundane maternal chore of childrearing" became "synonymous with the glorious sweep of onward human progress" (272). The regulatory function of developmental psychology, moreover, was heightened by its teleological character. Its norms were and are both synchronic and diachronic, having to do not only with capacities reached at particular ages but with an entire growth arc toward a state of completeness.[6]

In this way, childhood was refigured in terms of population studies, surveillance, medical management, and state regulation, a change that harmonized— though not entirely—with children's cultural status as the sentimental beating heart of middle-class domesticity. Children stood where biopolitics, in Foucault's sense of course, met domestic affect. But if, as Foucault writes, the biopolitical state manages information and resources in order to exercise its power "to make live and to let die" (*Society Must Be Defended* 241), then children were people desperately hoped to live and yet most likely to die, ensuring broad and even urgent participation in the biopolitical project. The biopolitics of childhood fueled the growth of disciplines, professions, sciences, and bureaucracies dedicated to studying and managing children as a population. The success of these in making children as a group more likely to live than they have been at any other moment in history has been truly extraordinary. In the case of children, the state's extension of its power through biopolitics has confirmed progressive models of history.

Biopolitics, in Foucault's account, covers a very wide array of state controls over the health and well-being of its population. In a narrower yet also critical sense, though, biopolitics bears on the formal political structures of citizenship. Constituted in developmental terms, children create a switchpoint between biopolitics and political liberalism, between the state's management of life and the modern forms of citizenship that define qualification in terms of reason and autonomy. Developmental psychology coalesced children's intellectual capacities into a developmental arc. It provided a language for reorganizing into rich narrative terms the line between incompetence and competence, between being incapable of rendering consent—to contracts, to sex, to being governed—to being capable. The developmental model took over the question of sexual consent so that it was no longer a question primarily of the status of children in relation to adults but rather one of the child's or adolescent's developmental cognitive and physiological capacity for consent. Development is also the key variable at play in recent theory and other scholarship about children's citizenship and exclusion from the franchise. Consider, for instance, children's rights theorist Claudio López-Guerra's contention that "the best available evidence on moral and cognitive development suggest that at ten years of age all normal children have the capacity to understand the idea of electing representatives and to adopt a position of their own, however rudimentary" (137). Rejecting the idea of a single-age threshold for civic competence, another children's rights theorist, Andrew Rehfeld, argues, "Children pose a specific problem for institutional design: they are a population that is incrementally developing among institutions that are all-inclusive or all-exclusive" (143). Specifying that he will "leave the developmental milestones to developmental psychologists," Rehfeld advocates "the establishment of precise age proxies for the stages of political maturity" that would be "tied to an empirical account of developmental psychology, as would the institutional recommendations that would follow" (144).

By linking increments of democratic inclusion to increments of development, accounts such as Rehfeld's produce not only a richer language for inclusion but also a more elaborated scientific justification for exclusion, since each new "milestone" marking a new threshold of inclusion would also entail marking a new exclusion. Such thinking invites an intensive scrutiny of voter qualification that could easily extend beyond the assessment of children's democratic inclusion to that of everyone else, because it links particular degrees of rights to particular degrees of capacity that, while they may be linked with age, are not entirely defined by it. As Brewer argues, when children were excluded from the capacity to consent because they "did not have reason," then "the emphasis on their informed consent provided an excuse to deny equality and consent to others on the same grounds" (341). A more elaborated developmental language of competence would generate as many reasons to deny equality to those deemed not to have the right kinds of competence as it would reasons to include children of a certain age who were deemed to possess them.

In *What Maisie Knew*, James makes the surveillance of child development and the question of competency's emergence into central principles of a literary narrative. The idea of doing so, however, came late in James's planning of the novel but was apparently necessary for him to write it at all. In his initial idea for a story about a custody battle, the emphasis was less on the child than on the power plays among the adults. The child was to be "a fresh bone of contention, a fresh source of dramatic situations, *du vivant* of the original parents"; the story would be one of "suspicion, jealousy, a fresh separation" among the adults, with "the innocent child in the midst" (*Notebooks* 71). The novel went nowhere though, until three years later, when James redefined his emphasis and began writing. The child would not be merely the bone of contention but the center of narrative perspective. As he wrote, he would "make [his] point of view, [his] *line*, the consciousness, the dim, sweet, sacred, wondering, clinging perception of the child" (*Notebooks* 148). James says little more about his plans for the novel in his notebooks, but in his 1907 preface to *What Maisie Knew* for the New York edition of his works, he writes that he found this new "line," as he first defined it, completely impossible to follow: "I recall that my first view of this neat possibility was as the attaching problem of the picture restricted (while yet achieving, as I say, completeness and coherency) to what the child might be conceived to have *understood*—to have been able to interpret and appreciate. Further reflexion and experiment showed me my subject strangled in that extreme rigour. The infant mind would at the best leave great gaps and voids; so that with a systemic surface possibly beyond reproach we should nevertheless fail of clearness of sense" (*What Maisie Knew* 27). The "infant mind," that is, makes so little sense of its world that the novel would make no sense at all. For this reason, James explains, he reconceived his project as one of surveillance. Instead of being confined to the limited subject matter that Maisie *understood*, the narrative would encompass what she *saw*: "a great deal of which quantity," as he wrote, "she either wouldn't understand at all or would quite misunderstand" (*What Maisie Knew* 27). The story would generate interest from the reader's ability to understand what Maisie only saw, because "we simply take advantage of these things better than she herself" (*What Maisie Knew* 27–28).

There is nothing unusual, of course, for James in particular or for fiction in general, about a protagonist whose knowledge is far outstripped by that of the narrator or reader, nor is there anything startling in the power of the irony to be derived from that fact. What distinguishes *What Maisie Knew* is that "we" understand more than Maisie for a very specific reason, because her perspective is limited not by her arrogance, innocence, or geography, but by the fact that she has a child's mind. Or, to be more precise, she has a child's mind *developing* toward competence. The narrative is driven less by the events that occur than by the narrowing gap between what Maisie understands and what the implicit, surveilling reader understands. We, that is, watch her become more like us, and the narrator's interventions make the steps in this process highly visible.

As the surveillance of Maisie's mind moves the novel forward, her limitations and her insights are put consistently in developmental terms. For instance, Maisie is at first confused by an exchange with her nurse. Maisie's father has instructed the nurse that she must tell Maisie that he wants the child to know that he feels burdened by her. Maisie notices that her nurse looks very strained when telling her this, though Maisie cannot understand why. At a later point, however, Maisie develops the ability to understand this nuance: "It was only after some time that she was able to attach to the picture of her father's sufferings, and more particularly to her nurse's manner about them, the meaning for which these things had waited" (41). What has intervened between the moment her father offered her this particular cruelty and her later comprehension of it is Maisie's intellectual development, which causes her to constantly reinterpret past events of her life in light of newly developed capacities. As the narrator writes, "By the time she had grown sharper . . . she found in her mind a collection of images and echoes to which meanings were attachable—images and echoes kept for her in the childish dusk, the dim closet, the high drawers, like games she wasn't big enough to play" (41). Maisie's development allows her to continuously rewrite her own past in light of her new understandings. She comes to see, in increasingly nuanced ways, just how odious her parents have been and are, and this growing ability to assess and reassess the actions of those who wield power over her later fuels her ability to grant meaningful consent to Mrs. Wix's guardianship.

The language of development, as its historians have claimed, has a normative effect (Stockton 6–11; Turmel 248–263). Developmental models of children's growth and cognition established norms for stages; both precocity and developmental delay were pathologized. Over the course of the novel, Maisie is constantly measured against such norms. At points, she perceives the world in a developmentally appropriate way, "with the acuteness of her years" (64); at other points, she is ahead of curve, perceiving "with a subtlety beyond her years" (58). Comprehending the power of these norms, Maisie fakes being less perceptive than she is so that she can escape her mother's questions about her father's household. Under such questioning, Maisie succeeds in achieving what the narrator archly calls "a hollowness beyond her years" (77). She is, in other words, a precocious performer who is ahead of the curve in her ability to fake being behind the curve. Shuttleworth, in reading *What Maisie Knew* through developmental psychology, notes how Maisie performs her childhood ignorance for the adults around her (325–334), foiling the linear narrative of development. Yet what is striking is that even Maisie's deceits have developmental implications; she pretends to be at stages that she is not rather than subverting the concept of stages altogether.

Taken in their totality, however, Maisie's deviations from the norms of development do less to prop up the idea of the norm than they do to complicate the equation between chronological age and competency. Maisie, the novel's conclusion would hold, is ready both earlier than and in defiance of any normative expectations about her ability to wield consent with the intellectual authority of an adult. As James explains in his 1907 preface, at the end of the novel, Maisie, though probably in her early teens, actually *is* an adult: "She wonders, in other words, to the end, to the death—the death of her childhood, properly speaking, after which (with the inevitable shift, sooner or later, of her point of view) her situation will change and become another affair, subject to other measurements and with a new centre altogether" (*What Maisie Knew* 28). Maisie's thinking, that is, kills her childhood; she wonders herself into adulthood and competency. And she does so well ahead of developmental schedule. Or rather, she does so in a way protected from the specifications of the developmental schedule. After the first several chapters, it becomes impossible to say exactly how old Maisie is. The novel summons the specters of developmental markers but never lets them become concrete or definitive. In this way, her narrative of development troubles the terms of the age of consent laws and laws of civic inclusion that would declare her incompetent on the basis of her chronological age.

At the same time that her narrative makes it possible to dispute the age at which people are considered competent to consent, however, the body of the narrative very thoroughly upholds the principle that proper consent is a factor of development. By rendering consent's development in such remarkable detail, it also upholds the principle that the ability to render proper consent is the signal attainment of a human subject and the factor that confers meaning and authority on its relations. Moreover, by making surveillance of the development of the mind toward its capacity to consent the motive drama of the novel, it enshrines that surveillance as a pleasure and a duty. The surveillance is self-justifying, revealing that the capacity to consent can only be discerned through such close surveillance. Competency's emergence in time is unpredictable; its emergence at all is unpredictable. The implications of this are dizzying. If it becomes impossible to *rule out* a legal minor's ability to offer developmentally mature consent, then it also becomes impossible to assert that any particular person, on the basis of age, *must* be competent, since competence has been severed from age. The open question of a child's competence in *Maisie*, that is, suggests the necessity of scrutinizing citizens more generally in order to determine their competence, because objective measures such as age have no reliable bearing on whether any particular person will meet the standard of competence to consent.

In putting the issue this way, however, I do not mean to lose sight of how the narrative form of child development affects people who are actually children. The narrative of development is teleological, meaning that everything that happens over its course is determined by its presumed endpoint in maturity and competence.[7] The child understood in terms of development is the means to an end rather than an end in itself; it is always a partial subject moving toward the horizon of completeness. As Sánchez-Eppler has noted, "The transitoriness of childhood is part of what gives it such emotional force" (xxxvi); childhood is a status, as she writes, "defined by its mutability—a stage inevitably passed through" (xxv). One way that political theorists have justified children's exclusion from democratic participation is by reference to this transitoriness; children's dispossession of agency, such theorists hold, is ameliorated by the fact that it will someday end. The claim that childhood is transitory, however, is something besides a statement of neutral fact. Adulthood is transitory and mutable as well. Being alive is transitory, but that does not mean we do not want power in the present. In fact, the present is the only time we actually possess any power; the rest is either power we once had or power we might someday have. The association of consensual competence with a finished developmental state—with a narrative closure—denies the political urgency of the present, both for children in their supposedly unfinished state and for people more generally.[8]

At the risk of putting far too much weight on the shoulders of Maisie Farange, however, I want to conclude by suggesting that James himself provides the ammunition for assailing the narrative closure of *What Maisie Knew*, upending the teleological character of its narrative of Maisie's development toward consensual competency. In a 1902 letter to his friend and literary ally William Dean Howells, James seems to say that he has been at war with several of his recent works, including not only *What Maisie Knew* but also *The Spoils of Poynton*, "The Turn of the Screw," and "various others," over the question of narrative closure. Complaining that these works grew well beyond the parameters he first conceived, James writes, "Several things of mine, in these last years, have paid the penalty of having been conceived only as the 'short story' that (alone, apparently) I could hope to work off somewhere (which I mainly failed of), and then *grew* by rank force of its own into something of which the idea had, modestly, never been to be a book" (*Letters* 251). These works grew bigger and bigger, he reports, as if by their own momentum, but in defiance of the marketing categories governing literary scale. They became too long to be short stories that could plausibly be placed in literary magazines. They grew in ways he had not anticipated and seemed to him entirely unjustified by the developmental arc he had imagined for each work's completion. As he castigates himself, "*given the tenuity of the idea*, the larger quantity of treatment hadn't been aimed at" (*Letters* 251). If he had had his aesthetic preference, he writes, that would have left *The Sacred Font* unfinished, "if . . . I were not always ridden by a superstitious terror of not finishing, for finishing's and for precedent's sake, what I have begun" (*Letters*

251). He imposes, that is, a teleology on the narrative and a teleology on the process of writing it.

James's gothic language here, his "superstitious terror of not finishing," is at once arch and apt. It suggests the monstrousness of a story growing beyond the proper boundaries by force of its own eerie power as well as the particular grotesqueness that belongs to the unfinished thing, be it the unshapeliness of the partial novel or the incompleteness of the mind and citizenship of a child understood to be a partial subject. His superstitious terror, that is, echoes Mrs. Beale's exclamation that Maisie's powers of consent are monstrous, though of course, unlike Mrs. Beale, the novel insists that Maisie is a finished subject, a completeness James made happen through forcing to conclude a story that had grown far beyond its intended bounds. But what if James had not forced the novel to this conclusion but had, rather, honored its apparent resistance to closure? Such a prospect is as ill a fit with the history of publishing and the novel more generally as children's partial subjecthood is with democratic inclusion. Like children, unfinished and unpublished manuscripts have little standing or authority; if they do not land in the fireplace or trash but somehow make it to the recesses of an archive, every word of them is marked by a profound interpretive uncertainty resulting from the fact that they lack the definitive conclusions that would contain the chaos of the sign within the teleology of narrative completion.

If in some alternative universe, however, *What Maisie Knew* had never been completed, and therefore Maisie's development toward consent was never completed, then perhaps her subjectivity would no longer look like one hurtling toward its completion but rather like one existing on its own terms in whatever way it did at any particular moment. She would never be "unfinished," to put it another way, because there would be no finished state toward which she was moving. If it were possible to see her struggles to understand her world and ameliorate her own sufferings without having also to see how she is ultimately saved through her capacity to consent and thus attain equality and mastery over her life, then the significance of her struggles would change in crucial ways. Instead of understanding her problems to be solved through her incorporation into the community of consent, we could be compelled rather to confront how children fundamentally do not fit into a political economy geared toward completeness as a qualification for full participation, rights, standing, and authority.[9] We might also have to face the necessary incompleteness of adults, whose subjectivities, in various ways, are always in flux. Maisie might then provide a model for a political subjectivity, open ended in its trajectory, that could help us rethink the terms of children's exclusion and trouble the modern parameters of consenting competence that leave so many without political power.

NOTES

1. On the relation of the body to consent in political philosophy, see in particular Elaine Scarry. Additionally, Holly Brewer considers the intertwining of these in Anglo-American law and practice from the sixteenth through the eighteenth centuries (particularly 288–337). Throughout *Public Vows*, Nancy Cott documents the connections between marital, sexual, and national consent.

2. As Brewer notes, Locke "crafted a different, narrower meaning of consent" (90) than did his predecessor in contract theory, Thomas Hobbes. While Hobbes bases both political and parental authority in the consent of the governed, he, unlike Locke, held that consent could be forced by a superior power. More broadly throughout Hobbes's work, the child is a confounding political entity, seen at once to consent to parents and to be subordinated by their physical vulnerability. For an account of the inconsistencies and contradictions in Hobbes's theory of children's consent to their parents' dominion, see Peter King.

3. My summary of the *Maiden Tribute Scandal* draws from accounts in Devereaux 11–15, Gorham 360–362, and Walkowitz 81–120.

4. For a discussion linking *What Maisie Knew*'s allusions to the "Maiden Tribute" scandal to a critique of middle-class morality, see DeVine.

5. *What Maisie Knew* is a bildungsroman in a very specific sense, a novel in which cognitive development and its telos in adulthood has a marked physiological character.

6. The developmental trajectory toward completeness, as Kathryn Bond Stockton reminds us, is widespread in cultural understandings of childhood more generally, not only in disciplinary investigations such as those conducted by developmental psychology. As Stockton holds and I will later discuss, childhood sexuality has been a particularly charged target of developmental norms. See Stockton 6–11.

7. Recently, Stockton has tried to overcome the teleology associated with children's developmental growth, particularly that into a normative adult sexuality, by proposing that "children grow sideways as well as up" (6), a formulation intended to create a more spacious, unpredictable, and distinctively queer conception of childhood sexuality.

8. For a fuller consideration of dangers of deferring children's rights to the future, see Murdy.

9. For a different but overlapping account of the subject states that do not fit with juridical notions of consent, see Judith Butler.

WORKS CITED

Brewer, Holly. *By Birth or Consent: Children, Law, and the Anglo-American Revolution in Authority*. U of North Carolina P, 2005.

Butler, Judith. "Sexual Consent: Some Thoughts on Psychoanalysis and the Law." *Columbia Journal of Gender and Law*, vol. 21, 2011, pp. 2–27.

Cott, Nancy. *Public Vows: A History of Marriage and the Nation*. Harvard UP, 2000.

Devereaux, Cecily. "'The Maiden Tribute' and the Rise of the White Slave in the Nineteenth Century: The Making of an Imperial Construct." *Victorian Review*, vol. 26, no. 2, 2000, pp. 1–23.

DeVine, Christine. "Marginalized Maisie: Social Purity and 'What Maisie Knew' (Henry James)." *Victorian Newsletter*, vol. 99, 2001, pp. 7–15.

Fliegelman, Jay. *Prodigals and Pilgrims: The American Revolution against Patriarchal Authority, 1750–1800*. Cambridge UP, 1982.

Foucault, Michel. *The History of Sexuality*. Translated by Robert Hurley, vol. 1, Vintage, 1978.

————. *Society Must Be Defended*. Translated by David Macey, Picador, 1997.

Gorham, Deborah. "The 'Maiden Tribute of Modern Babylon' Re-examined: Child Prostitution and the Idea of Childhood in Late-Victorian England." *Victorian Studies*, vol. 21, no. 3, spring 1978, pp. 353–379.

Hall, G. Stanley. *The Contents of Children's Minds on Entering School*, E. L. Kellogg, 1893.

James, Henry. *The Complete Notebooks of Henry James*. Oxford UP, 1987.

————. *Letters, Vol. IV, 1895–1916. Edited by Leon Edel*, Harvard UP, 1984.

————. *What Maisie Knew*. Penguin, 1985.

King, Peter. "Thomas Hobbes's Children." *The Philosopher's Child: Critical Perspectives in the Western Tradition*, edited by Susan M. Turner and Gareth B. Matthews, U of Rochester P, 1998, pp. 65–87.

López-Guerra, Claudio. "Enfranchising Minors and the Mentally Impaired." *Social Theory and Practice*, vol. 38, no. 1, Jan. 2012, pp. 115–138.

Murdy, Anne-Elizabeth. "Public Education and the Properties of Young People." *The Review of Education/Pedagogy/Cultural Studies*, vol. 18, no. 4, 1996, pp. 397–410.

Rehfeld, Andrew. "The Child as Democratic Citizen." *The ANNALS of the American Academy of Political and Social Sciences*, vol. 633, Jan. 2011, pp. 141–166.

Sánchez-Eppler, Karen. *Dependent States: The Child's Part in Nineteenth-Century American Culture*. U of Chicago P, 2005.

Scarry, Elaine. "Consent and the Body: Injury, Departure, and Desire." *New Literary History*, 1990, pp. 867–896.

Shuttleworth, Sally. *The Mind of the Child: Child Development in Literature, Science, and Medicine, 1840–1900*. Oxford UP, 2010.

Stockton, Kathryn Bond. *The Queer Child: On Growing Sideways in the Twentieth Century*. Duke UP, 2013.

Turmel, André. *A Historical Sociology of Childhood: Developmental Thinking, Categorization, and Graphic Visualization*. Cambridge UP, 2008.

Walkowitz, Judith R. *City of Dreadful Delight: Narratives of Sexual Danger in Late-Victorian London*. U of Chicago P, 1992.

NOTES ON CONTRIBUTORS

Trained in studio art in the United States and France, DREW DANIELLE BELSKY completed her master of arts in interdisciplinary studies at York University in 2013, focusing on critical disability studies and participatory/collaborative research methodologies in art practice. Drew is currently a doctoral student in science and technology studies. Her current project investigates the professionalization and practices of medical illustrators and the making of canonical bodies in twentieth-century North America.

JOSEPH J. FISCHEL is an associate professor of Women's, Gender, & Sexuality Studies at Yale University. His first two books, *Sex and Harm in the Age of Consent* (2016) and *Screw Consent: A Better Politics of Sexual Justice* (2018), level challenges against and propose alternatives to the consent paradigm of modern sex law and late modern sexual ethics. His next book project, *Against Nature: A Solicitation to Sodomitical Justice*, investigates the life and afterlife of sodomy law in New Orleans in order to reconsider the centrality of sex for projects of liberal and neoliberal governance.

CAROLINE GODART is an assistant professor of communication, Germanic languages, and cultural studies at IHECS (Brussels) and a dramaturge. She holds a PhD in comparative literature from Rutgers University and is the author of the book *The Dimensions of Difference: Space, Time, and Bodies in Women's Cinema and Continental Philosophy* (2016).

JORDANA GREENBLATT teaches English at York University and writing at the University of Toronto. Her research interests include sexuality, queer theory, contemporary literature and culture, and legal discourses. Her current book project addresses law, literature, consent, and perversion; previous publications include chapters on law, sadomasochism, and consent and articles on perverted poetics and affect, gender, and synthetic humans.

JUSTINE LEACH graduated with a PhD in English literature from University of Toronto in June 2017. Her dissertation, supervised by Ato Quayson, explores the ambiguation of sexual consent in depictions of sexual violence in world literature.

KARMEN MACKENDRICK is professor of philosophy at Le Moyne College. She works in philosophical theology but is influenced by any number of cross-disciplines and is especially fascinated by the interplay of words and bodies. Her most recent book is *The Matter of Voice* (2016).

BRIAN MARTIN is professor of French and comparative literature at Williams College. He is the author of the book *Napoleonic Friendship: Military Fraternity, Intimacy, and Sexuality in Nineteenth-Century France* (2011), a history of queer soldiers in the French military, from Napoleon to the First World War. Nominated for a Lambda Literary Prize in 2012, *Napoleonic Friendship* was awarded the Laurence Wylie Prize in French Cultural Studies in 2013. Martin's work focuses broadly on gender and sexuality in France and on Nordic masculinities from Scandinavia to Québec.

KIMBERLY O'DONNELL is a PhD candidate in the Department of English at Simon Fraser University. Her dissertation explores the relations between affect and ethics in the late Victorian novel.

VICTORIA OLWELL is an associate professor of English language and literature at the University of Virginia. She is the author of *The Genius of Democracy: Fictions of Gender and Citizenship in the United States, 1860–1945*, as well as of essays on American fiction, women's work, and democratic culture.

AMANDA PAXTON is an assistant professor in the English Department at Trent University, Durham. Specializing in nineteenth-century literature and culture, she has a forthcoming monograph on sadoeroticism in Victorian religious poetry. Her work appears in *European Romantic Review, Hopkins Quarterly*, the *Journal of Victorian Culture*, the *Journal of Pre-Raphaelite Studies*, and *Women Writing and Reading*.

ANNIE PFEIFER is an assistant professor of German studies at Tufts University. She has also taught at Rutgers University and the University of Bern (Switzerland). She received her PhD in comparative literature from Yale University in 2015. Her book project examines the relationship between the techniques of literary modernism and twentieth-century practices of collecting objects.

GRAHAM POTTS works as an assistant professor and instructor in communications, sociology, and other departments. His previous work can be found with *Architecture_MPS, CTheory, M/C Journal*, and the *International Journal of Baudrillard Studies*. He also recently coedited a book on architecture and lived space. He works at the intersection of everyday and popular (digital) objects, focusing on what they say about how we understand the self. However, he continues to channel his inner border collie into research areas ranging from architecture to (online) zoology.

MATTHIAS RUDOLF currently teaches literature and writing at Salem State University, with topical foci ranging from bioethics and biopolitics to guns, democracy, and matters of poetry. Rudolf received his PhD from the University of Wisconsin-Madison; he is the coeditor of the collection "Romanticism and Biopolitics" (RCPS) and has published on romanticism, postcolonial literature, and the political legacies of literary theory.

KEJA VALENS is professor of English at Salem State University. Her recent publications include *Desire between Women in Caribbean Literature* (2013), *The Barbara Johnson Reader* (2014), essays on Caribbean and African American literature in *Contemporary Women Writers* and *African American Review*, and a chapter on "Excruciating Impossibility and the Transgender Jamaican" in *Trans Studies: Beyond Hetero/Homo Normativities* (2016). She is currently working on a book on cookbooks and national culture in the Caribbean.

INDEX

CPSIA information can be obtained
at www.ICGtesting.com
Printed in the USA
LVOW10s1757300518

578580LV00001BA/1/P